Kaplan Publishing [illegible] tly finding new ways to [illegible] our studies and our exciting [illegible] y do offer something different [illegible] r exam success.

CW01652914

This book comes with free MyKaplan online resources so that you can study anytime, anywhere. This free online resource is not sold separately and is included in the price of the book.

Having purchased this book, you have access to the following online study materials:

CONTENT	ACCA (including FFA,FAB,FMA)		FIA (excluding FFA,FAB,FMA)	
	Text	Kit	Text	Kit
iPaper version of the book	✓	✓	✓	✓
Interactive electronic version of the book	✓			
Check Your Understanding Test with instant answers	✓			
Material updates	✓	✓	✓	✓
Latest official ACCA exam questions*		✓		
Extra question assistance using the signpost icon*		✓		
Timed questions with an online tutor debrief using the clock icon*		✓		
Interim assessment including questions and answers	✓		✓	
Technical articles	✓	✓	✓	✓

* Excludes F1, F2, F3, FFA, FAB, FMA

How to access your online resources

Kaplan Financial students will already have a MyKaplan account and these extra resources will be available to you online. You do not need to register again, as this process was completed when you enrolled. If you are having problems accessing online materials, please ask your course administrator.

If you are already a registered MyKaplan user go to www.MyKaplan.co.uk and log in. Select the 'add a book' feature and enter the ISBN number of this book and the unique pass key at the bottom of this card. Then click 'finished' or 'add another book'. You may add as many books as you have purchased from this screen.

If you purchased through Kaplan Flexible Learning or via the Kaplan Publishing website you will automatically receive an e-mail invitation to MyKaplan. Please register your details using this email to gain access to your content. If you do not receive the e-mail or book content, please contact Kaplan Flexible Learning.

If you are a new MyKaplan user register at www.MyKaplan.co.uk and click on the link contained in the email we sent you to activate your account. Then select the 'add a book' feature, enter the ISBN number of this book and the unique pass key at the bottom of this card. Then click 'finished' or 'add another book'.

Your Code and Information

This code can only be used once for the registration of one book online. This registration and your online content will expire when the final sittings for the examinations covered by this book have taken place. Please allow one hour from the time you submit your book details for us to process your request.

Please scratch the film to access your MyKaplan code.

Please be aware that this code is case-sensitive and you will need to include the dashes within the passcode, but not when entering the ISBN. For further technical support, please visit www.MyKaplan.co.uk

KAPLAN PUBLISHING

Professional Examinations

Paper F8

AUDIT AND ASSURANCE

EXAM KIT

KAPLAN
PUBLISHING

British Library Cataloguing-in-Publication Data

A catalogue record for this book is available from the British Library.

Published by:

Kaplan Publishing UK

Unit 2 The Business Centre

Molly Millar's Lane

Wokingham

Berkshire

RG41 2QZ

ISBN: 978-1-78415-230-7

Printed and bound in Great Britain

Acknowledgements

The past ACCA examination questions are the copyright of the Association of Chartered Certified Accountants. The original answers to the questions from June 1994 onwards were produced by the examiners themselves and have been adapted by Kaplan Publishing.

We are grateful to the Chartered Institute of Management Accountants and the Institute of Chartered Accountants in England and Wales for permission to reproduce past examination questions. The answers have been prepared by Kaplan Publishing.

CONTENTS

Features in this edition

In addition to providing a wide ranging bank of real past exam questions, we have also included in this edition:

- An analysis of all of the recent new syllabus examination papers.
- Paper specific information and advice on exam technique.
- Our recommended approach to make your revision for this particular subject as effective as possible.

  This includes step by step guidance on how best to use our Kaplan material (Complete text, pocket notes and exam kit) at this stage in your studies.
- Enhanced tutorial answers packed with specific key answer tips, technical tutorial notes and exam technique tips from our experienced tutors.
- Complementary online resources including full tutor debriefs and question assistance to point you in the right direction when you get stuck.

You will find a wealth of other resources to help you with your studies on the following sites:

www.MyKaplan.co.uk

www.accaglobal.com/students/

Quality and accuracy are of the utmost importance to us so if you spot an error in any of our products, please send an email to mykaplanreporting@kaplan.com with full details.

Our Quality Co-ordinator will work with our technical team to verify the error and take action to ensure it is corrected in future editions.

INDEX TO QUESTIONS AND ANSWERS

INTRODUCTION

The majority of the questions within the kit are past ACCA exam questions, the more recent questions are labelled as such in the index. Where changes have been made to the syllabus, the old ACCA questions within this kit have been adapted to reflect the new style of paper and the new guidance. If changed in any way from the original version, this is indicated in the end column of the index below with the mark *(A)*.

Note that

The specimen paper is included at the end of the kit.

KEY TO THE INDEX

PAPER ENHANCEMENTS

We have added the following enhancements to the answers in this exam kit:

Key answer tips

All answers include key answer tips to help your understanding of each question.

Tutorial note

All answers include more tutorial notes to explain some of the technical points in more detail.

Top tutor tips

For selected questions, we "walk through the answer" giving guidance on how to approach the questions with helpful 'tips from a top tutor', together with technical tutor notes.

These answers are indicated with the "footsteps" icon in the index.

ONLINE ENHANCEMENTS

Timed question with Online tutor debrief

For selected questions, we recommend that they are to be completed under full exam conditions (i.e. properly timed in a closed book environment).

In addition to the examiner's technical answer, enhanced with key answer tips and tutorial notes in this exam kit, you can find an answer debrief online by a top tutor that:

- works through the question in full
- discusses how to approach the question
- discusses how to ensure that the easy marks are obtained as quickly as possible
- emphasises how to tackle exam questions and exam technique.

These questions are indicated with the "clock" icon in the index.

Online question assistance

Have you ever looked at a question and not know where to start, or got stuck part way through?

For selected questions, we have produced "Online question assistance" offering different levels of guidance, such as:

- ensuring that you understand the question requirements fully, highlighting key terms and the meaning of the verbs used.
- how to read the question proactively, with knowledge of the requirements, to identify the topic areas covered.
- assessing the detailed content of the question body, pointing out key information and explaining why it is important.
- help to devise a plan of attack.

With this assistance, you should be able to attempt your answer confident that you know what is expected of you.

These questions are indicated with the "signpost" icon in the index.

SECTION A-TYPE QUESTIONS

SECTION B-TYPE QUESTIONS

Planning and risk assessment

Internal controls and audit evidence

Ethics

Corporate governance and internal audit

Review and Reporting

Audit framework

ANALYSIS OF PAST PAPERS

The table below summarises the key topics that have been tested in the new syllabus examinations to date.

	Specimen	June 11	Dec 11	June 12	Dec 12	June 13	Dec 13	June 14	Dec 14
Audit Framework									
Audit vs. assurance engagements				✓					
Statutory audits									
Benefits/limitations of an audit					✓				
The regulatory environment					✓				
Corporate governance			✓					✓	
Audit committee				✓					✓
Ethics	✓	✓	✓	✓	✓	✓	✓		
Acceptance							✓		
Engagement letter		✓							
Limited assurance engagements	✓								
Internal Audit									
Scope/limitations	✓				✓	✓			
Contrast with external audit	✓			✓					
Outsourcing internal audit		✓						✓	
Value for money								✓	
Planning and risk assessment									
Audit risk	✓	✓	✓		✓	✓	✓	✓	✓
Analytical procedures	✓			✓		✓			
Understanding the entity					✓				
Materiality						✓			
Fraud & error		✓		✓					✓
Laws & regulations			✓						
Audit strategy & plan	✓			✓			✓		

	Specimen	June 11	Dec 11	June 12	Dec 12	June 13	Dec 13	June 14	Dec 14
Interim & final	✓							✓	
Audit documentation				✓				✓	
Internal control									
Internal control questionnaires	✓	✓	✓		✓				
Systems/tests of controls:				✓					
– Revenue system	✓	✓					✓		✓
– Purchases system	✓					✓			
– Payroll system			✓					✓	
– Capital system	✓								
– Inventory system					✓				
– Cash system									
Systems documentation		✓					✓		
IT controls	✓					✓			
Audit Evidence									
Definitions: tests of controls and substantive	✓						✓		
ISA 500 Audit procedures		✓				✓			
Assertions	✓			✓					
Audit sampling				✓				✓	
Sufficient appropriate evidence	✓					✓	✓		
Use of experts	✓	✓		✓			✓		✓
Use of internal audit			✓						
Estimates									
CAAT's					✓				
The audit of specific items:									
– Sales		✓							✓
– Purchases		✓							
– Payroll			✓					✓	
– Trade receivables	✓	✓			✓		✓		
– Bank						✓			

	Specimen	June 11	Dec 11	June 12	Dec 12	June 13	Dec 13	June 14	Dec 14
– Non-current assets	✓			✓		✓	✓		✓
– Trade payables					✓				
– Provisions	✓		✓	✓	✓				
– Inventory			✓	✓	✓		✓	✓	✓
Completion & reporting									
Misstatements	✓	✓						✓	
Final review							✓		
Subsequent events	✓		✓			✓			✓
Going concern	✓			✓		✓		✓	
Written representations					✓				
Audit reports/opinions	✓	✓	✓	✓	✓	✓	✓	✓	✓
Reporting to those charged with governance						✓			

EXAM TECHNIQUE

- Use the allocated **15 minutes reading and planning time** at the beginning of the exam:
  - read the questions and examination requirements carefully, and
  - begin planning your answers.

  See the Paper Specific Information for advice on how to use this time for this paper.
- **Divide the time** you spend on questions in proportion to the marks on offer:
  - there are 1.8 minutes available per mark in the examination
  - within that, try to allow time at the end of each question to review your answer and address any obvious issues

  Whatever happens, always keep your eye on the clock and **do not over run on any part of any question!**
- **Objective testing questions:**
  - Don't leave any questions unanswered.
  - Try and identify the correct answer.
  - If you can't identify the correct answer, try and rule out the wrong answers.
  - If in doubt, guess.
- Spend the last **five minutes** of the examination:
  - reading through your answers, and
  - **making any additions or corrections**.
- If you **get completely stuck** with a question:
  - leave space in your answer book, and
  - **return to it later.**
- Stick to the question and **tailor your answer** to what you are asked.
  - pay particular attention to the verbs in the question.
- If you do not understand what a question is asking, **state your assumptions**.

  Even if you do not answer in precisely the way the examiner hoped, you should be given some credit, if your assumptions are reasonable.
- You should do everything you can to make things easy for the marker.

  The marker will find it easier to identify the points you have made if your **answers are legible**.
- **Written questions**:

  Your answer should:
  - Have a clear structure
  - Be concise: get to the point!
  - Address a broad range of points: it is usually better to write a little about a lot of different points than a great deal about one or two points.

- **Reports, memos and other documents**:

  Some questions ask you to present your answer in the form of a report, a memo, a letter or other document.

  Make sure that you use the correct format – there could be easy marks to gain here.

PAPER SPECIFIC INFORMATION

THE EXAM

FORMAT OF THE F8 EXAM

		Number of marks
Section A:	8 × 2 mark objective test questions	
	4 × 1 mark objective test questions	20
Section B:	4 × 10 mark questions (mainly scenario based)	40
	2 × 20 mark questions (mainly scenario based)	40
		100

Total time allowed: 3 hours plus 15 minutes reading and planning time.

Note that:

- Any part of the syllabus can be tested in any section.
- Section A objective test questions will be knowledge based and you will have to choose the correct answer from the options given.
- Section B will contain some knowledge based written questions. Requirements are typically 'list and explain', where you pick up ½ for listing the point and ½ for explaining it. Knowledge of ISAs is usually required in this question.
- The scenario based questions in Section B will require application of knowledge to the scenario provided. It is important you relate your answers to the scenario rather than just regurgitate rote-learned knowledge.
- For the scenario based questions it is important to read the information carefully and only use this information to generate your answers. There are unlikely to be any marks awarded to students creating their own scenario and generating answers from that.
- Most points of explanation, discussion or procedures are worth 1 mark.
- Only one syllabus area will be tested in any one 10 mark question.
- Two syllabus areas may be tested in a 20 mark question.
- 20 mark questions are likely to focus on planning and risk, controls and evidence.

PASS MARK

The pass mark for all ACCA Qualification examination papers is 50%.

READING AND PLANNING TIME

Remember that all three hour paper based examinations have an additional 15 minutes reading and planning time.

ACCA GUIDANCE

ACCA guidance on the use of this time is as follows:

This additional time is allowed at the beginning of the examination to allow candidates to read the questions and to begin planning their answers before they start to write in their answer books.

This time should be used to ensure that all the information and, in particular, the exam requirements are properly read and understood.

During this time, candidates may only annotate their question paper. They may not write anything in their answer booklets until told to do so by the invigilator.

KAPLAN GUIDANCE

As all questions are compulsory, there are no decisions to be made about choice of questions, other than in which order you would like to tackle them.

Therefore, in relation to F8, we recommend that you take the following approach with your reading and planning time:

- **Skim through the whole paper**, assessing the level of difficulty of each question.
- **Write down** on the question paper next to the mark allocation **the amount of time you should spend on each part.** Do this for each part of every question.
- **Decide the order** in which you think you will attempt each question:

  This is a personal choice and you have time on the revision phase to try out different approaches, for example, if you sit mock exams.

  A common approach is to tackle the question you think is the easiest and you are most comfortable with first.

  Others may prefer to tackle the longer questions first.

  It is usual, however, that students tackle their least favourite topic and/or the most difficult question last.

  Whatever your approach, you must make sure that you leave enough time to attempt all questions fully and be very strict with yourself in timing each question.

- **For each question** in turn, read the requirements and then the detail of the question carefully.

  Always read the requirement first as this enables you to **focus on the detail of the question with the specific task in mind**.

  For written questions:

  Take notice of the format required (e.g. letter, memo, notes) and identify the recipient of the answer . You need to do this to judge the level of sophistication required in your answer and whether the use of a formal reply or informal bullet points would be satisfactory.

  With F8, whilst there are occasions when you are requested to write a formal document, there are many times when you can use tables to present your answer. This is the case when you are asked to link answers together. Pay attention to the format of the answers in this text to help identify when such layouts are appropriate.

  Plan your beginning, middle and end and the key areas to be addressed and your use of titles and sub-titles to enhance your answer.

  For all questions:

  Spot the easy marks to be gained in a question.

  Make sure that you do these parts first when you tackle the question.

  Don't go overboard in terms of planning time on any one question – you need a good measure of the whole paper and a plan for all of the questions at the end of the 15 minutes.

  By covering all questions you can often help yourself as you may find that facts in one question may remind you of things you should put into your answer relating to a different question.

- With your plan of attack in mind, **start answering your chosen question** with your plan to hand, as soon as you are allowed to start.

- **Do not leave any multiple choice questions unanswered**. Start by looking for the correct answer. If you are not sure which answer is correct, try working out which answers are incorrect so you are left with the correct answer. Otherwise – guess!

Always keep your eye on the clock and do not over run on any part of any question!

DETAILED SYLLABUS

The detailed syllabus and study guide written by the ACCA can be found at:

www.accaglobal.com/students/

KAPLAN'S RECOMMENDED REVISION APPROACH

QUESTION PRACTICE IS THE KEY TO SUCCESS

Success in professional examinations relies upon you acquiring a firm grasp of the required knowledge at the tuition phase. In order to be able to do the questions, knowledge is essential.

However, the difference between success and failure often hinges on your exam technique on the day and making the most of the revision phase of your studies.

The **Kaplan complete text** is the starting point, designed to provide the underpinning knowledge to tackle all questions. However, in the revision phase, pouring over text books is not the answer.

Kaplan Online progress tests help you consolidate your knowledge and understanding and are a useful tool to check whether you can remember key topic areas.

Kaplan pocket notes are designed to help you quickly revise a topic area, however you then need to practice questions. There is a need to progress to full exam standard questions as soon as possible, and to tie your exam technique and technical knowledge together.

The importance of question practice cannot be over-emphasised.

The recommended approach below is designed by expert tutors in the field, in conjunction with their knowledge of the examiner and their recent real exams.

The approach taken for the fundamental papers is to revise by topic area. However, with the professional stage papers, a multi topic approach is required to answer the scenario based questions.

You need to practice as many questions as possible in the time you have left.

OUR AIM

Our aim is to get you to the stage where you can attempt exam standard questions confidently, to time, in a closed book environment, with no supplementary help (i.e. to simulate the real examination experience).

Practising your exam technique on real past examination questions, in timed conditions, is also vitally important for you to assess your progress and identify areas of weakness that may need more attention in the final run up to the examination.

In order to achieve this we recognise that initially you may feel the need to practice some questions with open book help and exceed the required time.

The approach below shows you which questions you should use to build up to coping with exam standard question practice, and references to the sources of information available should you need to revisit a topic area in more detail.

Remember that in the real examination, all you have to do is:

- attempt all questions required by the exam
- only spend the allotted time on each question, and
- get them at least 50% right!

Try and practice this approach on every question you attempt from now to the real exam.

EXAMINER COMMENTS

We have included the examiners comments to the specific new syllabus examination questions in this kit for you to see the main pitfalls that students fall into with regard to technical content.

However, too many times in the general section of the report, the examiner comments that students had failed due to:

- "misallocation of time"
- "running out of time" and
- showing signs of "spending too much time on an earlier questions and clearly rushing the answer to a subsequent question".

Good exam technique is vital.

THE KAPLAN PAPER F8 REVISION PLAN

Stage 1: Assess areas of strengths and weaknesses

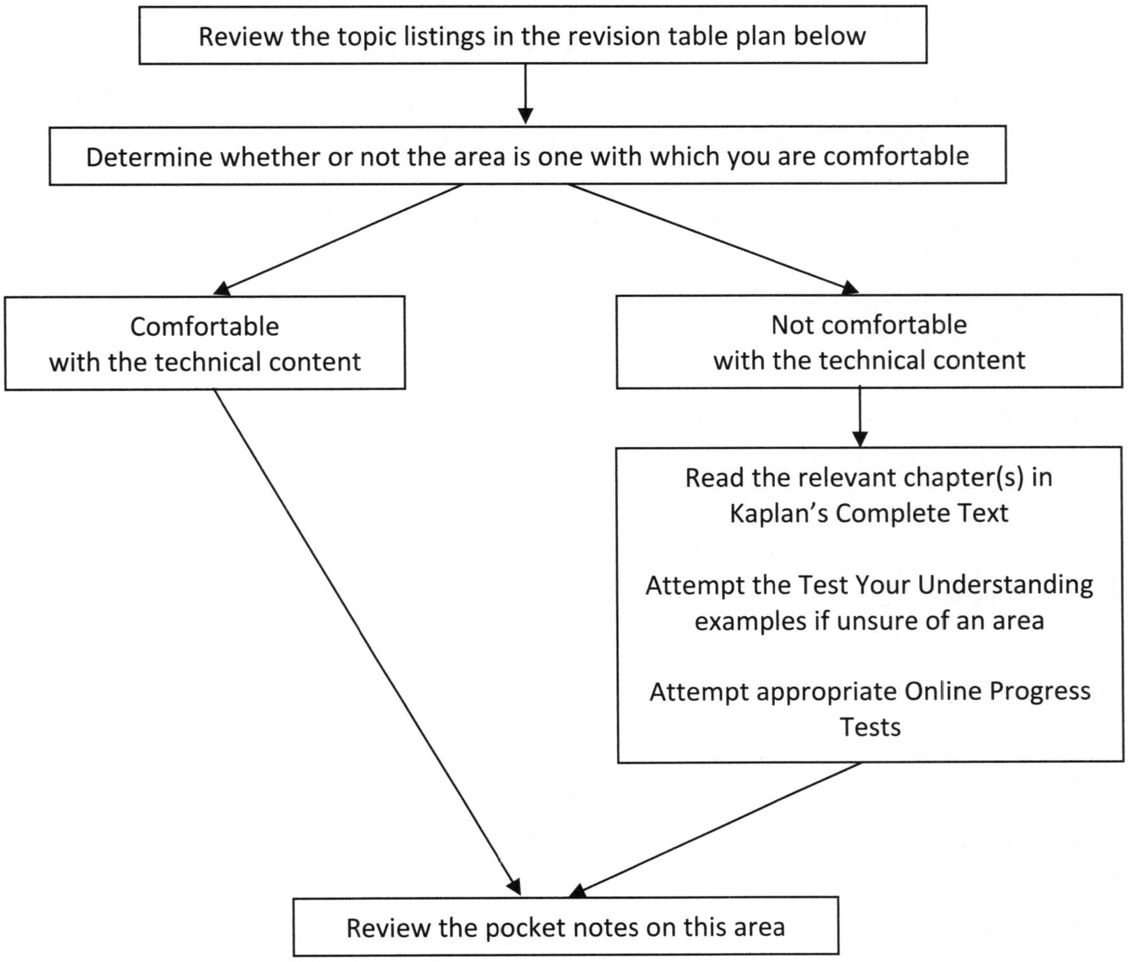

Stage 2: Practice questions

Follow the order of revision of topics as recommended in the revision table plan below and attempt the questions in the order suggested.

Try to avoid referring to text books and notes and the model answer until you have completed your attempt.

Try to answer the question in the allotted time.

Review your attempt with the model answer and assess how much of the answer you achieved in the allocated exam time.

Fill in the self-assessment box below and decide on your best course of action.

Comfortable with question attempt	Not comfortable with question attempts
Only revisit when comfortable with questions on all topic areas	Focus on these areas by: • Reworking test your understanding examples in Kaplan's Complete Text • Revisiting the technical content from Kaplan's pocket notes • Working any remaining questions on that area in the exam kit • Reattempting an exam standard question in that area, on a timed, closed book basis

Note that :

The "footsteps questions" give guidance on exam techniques and how you should have approached the question.

The "clock questions" have an online debrief where a tutor talks you through the exam technique and approach to that question and works the question in full.

Stage 3: Final pre-exam revision

We recommend that you **attempt at least one three hour mock examination** containing a set of previously unseen exam standard questions.

It is important that you get a feel for the breadth of coverage of a real exam without advanced knowledge of the topic areas covered – just as you will expect to see on the real exam day.

Ideally this mock should be sat in timed, closed book, real exam conditions and could be:

- a mock examination offered by your tuition provider, and/or
- the specimen paper in the back of this exam kit, and/or
- the last real examination paper (available shortly afterwards on MyKaplan with "enhanced walk through answers" and a full "tutor debrief").

KAPLAN'S DETAILED REVISION PLAN

Topics	*Complete Text (and Pocket Note) Chapter*	*Questions to attempt*	*Tutor guidance*	*Date attempted*	*Self assessment*
1 Audit framework and regulation	1, 2	202, 203, 204	You must also be able to discuss the purpose of assurance and the levels of assurance offered by accountants.		
2 Ethics	3	177, 180, 183	Make sure that you can define the elements of the Code of Ethics and that you practice applying the concepts to specific scenarios.		
3 Internal audit	11	186, 189	Questions tend to focus on: differences between internal and external auditors; how internal and external auditors interact; considerations before establishing an internal audit department; and advantages and disadvantages of outsourcing internal audit.		
4 Corporate governance	12	184, 185	You need to be able to identify and explain the main requirements of corporate governance regulations (e.g. UK Corporate Governance Code) and be able to identify when a company is not compliant with best practise.		
5 Understanding clients: risk assessment and planning	4 & 5	141, 144, 146	Audit risk is a vital concept. You need to be able to: discuss what it is, including materiality; perform risk assessment for a client; and discuss its impact on audit strategy.		

6 Internal controls	7	154, 155, 157, 158, 162	You need to know how a simple financial control system (e.g. sales, purchases, payroll etc.) operates. You may be asked to identify deficiencies in control systems and provide recommendations. You need to be able to state how those systems and controls should be tested, including CAATs.		
7 Audit evidence	6 & 8	164, 170, 174	It is vital that you are able to identify **specifically** what procedures are required (e.g. tests of control, analytical procedures) and what assertions are being tested (e.g. completeness, existence, accuracy) for a particular balance or issue given.		
8 Completion and review	9	190, 191	There are a wide range of issues that need to be considered at the completion phase of an audit. Typical examples include: subsequent events, going concern, written representations and evaluation of misstatements.		
9 Reporting	10	194, 198, 199	It is important that you are able to assess a scenario and identify how it might impact upon your audit report and opinion. You also need to be able to discuss the content and purpose of the sections of an audit report. You also need to be able to identify matters which should be reported to those charged with governance.		

The remaining questions are available in the kit for extra practise for those who require more question on some areas.

Section 1

MULTIPLE CHOICE QUESTIONS

PLANNING AND RISK ASSESSMENT

1 Which TWO of the following should be included in an audit engagement letter?

1 Objective and scope of the audit

2 Results of previous audits

3 Management's responsibilities

4 Need to maintain professional scepticism

A 1 and 2

B 1 and 3

C 2 and 4

D 3 and 4 **(2 marks)**

2 Which of the following amendments to the audit approach would reduce detection risk?

A Decrease in sample sizes

B Decrease the materiality level

C Decrease supervision **(1 mark)**

3 Which of the following is NOT a responsibility of the auditor?

A To provide an opinion on the truth and fairness of the financial statements

B To conduct an audit in accordance with International Standards on Auditing

C To express an opinion on the company's going concern status **(1 mark)**

4 Is the following statement true or false?

Audit risk is a function of two components, inherent risk and control risk.

A True

B False **(1 mark)**

5 Which of the following circumstances gives rise to an inherent risk?

A The audit client manufactures computer equipment

B Customers are allowed a $100,000 initial credit limit before a formal credit limit is agreed following credit checks

C The finance director has resigned and is yet to be replaced **(1 mark)**

6 Which of the following circumstances would increase control risk?

A The client operates in a highly regulated industry

B The auditor is relying on tests of controls and reducing substantive procedures accordingly

C There is a high turnover of staff in the finance department **(1 mark)**

7 Which of the following TWO matters must an engagement letter include?

1 The responsibilities of management

2 The period of engagement

3 Identification of an applicable financial reporting framework

4 The audit fee

A 1 and 2

B 1 and 3

C 2 and 4

D 3 and 4 **(2 marks)**

8 You are planning the audit of Veryan Co. This is the first year your firm has audited Veryan Co. Consequently there is a lack of cumulative audit knowledge and experience, increasing detection risk.

Which of the following is an appropriate auditor's response to the risk described?

A Extended controls testing should be performed.

B More time and resource will need to be devoted to obtaining an understanding of Veryan Co at the start of the audit.

C Reduce reliance on tests of controls.

D Consideration should be given to relying on an independent expert. **(2 marks)**

9 Which of the following would an auditor not obtain an understanding of at the planning stage?

A Laws and regulations applicable to the entity

B Events after the reporting period/subsequent events

C Financing structure of the entity

D Accounting policies used by the entity **(2 marks)**

10 Auditors must plan the audit so that it will be performed in an effective manner. Which of the following statements, if any, are correct?

1 Carrying out analytical procedures is required at the planning stage, but not as a substantive procedure.

2 Auditors are required to perform risk assessment procedures consisting of enquiries, analytical procedures, observation and inspection.

A 1 only

B 2 only

C Neither 1 nor 2

D Both 1 and 2 **(2 marks)**

11 It is vital that audit engagements are planned. Which of the following is not a purpose of planning an audit?

A To ensure that appropriate team members are selected to enable the development of their competencies and capabilities.

B To organise and manage the audit so that it is performed in an effective and efficient manner.

C To ensure that the client obtains added value from the audit to increase the chances of retaining the audit for next year.

D To reduce the risk of giving an inappropriate audit opinion to an acceptable level. **(2 marks)**

12 Which of the following would constitute material misstatement?

1 An error of $5,000 in relation to assets of $2m.

2 A payroll fraud of $100 in a company where profit before tax is $10,000.

3 Non-disclosure of a material uncertainty.

4 Financial statements have been prepared on a going concern basis when the company is in the process of being liquidated.

A 1 and 2

B 3 and 4

C 2 and 3

D 1 and 4 **(2 marks)**

13 Which is the correct definition of audit risk?

A The risk the auditor fails to detect material misstatements in the financial statements.

B The risk the auditor expresses an inappropriate opinion when the financial statements are materially misstated.

C The risk the auditor issues the correct opinion in the circumstances. **(1 mark)**

14 Which of the following is an example of an audit risk?

A The business is experiencing cash flow problems

B A customer has gone out of business

C A supplier has increased prices

D Inventory may be overstated due to damaged items being valued at cost instead of net realisable value **(2 marks)**

15 Which of the following is NOT an example of an audit risk?

A Intangibles may be overstated due to development costs not meeting the relevant criteria of IAS 38 *Intangibles*.

B Disclosures of going concern issues may not be adequate.

C The company may not be compliant with relevant laws and regulations.

D There is a tight reporting deadline which may mean there are material misstatements due to a higher number of estimates included in the financial statements. **(2 marks)**

16 Which of the following best describes the auditor's responsibilities in relation to laws and regulations?

A The auditor must consider whether the financial statements are materially misstated as a result of non-compliance with laws and regulations.

B The auditor must detect all instances of non-compliance and report them to the police.

D The auditor has no responsibility in respect of laws and regulations. **(1 mark)**

17 Which of the following is an example of an analytical procedure?

A Comparing gross profit margin to the prior year figure to identify significant changes

B Enquiries of management regarding the risks of the business

C Recalculation of a balance **(1 mark)**

18 Which of the following would NOT appear in the audit strategy?

A Results of substantive procedures

B Risk assessment and materiality

C Consideration of quality control procedures such as supervision and review **(1 mark)**

19 Which of the following best describes an audit risk?

A The risk profits will decrease as a result of intense competition in the market

B The risk a provision has not been recognised resulting in understatement of liabilities

C The risk a customer cannot pay their debts

D The risk the company's reputation may be damaged by a product recall **(2 marks)**

20 Calculate the receivables days ratio from the following information for a one year period:

Revenue	$1,267,000
Cost of sales	$1,013,000
Receivables	$121,000
Payables	$87,500
Inventory	$60,000

A 22

B 35

C 32

D 44 **(2 marks)**

21 Which of the following explanations is valid in respect of audit risk?

A Higher receivables days indicate a risk of understatement of receivables

B Higher payables days indicate a risk of understatement of payables

C Higher inventory days indicate that cost of sales may be overstated

D Higher gross profit margin indicates either overstatement or revenue or understatement of cost of sales **(2 marks)**

22 Which of the following is true in respect of responsibilities in relation to fraud and error?

A The auditor is responsible for preventing and detecting fraud.

B Management are responsible for preventing fraud and auditors are responsible for detecting fraud.

C Auditors should plan and perform their work to have a reasonable expectation of detecting material misstatement caused by fraud or error.

D The auditor has no responsibility for prevention or detection of fraud as this is solely management's responsibility. **(2 marks)**

23 Which of the following is true in respect of audit documentation?

A Auditors should keep audit files for at least 10 years from the end of the audit.

B Auditors must document every aspect of the audit in case of investigation at a later date.

C Auditors must destroy audit files once the audit report has been issued.

D Audit documentation is used to demonstrate the audit was planned and performed in accordance with ISA's and provides evidence for the basis of the audit opinion.

(2 marks)

INTERNAL CONTROL AND AUDIT EVIDENCE

24 Which of the following is NOT an audit software technique?

A Using computer programs to extract a sample for a receivables circularisation.

B Running a computer program to test the addition of the cash book.

C Using a computer to perform an analytical review comparison of administration expenses against the prior year.

D Entering a sample of dummy sales orders through the computer system which takes customers over their credit limit to ensure the system rejects the orders. **(2 marks)**

25 Which of the following is a DISADVANTAGE of recording accounting and control systems using internal control questionnaires?

A They may contain a large number of irrelevant controls

B It can be difficult to identify missing controls

C They are time consuming to complete **(1 mark)**

26 Which TWO of the following substantive procedures provide evidence over the EXISTENCE of trade receivables?

1 Agreeing a sample of goods despatched notes to sales invoices and to the sales ledger.

2 Undertaking a receivables circularisation.

3 Review of post year-end cash receipts, if these relate to year-end receivables follow through to the sales ledger.

4 Recalculating the allowance for uncollectible accounts.

A 1 and 3

B 2 and 4

C 2 and 3

D 1 and 4 **(2 marks)**

27 Which of the following procedures are TESTS OF CONTROL an auditor should perform in testing the inventory cycle of their client whilst attending the inventory count?

1. Observe whether the client's staff are following the inventory count instructions.
2. Review inventory present in the warehouse for evidence of damage or obsolescence.
3. Obtain a sample of the last goods received notes and goods despatched notes and follow through to ensure inclusion in the correct accounting period.
4. Inspect and review management's inventory count instructions.

A 2 and 3

B 1 and 4

C 1 and 2

D 3 and 4 **(2 marks)**

28 Which of the following is NOT an example of the use of audit software in the application of computer assisted audit techniques?

A Extracting samples according to specified criteria

B Stratification of data (such as invoices by customer or age)

D Submitting data with incorrect batch control totals **(1 mark)**

29 Which of the following sampling methods correctly describes monetary-unit sampling?

A A sampling method which is a type of value-weighted selection in which sample size, selection and evaluation results in a conclusion in monetary amounts.

B A sampling method which involves having a constant sampling interval, the starting point for testing is determined randomly.

C A sampling method in which the auditor does not use a structured technique but avoids bias or predictability. **(1 mark)**

30 In relation to audit evidence, is the following statement true or false?

Auditors can eliminate the need for substantive audit procedures entirely, if the tests of control performed provide sufficient appropriate evidence that the client's internal control system is designed and operating effectively.

A True

B False **(1 mark)**

31 Which of the following statements best defines audit sampling?

A The application of audit procedures to less than 100% of items within a population such that all sampling units have an equal chance of selection.

B The application of audit procedures to less than 100% of items within a population such that all sampling units have a chance of selection.

C The application of audit procedures to one or more items within a population.

(1 mark)

32 There are a number of possible ways in which the auditor can document internal control systems. The method adopted is a matter of judgment. In relation to documenting internal control systems, which method is described by the following statement?

A questionnaire listing control objectives, that requires the client to explain how they meet each objective.

A Narrative notes

B Internal Control Questionnaire

C Internal Control Evaluation Questionnaire **(1 mark)**

33 Which of the following is part of the control environment component within an internal control system as per ISA 315 *Identifying and assessing the risks of material misstatement through understanding the entity and its environment*?

A The attitude, actions and awareness of all personnel within an entity

B The governance and management function

C Segregation of duties **(1 mark)**

34 Which of the following is a type of control activity within an internal control system?

A Information processing

B Information system

C Risk assessment **(1 mark)**

35 Which of the following audit procedures could be used to verify the net realisable value of inventory?

A Inspect post-year end sales invoices for a sample of inventory items

B Inspect bank statements for a sample of payments to suppliers

C Inspect purchase invoices for a sample of inventory items **(1 mark)**

36 When placing reliance on evidence obtained from a service organisation is the following statement true or false?

The use of a service organisation may increase the reliability of the evidence obtained.

A True

B False **(1 mark)**

37 Which of the following substantive audit procedures would provide the best evidence over completeness of additions to tangible non-current assets?

A Review the list of additions and confirm they are assets rather than repairs and maintenance.

B Inspect title deeds for property additions to ensure they are in the name of the client.

C Select a sample of additions and agree the cost to supplier invoices.

D Obtain a breakdown of additions; cast the list and agree to the non-current asset register. **(2 marks)**

38 Which of the following substantive audit procedures could be used to verify the valuation of inventory?

A Trace the items counted during the inventory count to the final inventory list to ensure it is the same as the one used at the year-end and to ensure that any errors identified during the counting procedures have been rectified.

B Trace the goods received immediately prior to the year-end, to year-end payables and inventory balances.

C Inspect the ageing of inventory items to identify older/slow-moving amounts that may require allowance and discuss these with management.

D Perform a two-way test count: select a sample of items from the inventory count sheets and physically inspect the items in the warehouse and select a sample of physical items from the warehouse and trace them to the inventory count sheets to ensure they are recorded accurately. **(2 marks)**

39 An audit junior has been assigned to the audit of tangible assets of Poppy & Patch Co. He has obtained the following evidence:

1 Asset register reconciliation carried out by client management

2 Valuation report from an independent Chartered Surveyor

3 Depreciation proof in total carried out by the audit junior

4 Verbal confirmation from the directors that they plan to dispose of one of Poppy & Patch Co's buildings

What is the order of reliability of the audit evidence starting with the most reliable first?

A 4, 2, 1 and 3

B 2, 1, 4 and 3

C 4, 3, 2 and 1

D 2, 3, 1 and 4 **(2 marks)**

40 Which of the following substantive audit procedures could be used to verify the rights and obligations of receivables?

A Perform a positive receivables circularisation of a representative sample of the client's year-end balances, for any non-replies, with the client's permission, send a reminder letter to follow-up.

B Calculate average receivables days and compare this to prior year, investigate any significant differences.

C Select a sample of goods despatch notes before and just after the year-end and follow through to the sales invoice to ensure they are recorded in the correct accounting period.

D Review a sample of post year-end credit notes to identify any that relate to pre-year-end transactions to ensure that they have not been included in receivables.

(2 marks)

41 Which TWO of the following financials statement assertions relate to transactions and events?

1 Occurrence

2 Completeness

3 Valuation

4 Existence

A 1 and 2

B 2 and 3

C 3 and 4

D 2 and 4 **(2 marks)**

42 Which TWO of the following financial statement assertions are <u>most</u> relevant to the audit of inventory?

1 Cut-off

2 Existence

3 Occurrence

4 Accuracy

A 3 and 4

B 2 and 4

C 2 and 3

D 1 and 2 **(2 marks)**

43 All audit procedures have limitations, for example observation only provides evidence that a control was operating at the time of observation.

Which of the following best describes a limitation of the audit procedure, enquiry?

A It relies on the operating effectiveness of controls

B It relies on the integrity and knowledge of the source

C It only verifies existence (but may indicate impairment)

D It relies on the accuracy of the underlying data **(2 marks)**

44 Which of the following characteristics, if any, does statistical sampling have?

1 Random selection of samples

2 The use of probability theory to evaluate sample results

A 1 only

B 2 only

C Both 1 and 2

D Neither 1 nor 2 **(2 marks)**

45 General controls are policies and procedures that relate to many applications and support the effective functioning of application controls by helping to ensure the continued proper operation of information systems.

Which TWO of the following are general controls?

1 Regular back up of programs

2 Authorisation for the acquisition of new software

3 Sequence checks

4 Exception reporting

A 1 and 3

B 1 and 2

C 2 and 4

D 3 and 4 **(2 marks)**

46 Which TWO of the following are objectives of the controls in the revenue cycle?

1 Goods are only supplied to customers who pay promptly and in full.

2 All purchases are made with reliable and competitively priced suppliers.

3 Orders are despatched promptly and in full to the correct customer.

4 Only genuine employees are paid.

A 1 and 2

B 1 and 3

C 2 and 3

D 3 and 4 **(2 marks)**

47 Which TWO of the following are objectives of the controls in the payroll cycle?

1 Expenditure is recorded accurately and related payables are recorded at an appropriate value.

2 All purchases and related payables are recorded.

3 Correct amounts owed are recorded and paid to the taxation authorities.

4 Employees are paid at the correct rate of pay.

A 1 and 2

B 1 and 3

C 2 and 3

D 3 and 4 **(2 marks)**

48 You are the audit senior for the audit of Coastal Co and are reviewing the audit junior's documentation of the purchase cycle.

Which of the following two features of the purchase cycle described, if any, are a deficiency in the internal control system of Coastal Co?

1. Goods are counted and agreed to the supplier's delivery note before signing the delivery note to accept the goods.
2. The purchase invoice is matched to and filed with the relevant goods received note and purchase order, by the purchase ledger team in the finance department.

A 1 only

B 2 only

C Both 1 and 2

D Neither 2 nor 2 **(2 marks)**

49 You are the audit senior for the audit of Ocean Co and are reviewing the audit junior's documentation of the payroll cycle.

Which of the following two features of the payroll cycle described, if any, are a deficiency in the internal control system of Ocean Co?

1. Standing data files are sent to departmental managers on a quarterly basis for review.
2. Hours worked are entered onto a pre-printed payroll sheet by the wages clerk.

A 1 only

B 2 only

C Both 1 and 2

D Neither 1 nor 2 **(2 marks)**

50 You are the audit senior for the audit of Lighthouse Co and are reviewing the audit junior's documentation of the sales cycle.

Which of the following two features of the sales cycle described, if any, are a deficiency in the internal control system of Lighthouse Co?

1. A credit check is undertaken for all new customers. Once approved, customers are assigned a unique customer account number.
2. A copy of the customer's order is sent to the accounts team at head office and a sequentially numbered sales invoice is raised.

A 1 only

B 2 only

C Both 1 and 2

D Neither 1 nor 2 **(2 marks)**

51 Which TWO of the following controls in a purchase cycle could be implemented to reduce the risk of payment of goods not received?

1 Purchase requisitions are sequentially numbered and sequence checked.

2 Goods received notes are matched with purchase invoices.

3 Goods are agreed to purchase order before being accepted.

4 Inventory system is updated daily.

A 1 and 2

B 2 and 3

C 2 and 4

D 3 and 4 **(2 marks)**

52 Which TWO of the following controls in the purchase cycle could be implemented to reduce the risk of procurement of unnecessary goods and services?

1 Centralised purchasing department.

2 Sequentially pre-numbered purchase requisitions and sequence check.

3 Orders can only be placed with suppliers from the approved suppliers list.

4 All purchase requisitions are signed as authorised by an appropriate manager.

A 1 and 3

B 1 and 4

C 2 and 4

D 3 and 4 **(2 marks)**

53 Testing for overstatement addresses which of the following assertions?

1 Existence

2 Occurrence

3 Completeness

A 1 and 2 only

B All of the above

C 1 and 3 only **(1 mark)**

54 Which of the following is NOT a valid substantive test when testing a bank balance?

A Agree the balance per the bank statement to the bank confirmation letter

B Review the cash book around the year end for any unusual/large transactions

C Trace outstanding lodgements to the pre year-end bank statement

D Trace unpresented cheques to the post year-end bank statement **(2 marks)**

55 Which of the following is not a valid substantive test for trade receivables?

A Cast the aged receivables listing

B Inspect copies of credit checks carried out on new customers

C Agree invoices in year-end receivables to goods despatch notes

D Inspect board minutes for any evidence of disputes with customers **(2 marks)**

56 Which of the following risks require specific consideration for an audit of a not-for-profit organisation?

1 Fewer segregation of duties due to fewer paid staff.

2 Increased risk over the going concern due to uncertainty of income.

3 Complexity of taxation rules.

4 Competence of volunteer staff.

A 1, 2 and 3 only

B 1, 3 and 4 only

C All of the above

D 1 and 4 only **(2 marks)**

57 Which of the following is a reason why an audit of a not-for-profit organisation can differ from an audit of a for-profit company?

A Management of NFP's have no financial qualifications therefore greater risk of material misstatement.

B NFP's do not have shareholders therefore an audit is voluntary whereas an audit is a statutory requirement for a company of a certain size.

C There are fewer auditing standards applicable to audits of NFP's.

D An NFP has differing objectives to a profit making company and the financial statements will be used by different groups with different needs to those of a company. **(2 marks)**

58 Which of the following is not an additional reporting requirement for a not-for-profit organisation?

A Value for money audit

B Audit of performance indicators

C Regularity audit

D Due diligence **(2 marks)**

59 What does CAAT stand for?

A Computer assisted auditing techniques

B Computer automated audit testing

C Computer affected audit techniques **(1 mark)**

60 When using CAAT's, the auditor may use test data or audit software. Which of the following best describes test data?

A Scrutininising large volumes of transactions to increase the efficiency of the audit

B Testing the inputs and outputs of the clients systems

C Testing the computerised controls operating within the clients systems

D Scrutinising the source code of the system for errors in programming **(2 marks)**

61 Which of the following is not a benefit of using CAAT's?

A Greater volumes can be tested

B CAAT's are usually cheap to set up

C Aspects not which are not able to be tested by other means can be tested **(1 mark)**

62 Which of the following statements is not true in respect of using the work of others?

A The auditor should consider the competence and objectivity of the party whose work they wish to rely on.

B The auditor should make reference in the audit report to the fact they have relied on someone else's work.

C The auditor should evaluate the work before placing reliance on it to ensure it is good enough for audit purposes. **(1 mark)**

63 Which of the following statements is not true in respect of a company's internal audit department?

A The external auditor may use internal audit staff to perform some audit procedures under their supervision and review

B The external auditor may rely on the work the internal auditor has performed during the year if it is relevant to the external audit and has been considered reliable

C The external auditor can use the work performed by the internal auditor without checking it if the company has an audit committee in place responsible for overseeing the internal audit function

D All of the above **(2 marks)**

64 Which of the following best describes a test of control?

A A procedure performed by the external auditor to verify whether a control is in place and operating effectively

B A process implemented by the audited entity to mitigate a risk

C A procedure performed by the external auditor to detect material misstatement at an assertion level

D An evaluation of plausible relationships between financial and non-financial data **(2 marks)**

65 Which of the following is not a test of control?

A Inspection of capital expenditure forms for evidence that three quotations have been obtained to ensure the best price is paid

B Inspection of a title deed for the name of the client to confirm rights and obligations

C Inspection of the reconciliation of the non-current asset register with the physical assets to confirm the reconciliation has been performed on a regular basis

D Inspection of non-current assets for evidence of asset tags/barcodes that can be used to trace assets **(2 marks)**

66 Which of the following tests of control best provides evidence that a company performs regular credit checks on customers?

A Review of the aged receivables report to ensure no debts are overdue

B Enquiry of management to confirm credit checks are performed

C Review of the customer's account to verify that credit limits are in place

D Inspect of the customers file to ensure a credit report has been obtained and the date on the report is within the last year **(2 marks)**

67 Auditors are required to communicate deficiencies in internal control to those charged with governance and management in accordance with ISA 265 *Communicating deficiencies in internal control to those charged with governance and management*. Which of the following statements is true in respect of this communication?

A The auditor must communicate all deficiencies identified during the audit

B The auditor must communicate those deficiencies identified during the audit which they believe merit the attention of those charged with governance and management

C The auditor can communicate deficiencies in internal control verbally or in writing **(1 mark)**

68 Which of the following indicate the presence of a significant deficiency?

A Lack of oversight and scrutiny by management

B The presence of an audit committee

C Management implementation of controls to remedy control deficiencies once identified **(1 mark)**

69 Which of the following is not a substantive procedure relevant to purchases?

A Inspection of goods received notes around the year end to verify cut-off

B Inspection of purchase invoices to confirm accuracy of the purchase amount

C Inspection of payments made post year end to confirm a liability existed at the year end

D Calculation of the % change in purchases from last year and comparison with the % change in revenue **(2 marks)**

70 Which of the following procedures are analytical procedures?

1 Calculation of gross profit margin and comparison with prior year.

2 Proof in total calculation of depreciation charge for the year.

3 Recalculation of the non-current asset register.

4 Comparison of current year payroll with prior year payroll.

A 2, 3 and 4 only

B All of the above

C 1, 3 and 4 only

D 1, 2 and 4 only **(2 marks)**

71 According to ISA 610 (revised) *Using the work of internal auditors*, the external auditor must evaluate the internal audit function and the work performed by the internal auditor before placing reliance on the work of the internal auditor.

A False

A True **(1 mark)**

72 Which of the following is not a procedure for testing the valuation assertion?

A Inspection of inventory for evidence of damage

B Recalculation of depreciation of a non-current asset

C Inspection of sales invoices to verify net realisable value of inventory

D Inspection of purchase invoices to verify cost of purchases **(2 marks)**

73 With regard to inventories clients may use a continuous counting system rather than carrying out a full year-end count. Which of the following statements are correct?

1 The auditor must attend at least one count to ensure adequate controls are applied.

2 If no count is carried out at the year-end cut off testing need not be performed.

3 By the year-end all lines of inventory must have been counted at least twice.

A 1 only

B 1 and 3

C 2 and 3

D 1 and 2 **(2 marks)**

74 One audit test for accruals is to compare the list of accruals with the prior year. With regard to this procedure which of the following statements is NOT correct?

A This is an example of an analytical procedure

B This addresses the assertions of completeness and valuation

C Tests of detail must still be performed

D This could be the only form of substantive testing required if internal controls are reliable **(2 marks)**

75 Which of the following would be the most reliable source of audit evidence when auditing a legal provision?

A Board minutes

B Written representations from management

C Correspondence from the client's solicitors

D A numerical breakdown of the provision obtained from the financial controller

(2 marks)

76 When evaluating the adequacy of an expert's work, the auditor must consider the relevance and reasonableness of the experts findings and assumptions and methods used. True or false?

A True

B False **(1 mark)**

77 Which of the following statements is true in respect of a client which uses a service organisation for payroll processing?

1 The risk of material misstatement may be reduced as the service organisation may make fewer processing errors

2 Sufficient appropriate evidence may not be available if the service organisation or service organisation's auditors are not cooperative

A Neither

B 1 and 2

C 1 only

D 2 only **(2 marks)**

ETHICS

78 Auditors have a professional duty of confidentiality under ACCA's *Code of Ethics and Conduct*; voluntary disclosure of information may be necessary in certain situations.

For which TWO of the following situations should an auditor make VOLUNTARY disclosure?

1 If an auditor knows or suspects his client is engaged in money laundering.

2 Where disclosure is made to non-governmental bodies.

3 Where it is in the public interest to disclose.

4 If an auditor suspects his client has committed terrorist offences.

A 1 and 4

B 1 and 3

C 2 and 4

D 2 and 3 **(2 marks)**

79 **Which of the following best describes the fundamental principle of confidentiality?**

A Not disclosing any client information to anyone outside of the audit firm, unless with proper and specific authority or when there is a legal right or duty to do so.

B Not disclosing any client information to anyone outside of the engagement team, unless with proper and specific authority or when there is a legal right or duty to do so.

C Not disclosing any client information to anyone outside of the engagement team under any circumstances. **(1 mark)**

80 An ACCA member informed a friend of the difficulties faced by their audit client, a listed company. The friend held shares in the company – although the ACCA member was not aware of this – and following receipt of the information, sold their shares.

Which of the following fundamental principles has been breached by the ACCA member's actions?

A Objectivity

B Integrity

C Confidentiality **(1 mark)**

81 During disciplinary proceedings an ACCA member disclosed confidential client information as part of their defence.

Which of the following fundamental principles, if any, has been threatened or breached by the ACCA member's actions described above?

A Objectivity

B Professional behaviour

C Confidentiality

D There has been no breach of the fundamental principles **(2 marks)**

82 The audit senior has recently resigned and is now employed as financial controller of the audit client.

Which of the following threats to objectivity does the above circumstance give rise to?

1 Familiarity threat

2 Self-review threat

A 1 only

B 2 only

C Both 1 and 2

D Neither 1 nor 2 **(2 marks)**

83 Which TWO of the following safeguards could be implemented to address a self-review threat to objectivity?

1 Information barriers

2 Separate teams with separate reporting lines

3 Rotation of team members

4 Independent quality control reviews

A 1 and 3

B 1 and 4

C 2 and 4

D 3 and 4 **(2 marks)**

84 The auditor of Mawen Co has been invited to tender for the audit of Just Co. Mawen Co is a supplier of Just Co. Which of the following fundamental principles, if any, are threatened by the invitation to tender for the audit of Just Co?

1 Objectivity

2 Confidentiality

A 1 only

B 2 only

C Both 1 and 2

D Neither 1 nor 2 **(2 marks)**

85 Your audit firm has been invited to tender for the following engagements:

Company A has invited you to tender for their audit. An audit partner in your firm owns shares in Company A.

Company B has invited you to tender for their audit. You are already the auditor of a major competitor of Company B.

Which of the engagements, if any, must the audit firm decline?

1 Company A

2 Company B

A 1 only

B 2 only

C Both 1 and 2

D Neither 1 nor 2 **(2 marks)**

86 Which of the following threats to objectivity might arise if an audit team member is being interviewed for a job with an audit client?

A Self interest

B Advocacy

C Self review **(1 mark)**

87 Which of the following creates a presumption of fee dependency for a public interest/listed client?

A Fees from audit work exceed 15% of the firm's total fee income for one year.

B Fees from all services provided for the client exceed 15% of the firm's total fee income for one year.

C Fees from audit work exceed 15% of the firm's total fee income for two consecutive years.

D Fees from all services exceed 15% of the firm's total fee income for two consecutive years. **(2 marks)**

88 Which of the following best describes a conceptual framework approach to ethics?

A A set of laws for the auditor to follow

B A set of rules which must be strictly applied

C A set of guidelines which enable the auditor to use judgement to choose the most appropriate behaviour according to the specific circumstances

D A set of guidelines which the auditor can choose to apply at their own discretion **(2 marks)**

CORPORATE GOVERNANCE AND INTERNAL AUDIT

89 Which of the following is NOT an advantage of a company outsourcing its internal audit function?

A There will always be a reduction in costs

B Provides access to specialist skills

C Can provide access to an internal audit team immediately **(1 mark)**

90 Which of the following statements, if any, is/are correct?

1 Internal auditors should report to the finance director as they understand internal controls and are best placed to implement any recommendations in a timely manner.

2 Companies are not required to establish and maintain an internal audit function.

A 1 only

B 2 only

C Both 1 and 2

D Neither 1 nor 2 **(2 marks)**

91 Which of the following best describes the aim of corporate governance?

A To ensure that companies are well run in the interests of their shareholders and the wider community.

B To ensure that the wealth of companies contributes to the health of the economies where their shares are traded.

C To ensure that companies have a positive impact on the environment, stakeholders and the wider society. **(1 mark)**

92 Value for money is often referred to as the three 'Es': Economy, Efficiency and Effectiveness. In relation to value for money, which term does the following statement define?

'Achievement of goals and targets.'

A Economy

B Efficiency

C Effectiveness

D Value for money **(2 marks)**

93 Moyles Co operate a chain of car dealerships and have a large internal audit department in place. The management of Moyles Co are keen to increase the range of assignments that internal audit undertake.

Which TWO of the following assignments could the internal audit department of Moyles Co be asked to perform by management?

1 Fill a temporary vacancy in the credit control department on a rotational basis.

2 Under the external auditor's supervision, assist the external auditors by evaluating returns from the receivables circularisation.

3 Implement a new inventory control system.

4 Evaluate the inventory count instructions.

A 1 and 2

B 3 and 4

C 2 and 4

D 1 and 3 **(2 marks)**

94 Which of the following statements in relation to listed companies, if any, are correct?

1 Listed companies, i.e. companies whose shares are publicly traded, are normally required to have an internal audit function.

2 Listed companies, i.e. companies whose shares are publicly traded, are normally required to have an audit committee.

A 1 only

B 2 only

C Both 1 and 2

D Neither 1 nor 2 **(2 marks)**

95 Which of the following options correctly summarises the committees recommended as part of the UK Corporate Governance Code?

A Audit committee, Remuneration Committee, Nomination Committee

B Remuneration Committee, Nomination Committee, Financial Reporting Committee

C Corporate Social Responsibility Committee, Audit committee, Remuneration Committee

D Remuneration Committee, Controls Committee, Nomination Committee **(2 marks)**

96 When auditing a company that is compliant with corporate governance codes which TWO of the following statements are correct?

1 The control environment is likely to be stronger.

2 The level of inherent risk would be lower.

3 External auditors can raise issues with an Audit Committee.

4 The auditors are more likely to be reappointed each year.

A 1 and 2

B 1 and 3

C 1 and 4

D 2 and 3 **(2 marks)**

97 Which TWO of the following statements are correct?

1 Internal auditors always report directly to shareholders.

2 The format of external audit reports is determined by management.

3 Internal auditors work may be programmed for them by the board of directors.

4 All external audits must be planned in accordance with International Auditing Standards and other regulatory requirements.

A 3 and 4

B 1 and 4

C 1 and 3

D 2 and 3 **(2 marks)**

98 Which TWO of the following are advantages of outsourcing internal audit functions?

1 The outsourced firm will have a greater awareness of the client's business risks.

2 It improves independence.

3 Risk of staff turnover is passed to the outsourced firm.

4 Enhanced flexibility and availability of internal audit staff.

A 2 and 4

B 1 and 2

C 2 and 3

D 3 and 4 **(2 marks)**

99 Portland Co has a well-established internal audit department consisting of staff that have an average length of service of six years. The scope of the internal auditors work is determined by the Chief Financial Officer (CFO). For some projects the internal audit teams review their own work. Which of the following statements are correct?

1 The independence of the internal audit department could be enhanced if another member of the finance team was involved in determining the scope of their work.

2 Staff should be rotated on a regular basis to reduce the familiarity threat associated with the long length of service.

A Both 1 and 2

B Neither

C 1 only

D 2 only **(2 marks)**

100 Which of the following cannot be performed by the internal audit function?

A Risk identification and monitoring

B Expressing an audit opinion to the shareholders on whether the financial statements give a true and fair view

C Assessment of compliance with laws and regulations

D Evaluation of the effectiveness of internal controls **(2 marks)**

REVIEW AND REPORTING

101 ISA 580 *Written Representations* require auditors to obtain written representations to support other evidence.

For which of the following matters would a written representation NOT be suitable as audit evidence?

A That all deficiencies in internal control known to management have been communicated to the auditor.

B That subsequent events requiring adjustment or disclosure in the financial statements have been dealt with appropriately.

C That the payroll charge for three months of the year when the accounting records were unavailable is correctly stated.

D That management has fulfilled their responsibility for the preparation and presentation of the financial statements. **(2 marks)**

102 Which of the following statements, relating to the auditor's reporting responsibilities for going concern, if any, is/are correct?

1 Where management is unwilling to make their assessment of the company's ability to continue as a going concern, the auditor should include an emphasis of matter paragraph in the audit report.

2 Where the use of the going concern assumption is inappropriate, the auditor should include a qualified opinion in the audit report.

A 1 only

B 2 only

C Both 1 and 2

D Neither 1 nor 2 **(2 marks)**

103 For which of the following matters would it be inappropriate for the auditor to request a written representation?

A Confirmation that all information in relation to alleged or suspected fraud affecting the financial statements has been disclosed to the auditor.

B Plans or intentions that may affect the carrying value of assets or liabilities.

C To verify the quantity of inventory held by third parties.

D Confirmation that management, and those charged with governance, have fulfilled their responsibility for the preparation of the financial statements. **(2 marks)**

104 As part of a subsequent events review, the auditor must obtain sufficient appropriate evidence about whether events that require adjustment of, or disclosure in, the financial statements are appropriately reflected in those financial statements in accordance with the applicable financial reporting framework.

Which of the following is the definition of subsequent events, in accordance with ISA 560 *Subsequent Events*?

A Events occurring between the first day of the financial year and the date of the auditor's report, and facts that become known to the auditor after the date of the auditor's report.

B Events occurring between the date the financial statements are approved and the date of the auditor's report, and facts that become known to the auditor after the date of the auditor's report.

C Events occurring between the date of the financial statements and the date of the auditor's report, and facts that become known to the auditor after the date of the auditor's report.

D Events occurring between the date of the financial statements and the date of the auditor's report, and facts that become known to the auditor before the date of the auditor's report. **(2 marks)**

105 Which TWO of the following are potential indicators that an entity is not a going concern?

1 Net current liabilities (or net liabilities overall).

2 Borrowing facilities not agreed or close to expiry of current agreement.

3 A broad customer base.

4 Prioritisation of payments to tax authorities.

A 1 and 2

B 1 and 3

C 2 and 3

D 3 and 4 **(2 marks)**

106 In which of the following circumstances would a 'Basis for opinion' paragraph be included in the audit report?

A All audit reports

B Unmodified audit reports

C Audit reports with a modified audit opinion

D All modified audit reports **(2 marks)**

107 Which TWO of the following are reasons why an auditor would need to modify the audit opinion?

1 They conclude that there is a material inconsistency between the audited financial statements and the other information contained in the annual report.

2 They wish to draw attention to a matter that is fundamental to the users' understanding of the financial statements.

3 They conclude that the financial statements as a whole are not free from material misstatement.

4 They have been unable to obtain sufficient appropriate evidence to conclude that the financial statements as a whole are free from material misstatement.

A 1 and 2

B 2 and 3

C 2 and 4

D 3 and 4 **(2 marks)**

108 Which of the following circumstances would lead the auditor to give a qualified opinion?

A The matter represents a substantial proportion of the financial statements

B The matter is not confined to specific elements of the financial statements

C The matter is material to the financial statements

D The matter relates to a disclosure that is fundamental to the users' understanding of the financial statements **(2 marks)**

109 An other matter paragraph is used in an audit report to draw attention to a matter that does not affect the financial statements. Which of the following are correct in relation to an Other Matter Paragraph in the Auditor's Report?

A The matter is deemed to be fundamental to the users' understanding of the financial statements

B It is used to communicate a matter relevant to users' understanding of the audit, the auditor's responsibilities or the audit report

C The audit report is referred to as an unmodified report

D It is used as an alternative to a qualified opinion **(2 marks)**

110 The audit of Hadley Co's financial statements has been completed. A material non-adjusting event has occurred after the reporting period which has not been disclosed in the notes to the financial statements. What impact, if any, should this have on the audit report?

A No impact, the audit report should be unmodified

B An emphasis of matter paragraph

C A qualified opinion due to material misstatement

D An adverse opinion **(2 marks)**

111 Which TWO of the following elements must an unmodified auditor's report include, at a minimum?

1 An emphasis of matter paragraph.

2 A description of the responsibilities of management.

3 A reference to International Standards on Auditing and the law or regulation.

4 The auditor's telephone number.

A 1 and 3

B 2 and 3

C 2 and 4

D 3 and 4 **(2 marks)**

112 Which of the following phrases would be included in an unmodified audit opinion?

A The financial statements present fairly, in all material respects...

B Nothing has come to our attention to suggest that the financial statements do not present fairly, in all material respects...

C The financial statements are free from material misstatement... **(1 mark)**

113 In which section of the audit report should the following phrase be included?

'We conducted our audit in accordance with International Standards on Auditing'

A Auditor's responsibility

B Auditor's opinion

C Introductory paragraph **(1 mark)**

114 In which section of the audit report should the following phrase be included?

'We have audited the accompanying financial statements of ABC Company, which comprise...'

A Auditor's responsibility

B Auditor's opinion

C Introductory paragraph **(1 mark)**

115 Which type of audit opinion is illustrated by the following phrase?

'We do not express an opinion on the financial statements'

A Unmodified opinion

B Adverse opinion

C Disclaimer of opinion **(1 mark)**

116 Austin Co manufactures air conditioning units for use in large office developments. Included in inventory as at 31st March was a system that cost $400,000 to manufacture. In April the system was sold for $410,000 but this was after modification work was performed costing $50,000. Austin Co's profit before tax for the year ended 31st March was $800,000. Which type of audit report/opinion would be most appropriate for Austin Co, assuming the directors refused to make any adjustments in respect of the above?

A Unmodified report, as the sale happened after the year end

B Unmodified report with an emphasis of matter paragraph

C Modified Opinion – Adverse

D Modified Opinion – Except For (Qualified) **(2 marks)**

117 Grapefruit Co is being sued by a competitor for stealing trade secrets. The court case would bankrupt Grapefruit if they were to lose the case. The company lawyers are uncertain as to the likely outcome but the directors have decided to include a note to the accounts describing the potential liability. The auditors are satisfied the wording of the note is adequate.

Which type of audit report/opinion would be most appropriate for Grapefruit Co?

A Modified Opinion – Adverse

B Unmodified audit report

C Unmodified report with an 'other matter' paragraph

D Modified audit report with an unmodified opinion **(2 marks)**

118 Which of the following procedures would NOT be performed by the auditor during their final, overall review of the financial statements?

A Analytical procedures

B Inspection of board minutes

C Review of the financial statements using a disclosure checklist **(1 mark)**

119 Analytical procedures must be performed at the completion stage of the audit to ensure the financial statements are consistent with the auditor's knowledge and understanding of the performance and position of the company. True or false?

A True

B False **(1 mark)**

120 Which of the following statements is true in respect of uncorrected misstatements?

A All uncorrected misstatements must be adjusted in order for an unmodified opinion to be issued

B Only the material misstatements must be communicated to management and requested to be adjusted

C All uncorrected misstatements must be communicated to management and requested to be adjusted

D All uncorrected misstatements must be communicated to shareholders **(2 marks)**

121 A material uncertainty regarding the going concern status of a company would require a modified opinion due to the auditor being unable to obtain sufficient appropriate evidence. True or false?

A True

B False **(1 mark)**

122 The directors of a company are refusing to sign the written representation letter. Which opinion is most likely to be issued?

A Disclaimer of opinion

B Adverse opinion

C Unmodified opinion **(1 mark)**

AUDIT FRAMEWORK

123 Which of the following is the correct definition of an assurance engagement?

A 'An engagement in which a responsible party expresses a conclusion designed to enhance the degree of confidence of the intended users about the outcome of the evaluation or measurement of a subject matter against criteria.'

B 'An engagement in which a practitioner expresses a conclusion designed to enhance the degree of confidence of the intended users other than the responsible party about the outcome of the evaluation or measurement of a subject matter against criteria.'

C 'An engagement in which a practitioner expresses a conclusion designed to enhance the degree of confidence of the intended users other than the responsible party about a subject matter.' **(1 mark)**

124 In relation to the meaning of 'true and fair, is the following statement true or false?

There is no definition in the International Standards on Auditing of true and fair, but it is generally considered to have the following meaning:

True: Factual, conforms with accounting standards and relevant legislation and agrees with underlying records.

Fair: Clear, impartial and unbiased and reflects the commercial substance of the transactions of the entity.

A True

B False **(1 mark)**

125 International Standards on Auditing are developed and promoted by the International Audit and Assurance Standards Board; a subsidiary of the International Federation of Accountants.

Which of the following statements is correct in relation to the International Standards on Auditing ('ISAs')?

A ISAs are written for the audit of financial statements and cannot be applied to the audit or review of any other financial information

B ISAs are written in the context of an audit of financial statements but can be applied to the audit of other historical financial information

C ISAs can be applied to the audit or review of any financial information, prospective or historical **(1 mark)**

126 One of the primary sources of information about a company is the financial statements. The directors are responsible for preparing the financial statements.

Which of the following is one explanation of the need for an independent audit of these financial statements?

A The directors may lack the necessary skills or knowledge to prepare financial statements that are true and fair.

B All companies are required by law to have their financial statements audited by an independent, professionally qualified accountant.

C An independent audit will ensure that the correct tax is paid to the tax authorities.

D The directors often directly benefit from reporting higher profits as director's remuneration may include bonuses linked to the level of profits achieved. This creates a conflict of interest. **(2 marks)**

127 Which TWO of the following are elements of an assurance engagement?

1 Shareholders

2 An appropriate subject matter

3 A registered auditor

4 A written assurance report in an appropriate form

A 1 and 3

B 2 and 3

C 2 and 4

D 3 and 4 **(2 marks)**

128 Which of the following is a benefit of an audit?

A An audit may reduce the risk of management bias, fraud and error by acting as a deterrent.

B An audit will detect any material frauds.

C An auditor will prevent fraud by identifying any deficiencies in the internal control system and designing controls to address deficiencies.

D An auditor will report any fraud detected to the police to enable appropriate criminal action to be taken. **(2 marks)**

129 Which of the following statements is correct? In a limited assurance engagement….

A …the practitioner gathers sufficient appropriate evidence to be able to draw reasonable conclusions

B …the practitioner gives a positively worded assurance opinion

C …the procedures performed are normally restricted to enquiry and analytical procedures

D …the practitioner will state whether the subject matter conforms with the identified suitable criteria, in all material respects **(2 marks)**

130 Which of the following appropriately explains the difference between a limited assurance engagement and a reasonable assurance engagement?

A Limited assurance is given when a material misstatement has been identified in the subject matter but some assurance can still be given, where as reasonable assurance is given when no material misstatements have been identified.

B In a limited assurance engagement, the practitioner will gather limited evidence. In a reasonable assurance engagement the practitioner will gather sufficient appropriate evidence.

C In a reasonable assurance engagement, the practitioner is fully liable if the financial statements are later found to contain a material misstatement; in a limited assurance engagement, the practitioner has limited liability.

D In a limited assurance engagement the practitioner will conclude whether the subject matter, with respect to identified suitable criteria, is plausible in the circumstances. In a reasonable assurance engagement the practitioner will conclude whether the subject matter conforms in all material respects, with identified suitable criteria.

(2 marks)

131 The expectation gap is the difference between what the general public believe the auditor's responsibilities and function to be and the auditor's actual responsibilities.

Which TWO of the following beliefs are examples of the expectations gap?

1 Auditors test all transactions and balances.

2 An audit gives reasonable assurance that the financial statements are free from material misstatement.

3 Auditors are responsible for the detection of fraud.

4 A modified audit report does not mean that the financial statements are unreliable.

A 1 and 2

B 1 and 3

C 1 and 4

D 2 and 3 **(2 marks)**

132 National regulatory bodies enforce the implementation of auditing standards, have disciplinary powers to enforce quality of audit work and have rights to inspect audit files to monitor audit quality.

Which of the following statements, if any, are true?

1 All countries must use International Standards on Auditing.

2 National standard setters cannot modify International Standards on Auditing before adopting and implementing them.

A Neither 1 nor 2

B Both 1 and 2

C 1 only

D 2 only **(2 marks)**

133 **Which TWO of the following are rights that enable auditors to carry out their duties?**

1 To notify ACCA of their resignation or removal before the end of their term of office.

2 To receive information and explanations necessary for the audit.

3 To receive notice of and attend any general meeting of members of the company.

4 To deposit a statement of circumstances surrounding their resignation/removal at the company's registered office.

A 1 and 3

B 2 and 3

C 2 and 4

D 3 and 4 **(2 marks)**

134 Which THREE of the following are parties involved within an assurance engagement?

1 Directors

2 Auditors

3 Responsible Party

4 Practitioner

5 Intended users

A 1, 2, and 5

B 2, 3, and 5

C 3, 4, and 5

D 1, 3, and 4 **(2 marks)**

135 In a statutory audit engagement the audit practitioner should gather sufficient appropriate evidence to be able to:

A Draw plausible conclusions

B Draw reasonable conclusions

D Draw limited conclusions **(1 mark)**

136 In terms of assurance engagements is the following statement true or false?

A limited assurance engagement provides users with a low level of confidence in relation to the subject matter?

A True

B False **(1 mark)**

137 Which of the following are benefits of statutory audit engagements?

1 Improvements in quality and reliability of reported information.

2 Internal control deficiencies may be highlighted by the auditor.

3 Credibility of financial information is weakened.

4 Management is more likely to commit fraud to improve reported financial information.

5 Cost of financial reporting is decreased.

A 1 and 2 only

B 1, 2 and 3

C 3, 4 and 5

D 1, 2 and 4 **(2 marks)**

138 Under which circumstance is an auditor required to present a statement of circumstances at the company's registered office?

1 Removed as auditor.

2 Resigned as auditor.

3 Retired as auditor.

A 1 only

B 2 and 3 only

C 1 and 3 only

D 1, 2 and 3 **(2 marks)**

139 It is a legal requirement for all companies to have an external audit. True or false?

A True

B False **(1 mark)**

140 Where there is a conflict between national regulations and international auditing standards, which of the following statements is correct?

A The auditor may choose which regulations to follow

B National regulations take precedence

C International regulations take precedence **(1 mark)**

Section 2

PRACTICE QUESTIONS

PLANNING AND RISK ASSESSMENT

141 SEAGULL *Walk in the footsteps of a top tutor*

You are the audit supervisor of Seagull & Co and are currently planning the audit of your existing client, Eagle Heating Co (Eagle), for the year ending 31 December. Eagle manufactures and sells heating and plumbing equipment to a number of home improvement stores across the country.

Eagle has experienced increased competition and as a result, in order to maintain its current levels of sales, it has decreased the selling price of its products significantly since September. The finance director has informed your audit manager that he expects increased inventory levels at the year end. He also notified your manager that one of Eagle's key customers has been experiencing financial difficulties. Therefore, Eagle has agreed that the customer can take a six-month payment break, after which payments will continue as normal. The finance director does not believe that any allowance is required against this receivable.

In October the financial controller of Eagle was dismissed. He had been employed by the company for over 20 years, and he has threatened to sue the company for unfair dismissal. The role of financial controller has not yet been filled and so his tasks have been shared between the existing finance department team. In addition, the purchase ledger supervisor left in August and a replacement has been appointed in the last week. However, for this period no supplier statement reconciliations or purchase ledger control account reconciliations were performed.

You have undertaken a preliminary analytical review of the draft year to date statement of profit or loss, and you are surprised to see a significant fall in administration expenses.

Required:

Explain FIVE audit risks, and the auditor's response to each risk, in planning the audit of Eagle Heating Co.

(Total: 10 marks)

142 RECORDER COMMUNICATIONS *Walk in the footsteps of a top tutor*

Recorder Communications Co (Recorder) is a large mobile phone company which operates a network of stores in countries across Europe. The company's year end is 30 June. You are the audit senior of Piano & Co. Recorder is a new client and you are currently planning the audit with the audit manager. You have been provided with the following planning notes from the audit partner following his meeting with the finance director.

Recorder purchases goods from a supplier in South Asia and these goods are shipped to the company's central warehouse. The goods are usually in transit for two weeks and the company correctly records the goods when received. Recorder does not undertake a year-end inventory count, but carries out monthly continuous (perpetual) inventory counts and any errors identified are adjusted in the inventory system for that month.

During the year the company introduced a bonus based on sales for its sales persons. The bonus target was based on increasing the number of customers signing up for 24-month phone line contracts. This has been successful and revenue has increased by 15%, especially in the last few months of the year. The level of receivables is considerably higher than last year and there are concerns about the creditworthiness of some customers.

Recorder has a policy of revaluing its land and buildings and this year has updated the valuations of all land and buildings.

During the year the directors have each been paid a significant bonus, and they have included this within wages and salaries. Separate disclosure of the bonus is required by local legislation.

Required:

Describe FIVE audit risks, and explain the auditor's response to each risk, in planning the audit of Recorder Communications Co.

(Total: 10 marks)

143 MINTY COLA *Walk in the footsteps of a top tutor*

Minty Cola Co (Minty) manufactures fizzy drinks such as cola and lemonade as well as other soft drinks and its year end is 31 December 2013. You are the audit manager of Parsley & Co and are currently planning the audit of Minty. You attended the planning meeting with the engagement partner and finance director last week and recorded the minutes from the meeting shown below. You are reviewing these as part of the process of preparing the audit strategy.

Minutes of planning meeting for Minty

Minty's trading results have been strong this year and the company is forecasting revenue of $85 million, which is an increase from the previous year. The company has invested significantly in the cola and fizzy drinks production process at the factory. This resulted in expenditure of $5 million on updating, repairing and replacing a significant amount of the machinery used in the production process.

As the level of production has increased, the company has expanded the number of warehouses it uses to store inventory. It now utilises 15 warehouses; some are owned by Minty and some are rented from third parties. There will be inventory counts taking place at all 15 of these sites at the year end.

A new accounting general ledger has been introduced at the beginning of the year, with the old and new systems being run in parallel for a period of two months.

As a result of the increase in revenue, Minty has recently recruited a new credit controller to chase outstanding receivables. The finance director thinks it is not necessary to continue to maintain an allowance for receivables and so has released the opening allowance of $1.5 million.

In addition, Minty has incurred expenditure of $4.5 million on developing a new brand of fizzy soft drinks. The company started this process in January 2013 and is close to launching their new product into the market place.

The finance director stated that there was a problem in November in the mixing of raw materials within the production process which resulted in a large batch of cola products tasting different. A number of these products were sold; however, due to complaints by customers about the flavour, no further sales of these goods have been made. No adjustment has been made to the valuation of the damaged inventory, which will still be held at cost of $1 million at the year end.

As in previous years, the management of Minty is due to be paid a significant annual bonus based on the value of year-end total assets.

Required:

(a) Using the minutes provided, identify and describe SIX audit risks, and explain the auditor's response to each risk, in planning the audit of Minty Cola Co. (12 marks)

(b) Identify the main areas, other than audit risks, that should be included within the audit strategy document for Minty Cola Co; and for each area provide an example relevant to the audit. (4 marks)

(c) Describe substantive procedures the audit team should perform to obtain sufficient and appropriate audit evidence in relation to the following matters:

(i) The release of the $1.5 million allowance for receivables; and

(ii) The damaged inventory.

Note: The total marks will be split equally between each part. (4 marks)

(Total: 20 marks)

144 KANGAROO CONSTRUCTION *Walk in the footsteps of a top tutor*

(a) Explain the concepts of materiality and performance materiality in accordance with ISA 320 *Materiality in Planning and Performing an Audit*. (5 marks)

(b) You are the audit senior of Rhino & Co and you are planning the audit of Kangaroo Construction Co (Kangaroo) for the year ended 31 March 2013. Kangaroo specialises in building houses and provides a five-year building warranty to its customers. Your audit manager has held a planning meeting with the finance director. He has provided you with the following notes of his meeting and financial statement extracts:

Kangaroo has had a difficult year; house prices have fallen and, as a result, revenue has dropped. In order to address this, management has offered significantly extended credit terms to their customers. However, demand has fallen such that there are still some completed houses in inventory where the selling price may be below cost. During the year, whilst calculating depreciation, the directors extended the useful lives of plant and machinery from three years to five years. This reduced the annual depreciation charge.

The directors need to meet a target profit before interest and taxation of $0.5 million in order to be paid their annual bonus. In addition, to try and improve profits, Kangaroo changed their main material supplier to a cheaper alternative. This has resulted in some customers claiming on their building warranties for extensive repairs. To help with operating cash flow, the directors borrowed $1 million from the bank during the year. This is due for repayment at the end of 2013.

Financial statement extracts for year ended 31 March

	DRAFT	*ACTUAL*
	2013	*2012*
	$m	$m
Revenue	12.5	15.0
Cost of sales	(7.0)	(8.0)
Gross profit	5.5	7.0
Operating expenses	(5.0)	(5.1)
Profit before interest and taxation	0.5	1.9
Inventory	1.9	1.4
Receivables	3.1	2.0
Cash	0.8	1.9
Trade payables	1.6	1.2
Loan	1.0	–

Required:

Using the information above:

(i) Calculate FIVE ratios, for BOTH years, which would assist the audit senior in planning the audit; and (5 marks)

(ii) Using the information provided and the ratios calculated, identify and describe FIVE audit risks and explain the auditor's response to each risk in planning the audit of Kangaroo Construction Co. (10 marks)

(Total: 20 marks)

145 SUNFLOWER STORES *Walk in the footsteps of a top tutor*

Sunflower Stores Co (Sunflower) operates 25 food supermarkets. The company's year end is 31 December 2012. The audit manager and partner recently attended a planning meeting with the finance director and have provided you with the planning notes below.

You are the audit senior, and this is your first year on this audit. In order to familiarise yourself with Sunflower, the audit manager has asked you to undertake some research in order to gain an understanding of Sunflower, so that you are able to assist in the planning process. He has then asked that you identify relevant audit risks from the notes below and also consider how the team should respond to these risks.

Sunflower has spent $1.6 million in refurbishing all of its supermarkets; as part of this refurbishment programme their central warehouse has been extended and a smaller warehouse, which was only occasionally used, has been disposed of at a profit. In order to finance this refurbishment, a sum of $1.5 million was borrowed from the bank. This is due to be repaid over five years.

The company will be performing a year-end inventory count at the central warehouse as well as at all 25 supermarkets on 31 December. Inventory is valued at selling price less an average profit margin as the finance director believes that this is a close approximation to cost.

Prior to 2012, each of the supermarkets maintained their own financial records and submitted returns monthly to head office. During 2012 all accounting records have been centralised within head office. Therefore at the beginning of the year, each supermarket's opening balances were transferred into head office's accounting records. The increased workload at head office has led to some changes in the finance department and in November 2012 the financial controller left. His replacement will start in late December.

Required:

(a) List FIVE sources of information that would be of use in gaining an understanding of Sunflower Stores Co, and for each source describe what you would expect to obtain. (5 marks)

(b) Using the information provided, describe FIVE audit risks and explain the auditor's response to each risk in planning the audit of Sunflower Stores Co. (10 marks)

(c) The finance director of Sunflower Stores Co is considering establishing an internal audit department.

Required:

Describe the factors the finance director should consider before establishing an internal audit department. (5 marks)

(Total: 20 marks)

146 ABRAHAMS *Walk in the footsteps of a top tutor*

(a) Explain the components of audit risk and, for each component, state an example of a factor which can result in increased audit risk. (6 marks)

Abrahams Co develops, manufactures and sells a range of pharmaceuticals and has a wide customer base across Europe and Asia. You are the audit manager of Nate & Co and you are planning the audit of Abrahams Co whose financial year end is 31 January. You attended a planning meeting with the finance director and engagement partner and are now reviewing the meeting notes in order to produce the audit strategy and plan. Revenue for the year is forecast at $25 million.

During the year the company has spent $2.2 million on developing several new products. Some of these are in the early stages of development whilst others are nearing completion. The finance director has confirmed that all projects are likely to be successful and so he is intending to capitalise the full $2.2 million.

Once products have completed the development stage, Abrahams begins manufacturing them. At the year end it is anticipated that there will be significant levels of work in progress. In addition the company uses a standard costing method to value inventory; the standard costs are set when a product is first manufactured and are not usually updated. In order to fulfil customer orders promptly, Abrahams Co has warehouses for finished goods located across Europe and Asia; approximately one third of these are third party warehouses where Abrahams just rents space.

In September a new accounting package was introduced. This is a bespoke system developed by the information technology (IT) manager. The old and new packages were not run in parallel as it was felt that this would be too onerous for the accounting team. Two months after the system changeover the IT manager left the company; a new manager has been recruited but is not due to start work until January.

In order to fund the development of new products, Abrahams has restructured its finance and raised $1 million through issuing shares at a premium and $2.5 million through a long-term loan. There are bank covenants attached to the loan, the main one relating to a minimum level of total assets. If these covenants are breached then the loan becomes immediately repayable. The company has a policy of revaluing land and buildings, and the finance director has announced that all land and buildings will be revalued as at the year end.

The reporting timetable for audit completion of Abrahams Co is quite short, and the finance director would like to report results even earlier this year.

Required:

(b) Using the information provided, identify and describe FIVE audit risks and explain the auditor's response to each risk in planning the audit of Abrahams Co. (10 marks)

(c) Describe substantive procedures you should perform to obtain sufficient appropriate evidence in relation to:

(i) Inventory held at the third party warehouses; and

(ii) Use of standard costs for inventory valuation. (4 marks)

(Total: 20 marks)

147 REDSMITH *Walk in the footsteps of a top tutor*

(a) In agreeing the terms of an audit engagement, the auditor is required to agree the basis on which the audit is to be carried out. This involves establishing whether the preconditions for an audit are present and confirming that there is a common understanding between the auditor and management of the terms of the engagement.

Required:

Describe the process the auditor should undertake to assess whether the PRECONDITIONS for an audit are present. (3 marks)

(b) List FOUR examples of matters the auditor may consider when obtaining an understanding of the entity. (2 marks)

(c) You are the audit senior of White & Co and are planning the audit of Redsmith Co for the year ended 30 September 2010. The company produces printers and has been a client of your firm for two years; your audit manager has already had a planning meeting with the finance director. He has provided you with the following notes of his meeting and financial statement extracts.

Redsmith's management were disappointed with the 2009 results and so in 2010 undertook a number of strategies to improve the trading results. This included the introduction of a generous sales-related bonus scheme for their salesmen and a high profile advertising campaign. In addition, as market conditions are difficult for their customers, they have extended the credit period given to them.

The finance director of Redsmith has reviewed the inventory valuation policy and has included additional overheads incurred this year as he considers them to be production related. He is happy with the 2010 results and feels that they are a good reflection of the improved trading levels.

Financial statement extracts for year ended 30 September

	DRAFT 2010	*ACTUAL 2009*
	$m	$m
Revenue	23.0	18.0
Cost of Sales	(11.0)	(10.0)
Gross profit	12.0	8.0
Operating expenses	(7.5)	(4.0)
Profit before interest and taxation	4.5	4.0
Inventory	2.1	1.6
Receivables	4.5	3.0
Cash	–	2.3
Trade payables	1.6	1.2
Overdraft	0.9	–

Required:

Using the information above:

(i) Calculate FIVE ratios, for BOTH years, which would assist the audit senior in planning the audit; and (5 marks)

(ii) From a review of the above information and the ratios calculated, explain the audit risks that arise and describe the appropriate response to these risks. (10 marks)

(Total: 20 marks)

148 SPECS4YOU *Walk in the footsteps of a top tutor*

ISA 230 *Audit Documentation* establishes standards and provides guidance regarding documentation in the context of the audit of financial statements.

Required:

(a) List the purposes of audit working papers. (3 marks)

(b) You have recently been promoted to audit manager in the audit firm of Trums & Co. As part of your new responsibilities, you have been placed in charge of the audit of Specs4You Co, a long established audit client of Trums & Co. Specs4You Co sells spectacles; the company owns 42 stores where customers can have their eyes tested and choose from a range of frames.

Required:

List the documentation that should be of assistance to you in familiarising yourself with Specs4You Co. Describe the information you should expect to obtain from each document. (8 marks)

(c) The time is now towards the end of the audit, and you are reviewing working papers produced by the audit team. An example of a working paper you have just reviewed is shown below.

Client Name **Specs4You Co**	Year **end 30 April**	Page **xxxxxxx**
Working paper **Payables transaction testing**		
	Prepared by	Date
	Reviewed by **CW**	Date **12 June 2007**

Audit assertion: To make sure that the purchases day book is correct.

Method: Select a sample of 15 purchase orders recorded in the purchase order system. Trace details to the goods received note (GRN), purchase invoice (PI) and the purchase day book (PDB) ensuring that the quantities and prices recorded on the purchase order match those on the GRN, PI and PDB.

Test details: In accordance with audit risk, a sample of purchase orders were selected from a numerically sequenced purchase order system and details traced as stated in the method. Details of items tested can be found on another working paper.

Results: Details of purchase orders were normally correctly recorded through the system. Five purchase orders did not have any associated GRN, PI and were not recorded in the PDB. Further investigation showed that these orders had been cancelled due to a change in spectacle specification. However, this does not appear to be a system deficiency as the internal controls do not allow for changes in specification.

Conclusion: Purchase orders are completely recorded in the purchase day book.

Required:

Explain why the working paper shown above does not meet the standards normally expected of a working paper. *Note:* You are not required to reproduce the working paper. **(9 marks)**

(Total: 20 marks)

149 DOCUMENTATION/PLANNING

(a) ISA 230 *Audit Documentation* deals with the auditor's responsibility to prepare audit documentation for an audit of financial statements.

Required:

State THREE benefits of documenting audit work. **(3 marks)**

(b) Explain the purpose of FOUR items that should be included on every working paper prepared by the audit team. **(4 marks)**

(c) Describe the two main planning documents prepared by the auditor and briefly explain the relationship between them. **(3 marks)**

(Total: 10 marks)

150 AUDITOR RESPONSIBILITIES *Walk in the footsteps of a top tutor*

(a) Explain the auditor's responsibility for the prevention and detection of fraud and error. **(5 marks)**

(b) Explain the auditor's responsibility to consider laws and regulations **(5 marks)**

(Total: 10 marks)

151 ENGAGEMENT LETTERS/PLANNING

(a) ISA 300 *Planning an Audit of Financial Statements* provides guidance to assist auditors in planning an audit.

Required:

Explain the benefits of audit planning. **(5 marks)**

(b) ISA 210 *Agreeing the Terms of Audit Engagements* provides guidance on the content of engagement letters and deals with the auditor's responsibilities in agreeing the terms of the audit engagement with management.

Required:

(i) State the purpose of an engagement letter. **(2 mark)**

(ii) List SIX matters that should be included within an audit engagement letter. **(3 marks)**

(Total: 10 marks)

152 ACCEPTANCE *Walk in the footsteps of a top tutor*

(a) **Describe the steps that an audit firm should take:**

(i) **Prior to accepting the audit; and** **(5 marks)**

(ii) **To confirm whether the preconditions for the audit are in place.** **(3 marks)**

(b) **State FOUR matters that should be included within an audit engagement letter.** **(2 marks)**

(Total: 10 marks)

153 SWANDIVE *Walk in the footsteps of a top tutor*

(a) ISA 300 *Planning an Audit of Financial Statements* provides guidance to auditors. Planning an audit involves establishing the overall audit strategy for the engagement and developing an audit plan. Adequate planning benefits the audit of financial statements in several ways.

Required:

Explain the importance of audit planning. **(5 marks)**

(b) You are the audit senior in charge of the audit of Swandive Co (Swandive), and have been informed by your audit manager that during the year a fraud occurred at the client. A payroll clerk set up fictitious employees and the wages were paid into the clerk's own bank account. This clerk has subsequently left the company, but the audit manager is concerned that additional frauds have taken place in the wages department.

Required:

Describe procedures which should be undertaken during the audit of wages as a result of the manager's assessment of the increased risk of fraud. **(5 marks)**

(Total: 10 marks)

INTERNAL CONTROLS AND AUDIT EVIDENCE

154 HUMMINGBIRD *Walk in the footsteps of a top tutor*

Hummingbird Scents Co (Hummingbird) manufactures and sells luxury toiletries; they have been trading for over 20 years and the company's year end is 30 September 2014. Hummingbird sells products to trade customers via its own website; this represents 60% of revenue. Remaining revenue is generated by contracts to supply toiletries to hotels. Below is a description of the sales system.

Hotel revenue

The hotel revenue is made up of four key customers. Hummingbird has one sales clerk, Brenda, who maintains all aspects of this revenue stream; Brenda receives customer orders, raises sales invoices and processes payments. In raising invoices, the sales system automatically inserts the online trade customer prices for products. However, each hotel customer has contracted prices which are lower than the online prices and hence Brenda manually edits the invoices prior to despatch.

Online revenue

New trade customers are set up in the sales ledger master file upon passing suitable credit checks, and a credit limit is set at this stage by the finance director. Customers place online orders up to their pre-set credit limit; they receive an email confirmation and the sales order interfaces into the despatch system. The order number is linked to the customer account number. Goods are despatched daily with a goods despatched note which is referenced to the sales order number but are not sequentially numbered. Hummingbird used to despatch goods via a reliable national courier company. However, to reduce costs they have changed to a cheaper local courier and some orders have been delivered to customers late.

Trade customers' sales invoices are automatically generated by the system on the day the online order is placed. The prices are inserted in accordance with the website rates. Occasionally Hummingbird makes special offers or discounts sales; when this occurs the master file data has to be amended to ensure that the correct prices are used on invoices. This task is usually performed by a senior sales ledger clerk.

Revenue and receivables records

On a monthly basis statements are sent to the hotel customers; a number of trade customers have been requesting monthly statements and Hummingbird is considering this request. The company only reconciles the sales ledger control account at the end of September in order to verify the year-end balance.

Required:

(a) As the external auditor of Hummingbird Co, write a report to management in respect of the sales system described above which:

(i) Identifies and explains SEVEN deficiencies in the sales system; and

(ii) Provides a recommendation to address each of these deficiencies.

A covering letter IS required.

Note: Up to two marks will be awarded within this requirement for presentation and the remaining marks will be split equally between each part. (16 marks)

(b) Describe substantive procedures the auditor should perform to confirm Hummingbird Co's revenue. (4 marks)

(Total: 20 marks)

155 TROMBONE *Walk in the footsteps of a top tutor*

Trombone Co (Trombone) operates a chain of hotels across the country. Trombone employs in excess of 250 permanent employees and its year end is 31 August. You are the audit supervisor of Viola & Co and are currently reviewing the documentation of Trombone's payroll system, detailed below, in preparation for the interim audit.

Trombone's payroll system

Permanent employees work a standard number of hours per week as specified in their employment contract. However, when the hotels are busy, staff can be requested by management to work additional shifts as overtime. This can either be paid on a monthly basis or taken as days off.

Employees record any overtime worked and days taken off on weekly overtime sheets which are sent to the payroll department. The standard hours per employee are automatically set up in the system and the overtime sheets are entered by clerks into the payroll package, which automatically calculates the gross and net pay along with relevant deductions. These calculations are not checked at all. Wages are increased by the rate of inflation each year and the clerks are responsible for updating the standing data in the payroll system.

Employees are paid on a monthly basis by bank transfer for their contracted weekly hours and for any overtime worked in the previous month. If employees choose to be paid for overtime, authorisation is required by department heads of any overtime in excess of 30% of standard hours. If employees choose instead to take days off, the payroll clerks should check back to the 'overtime worked' report; however, this report is not always checked.

The 'overtime worked' report, which details any overtime recorded by employees, is run by the payroll department weekly and emailed to department heads for authorisation. The payroll department asks department heads to only report if there are any errors recorded. Department heads are required to arrange for overtime sheets to be authorised by an alternative responsible official if they are away on annual leave; however, there are instances where this arrangement has not occurred.

The payroll package produces a list of payments per employee; this links into the bank system to produce a list of automatic payments. The finance director reviews the total list of bank transfers and compares this to the total amount to be paid per the payroll records; if any issues arise then the automatic bank transfer can be manually changed by the finance director.

Required:

(a) In respect of the payroll system of Trombone Co:

(i) Identify and explain FIVE deficiencies;

(ii) Recommend a control to address each of these deficiencies; and

(iii) Describe a test of control Viola & Co should perform to assess if each of these controls is operating effectively.

Note: The total marks will be split equally between each part. (15 marks)

(b) Describe substantive procedures you should perform at the final audit to confirm the completeness and accuracy of Trombone Co's payroll expense. (5 marks)

(Total: 20 marks)

156 OREGANO *Walk in the footsteps of a top tutor*

You are a member of the recently formed internal audit department of Oregano Co (Oregano). The company manufactures tinned fruit and vegetables which are supplied to large and small food retailers. Management and those charged with governance of Oregano have concerns about the effectiveness of their sales and despatch system and have asked internal audit to document and review the system.

Sales and despatch system

Sales orders are mainly placed through Oregano's website but some are made via telephone. Online orders are automatically checked against inventory records for availability; telephone orders, however, are checked manually by order clerks after the call. A follow-up call is usually made to customers if there is insufficient inventory. When taking telephone orders, clerks note down the details on plain paper and afterwards they complete a three part pre-printed order form. These order forms are not sequentially numbered and are sent manually to both despatch and the accounts department.

As the company is expanding, customers are able to place online orders which will exceed their agreed credit limit by 10%. Online orders are automatically forwarded to the despatch and accounts department.

A daily pick list is printed by the despatch department and this is used by the warehouse team to despatch goods. The goods are accompanied by a despatch note and all customers are required to sign a copy of this. On return, the signed despatch notes are given to the warehouse team to file.

The sales quantities are entered from the despatch notes and the authorised sales prices are generated by the invoicing system. If a discount has been given, this has to be manually entered by the sales clerk onto the invoice. Due to the expansion of the company, and as there is a large number of sale invoices, extra accounts staff have been asked to help out temporarily with producing the sales invoices. Normally it is only two sales clerks who produce the sales invoices.

Required:

(a) **Describe TWO methods for documenting the sales and despatch system; and for each explain an advantage and a disadvantage of using this method. (6 marks)**

(b) **List TWO control objectives of Oregano Co's sales and despatch system. (2 marks)**

(c) **Identify and explain SIX deficiencies in Oregano Co's sales and despatch system and provide a recommendation to address each of these deficiencies. (12 marks)**

(Total: 20 marks)

Substantive procedures for payroll

Add up
Recalculate
Analytical Procedures
Proof in total
Agree draft F/S wages to [illegible]

157 FOX INDUSTRIES *Walk in the footsteps of a top tutor*

Introduction

Fox Industries Co (Fox) manufactures engineering parts. It has one operating site and a customer base spread across Europe. The company's year end was 30 April 2013. Below is a description of the purchasing and payments system.

Purchasing system

Whenever production materials are required, the relevant department sends a requisition form to the ordering department. An order clerk raises a purchase order and contacts a number of suppliers to see which can despatch the goods first. This supplier is then chosen. The order clerk sends out the purchase order. This is not sequentially numbered and only orders above $5,000 require authorisation.

Purchase invoices are input daily by the purchase ledger clerk, who has been in the role for many years and, as an experienced team member, he does not apply any application controls over the input process. Every week the purchase day book automatically updates the purchase ledger, the purchase ledger is then posted manually to the general ledger by the purchase ledger clerk.

Payments system

Fox maintains a current account and a number of saving (deposit) accounts. The current account is reconciled weekly but the saving (deposit) accounts are only reconciled every two months.

In order to maximise their cash and bank balance, Fox has a policy of delaying payments to all suppliers for as long as possible. Suppliers are paid by a bank transfer. The finance director is given the total amount of the payments list, which he authorises and then processes the bank payments.

Required:

(a) **As the external auditors of Fox Industries Co, write a report to management in respect of the purchasing and payments system described above which:**

(i) **Identifies and explains FIVE deficiencies in the system; and**

(ii) **Explains the possible implication of each deficiency; and**

(iii) **Provides a recommendation to address each deficiency.**

A covering letter IS required.

Note: Up to two marks will be awarded within this requirement for presentation and the remaining marks will be split equally between each part. (17 marks)

(b) **Identify and explain THREE application controls that should be adopted by Fox Industries Co to ensure the completeness and accuracy of the input of purchase invoices. (3 marks)**

(Total: 20 marks)

158 LILY WINDOW GLASS *Walk in the footsteps of a top tutor*

Lily Window Glass Co (Lily) is a glass manufacturer, which operates from a large production facility, where it undertakes continuous production 24 hours a day, seven days a week. Also on this site are two warehouses, where the company's raw materials and finished goods are stored. Lily's year end is 31 December.

Lily is finalising the arrangements for the year-end inventory count, which is to be undertaken on 31 December 2012. The finished windows are stored within 20 aisles of the first warehouse. The second warehouse is for large piles of raw materials, such as sand, used in the manufacture of glass. The following arrangements have been made for the inventory count:

The warehouse manager will supervise the count as he is most familiar with the inventory. There will be ten teams of counters and each team will contain two members of staff, one from the finance and one from the manufacturing department. None of the warehouse staff, other than the manager, will be involved in the count.

Each team will count an aisle of finished goods by counting up and then down each aisle. As this process is systematic, it is not felt that the team will need to flag areas once counted. Once the team has finished counting an aisle, they will hand in their sheets and be given a set for another aisle of the warehouse. In addition to the above, to assist with the inventory counting, there will be two teams of counters from the internal audit department and they will perform inventory counts.

The count sheets are sequentially numbered, and the product codes and descriptions are printed on them but no quantities. If the counters identify any inventory which is not on their sheets, then they are to enter the item on a separate sheet, which is not numbered. Once all counting is complete, the sequence of the sheets is checked and any additional sheets are also handed in at this stage. All sheets are completed in ink.

Any damaged goods identified by the counters will be too heavy to move to a central location, hence they are to be left where they are but the counter is to make a note on the inventory sheets detailing the level of damage.

As Lily undertakes continuous production, there will continue to be movements of raw materials and finished goods in and out of the warehouse during the count. These will be kept to a minimum where possible.

The level of work-in-progress in the manufacturing plant is to be assessed by the warehouse manager. It is likely that this will be an immaterial balance. In addition, the raw materials quantities are to be approximated by measuring the height and width of the raw material piles. In the past this task has been undertaken by a specialist; however, the warehouse manager feels confident that he can perform this task.

Required:

(a) For the inventory count arrangements of Lily Window Glass Co:

(i) Identify and explain SEVEN deficiencies; and

(ii) Provide a recommendation to address each deficiency.

The total marks will be split equally between each part (14 marks)

You are the audit senior of Daffodil & Co and are responsible for the audit of inventory for Lily. You will be attending the year-end inventory count on 31 December 2012.

In addition, your manager wishes to utilise computer-assisted audit techniques for the first time for controls and substantive testing in auditing Lily Window Glass Co's inventory.

Required:

(b) Describe the procedures to be undertaken by the auditor DURING the inventory count of Lily Window Glass Co in order to gain sufficient appropriate audit evidence. (6 marks)

(Total: 20 marks)

159 PEAR INTERNATIONAL *Walk in the footsteps of a top tutor*

Pear International Co (Pear) is a manufacturer of electrical equipment. It has factories across the country and its customer base includes retailers as well as individuals, to whom direct sales are made through their website. The company's year end is 30 September 2012. You are an audit supervisor of Apple & Co and are currently reviewing documentation of Pear's internal control in preparation for the interim audit.

Pear's website allows individuals to order goods directly, and full payment is taken in advance. Currently the website is not integrated into the inventory system and inventory levels are not checked at the time when orders are placed.

Goods are despatched via local couriers; however, they do not always record customer signatures as proof that the customer has received the goods. Over the past 12 months there have been customer complaints about the delay between sales orders and receipt of goods. Pear has investigated these and found that, in each case, the sales order had been entered into the sales system correctly but was not forwarded to the despatch department for fulfilling.

Pear's retail customers undergo credit checks prior to being accepted and credit limits are set accordingly by sales ledger clerks. These customers place their orders through one of the sales team, who decides on sales discount levels.

Raw materials used in the manufacturing process are purchased from a wide range of suppliers. As a result of staff changes in the purchase ledger department, supplier statement reconciliations are no longer performed. Additionally, changes to supplier details in the purchase ledger master file can be undertaken by purchase ledger clerks as well as supervisors.

In the past six months Pear has changed part of its manufacturing process and as a result some new equipment has been purchased, however, there are considerable levels of plant and equipment which are now surplus to requirement. Purchase requisitions for all new equipment have been authorised by production supervisors and little has been done to reduce the surplus of old equipment.

Required:

(a) In respect of the internal control of Pear International Co:

(i) Identify and explain FIVE deficiencies

(ii) Recommend a control to address each of these deficiencies; and

(iii) Describe a test of control Apple & Co would perform to assess if each of these controls is operating effectively. (15 marks)

Pear's directors are considering establishing an internal audit department next year, and the finance director has asked what impact, if any, establishing an internal audit department would have on future external audits performed by Apple & Co.

Required:

(b) Explain the potential impact on the work performed by Apple & Co during the interim and final audits, if Pear International Co was to establish an internal audit department. (5 marks)

(Total: 20 marks)

160 GREYSTONE WALK IN THE FOOTSTEPS OF A TOP TUTOR

(a) Auditors have a responsibility under ISA 265 *Communicating Deficiencies in Internal Control to those Charged with Governance and Management,* to communicate deficiencies in internal controls. In particular SIGNIFICANT deficiencies in internal controls must be communicated in writing to those charged with governance.

Required:

Explain examples of matters the auditor should consider in determining whether a deficiency in internal controls is significant. (3 marks)

Greystone Co is a retailer of ladies clothing and accessories. It operates in many countries around the world and has expanded steadily from its base in Europe. Its main market is aimed at 15 to 35 year olds and its prices are mid to low range. The company's year end was 30 September 2010.

In the past the company has bulk ordered its clothing and accessories twice a year. However, if their goods failed to meet the key fashion trends then this resulted in significant inventory write downs. As a result of this the company has recently introduced a just in time ordering system. The fashion buyers make an assessment nine months in advance as to what the key trends are likely to be, these goods are sourced from their suppliers but only limited numbers are initially ordered.

Greystone Co has an internal audit department but at present their only role is to perform regular inventory counts at the stores.

Ordering process

Each country has a purchasing manager who decides on the initial inventory levels for each store, this is not done in conjunction with store or sales managers. These quantities are communicated to the central buying department at the head office in Europe. An ordering clerk amalgamates all country orders by specified regions of countries, such as Central Europe and North America, and passes them to the purchasing director to review and authorise.

As the goods are sold, it is the store manager's responsibility to re-order the goods through the purchasing manager; they are prompted weekly to review inventory levels as although the goods are just in time, it can still take up to four weeks for goods to be received in store.

It is not possible to order goods from other branches of stores as all ordering must be undertaken through the purchasing manager. If a customer requests an item of clothing, which is unavailable in a particular store, then the customer is provided with other branch telephone numbers or recommended to try the company website.

Goods received and invoicing

To speed up the ordering to receipt of goods cycle, the goods are delivered directly from the suppliers to the individual stores. On receipt of goods the quantities received are checked by a sales assistant against the supplier's delivery note, and then the assistant produces a goods received note (GRN). This is done at quiet times of the day so as to maximise sales. The checked GRNs are sent to head office for matching with purchase invoices.

As purchase invoices are received they are manually matched to GRNs from the stores, this can be a very time consuming process as some suppliers may have delivered to over 500 stores. Once the invoice has been agreed then it is sent to the purchasing director for authorisation. It is at this stage that the invoice is entered onto the purchase ledger.

Required:

(b) In respect of the purchasing system above:

(i) Identify and explain SIX deficiencies in that system

(ii) Provide a recommendation to address each deficiency **(12 marks)**

(c) Describe substantive procedures the auditor should perform on the year-end trade payables of Greystone Co. **(5 marks)**

(Total: 20 marks)

161 SMOOTHBRUSH PAINTS *Walk in the footsteps of a top tutor*

Introduction and client background

You are an audit senior in Staple and Co and you are commencing the planning of the audit of Smoothbrush Paints Co for the year ending 31 August 2010.

Smoothbrush Paints Co is a paint manufacturer and has been trading for over 50 years, it operates from one central site, which includes the production facility, warehouse and administration offices.

To avoid the disruption of a year end inventory count, Smoothbrush has this year introduced a continuous/perpetual inventory counting system. The warehouse has been divided into 12 areas and these are each to be counted once over the year. The counting team includes a member of the internal audit department and a warehouse staff member. The following procedures have been adopted:

(1) The team prints the inventory quantities and descriptions from the system and these records are then compared to the inventory physically present.

(2) Any discrepancies in relation to quantities are noted on the inventory sheets, including any items not listed on the sheets but present in the warehouse area.

(3) Any damaged or old items are noted and they are removed from the inventory sheets.

(4) The sheets are then passed to the finance department for adjustments to be made to the records when the count has finished.

(5) During the counts there will continue to be inventory movements with goods arriving and leaving the warehouse.

At the year end it is proposed that the inventory will be based on the underlying records.

Required:

List and explain suitable controls that should operate over the continuous/perpetual inventory counting system, to ensure the completeness and accuracy of the existing inventory records at Smoothbrush Paints Co.

(Total: 10 marks)

162 SHINY HAPPY WINDOWS *Walk in the footsteps of a top tutor*

(a) **Explain the terms 'control objectives' and 'control procedures' and explain the relationship between them.** **(3 marks)**

(b) Shiny Happy Windows Co (SHW) is a window cleaning company. Customers' windows are cleaned monthly, the window cleaner then posts a stamped addressed envelope for payment through the customer's front door.

SHW has a large number of receivable balances and these customers pay by cheque or cash, which is received in the stamped addressed envelopes in the post. The following procedures are applied to the cash received cycle:

(1) A junior clerk from the accounts department opens the post and if any cheques or cash have been sent, she records the receipts in the cash received log and then places all the monies into the locked small cash box.

(2) The contents of the cash box are counted each day and every few days these sums are banked by which ever member of the finance team is available.

(3) The cashier records the details of the cash received log into the cash receipts day book and also updates the sales ledger.

(4) Usually on a monthly basis the cashier performs a bank reconciliation, which he then files, if he misses a month then he catches this up in the following month's reconciliation.

Required:

For the cash cycle of SHW:

(i) Identify and explain FOUR deficiencies in the system **(4 marks)**

(ii) Suggest controls to address each of these deficiencies; and **(4 marks)**

(iii) List tests of controls the auditor of SHW would perform to assess if the controls are operating effectively. **(4 marks)**

(c) **Describe substantive procedures an auditor would perform in verifying a company's bank balance.** **(5 marks)**

(Total: 20 marks)

163 MATALAS *Walk in the footsteps of a top tutor*

Matalas Co sells cars, car parts and petrol from 25 different locations in one country. Each branch has up to 20 staff working there, although most of the accounting systems are designed and implemented from the company's head office. All accounting systems, apart from petty cash, are computerised, with the internal audit department frequently advising and implementing controls within those systems.

You are an audit manager in the internal audit department of Matalas. You are currently auditing the petty cash systems at the different branches. Your initial systems notes on petty cash contain the following information:

(1) The average petty cash balance at each branch is $5,000.

(2) Average monthly expenditure is $1,538, with amounts ranging from $1 to $500.

(3) Petty cash is kept in a lockable box on a bookcase in the accounts office.

(4) Vouchers for expenditure are signed by the person incurring that expenditure to confirm they have received re-imbursement from petty cash.

(5) Vouchers are recorded in the petty cash book by the accounts clerk; each voucher records the date, reason for the expenditure, amount of expenditure and person incurring that expenditure.

(6) Petty cash is counted every month by the accounts clerk, who is in charge of the cash. The petty cash balance is then reimbursed using the 'imprest' system and the journal entry produced to record expenditure in the general ledger.

(7) The cheque to reimburse petty cash is signed by the accountant at the branch at the same time as the journal entry to the general ledger is reviewed.

Required:

Explain the internal control deficiencies in the petty cash system at Matalas Co. For each deficiency, recommend a control to overcome that deficiency.

(Total: 10 marks)

164 JACKDAW MOTORS *Walk in the footsteps of a top tutor*

Jackdaw Motor Cars Co (Jackdaw) manufactures a range of motor cars and its year end is 31 January 2015. You are the audit supervisor of Puffin & Co and are currently preparing the audit programmes for the year-end audit of Jackdaw. You have had a meeting with your audit manager and he has notified you of a number of issues identified during the audit risk assessment process.

Land and buildings

Jackdaw have a policy of revaluing land and buildings, this is undertaken on a rolling basis over a five-year period. During the year Jackdaw requested an external valuer to revalue a number of properties, including a warehouse purchased in May 2014. Depreciation is charged on a pro rata basis.

Work in progress

Jackdaw undertakes continuous production of cars, 24 hours a day, seven days a week. An inventory count is to be undertaken at the year end and Puffin & Co will attend. You are responsible for the audit of work in progress (WIP) and will be part of the team attending the count as well as the final audit. WIP constitutes the partly assembled cars at the year end and this balance is likely to be material. Jackdaw values WIP according to percentage of completion, and standard costs are then applied to these percentages.

Required:

(a) **Explain the factors Puffin & Co should consider when placing reliance on the work of the independent valuer.** **(5 marks)**

(b) **Describe the substantive procedures the auditor should perform to obtain sufficient and appropriate audit evidence in relation to:**

  (i) **The revaluation of land and buildings and the recently purchased warehouse; and** **(6 marks)**

  (ii) **The valuation of work in progress.** **(4 marks)**

(c) During the audit, your team has identified an error in the valuation of work in progress, as a number of the assumptions contain out of date information. The directors of Jackdaw have indicated that they do not wish to amend the financial statements.

Required:

Explain the steps Puffin & Co should now take and the impact on the audit report in relation to the directors' refusal to amend the financial statements. **(5 marks)**

(Total: 20 marks)

165 ROSE LEISURE CLUB *Walk in the footsteps of a top tutor*

Rose Leisure Club Co (Rose) operates a chain of health and fitness clubs. Its year end was 31 October 2012. You are the audit manager and the year-end audit is due to commence shortly. The following matters have been brought to your attention.

(i) **Trade payables and accruals**

Rose's finance director has notified you that an error occurred in the closing of the purchase ledger at the year end. Rather than it closing on 1 November, it accidentally closed one week earlier on 25 October. All purchase invoices received between 25 October and the year end have been posted to the 2013 year-end purchase ledger. **(5 marks)**

(ii) **Receivables**

Rose's trade receivables have historically been low as most members pay monthly in advance. However, during the year a number of companies have taken up group memberships at Rose and hence the receivables balance is now material. The audit senior has undertaken a receivables circularisation for the balances at the year end; however, there are a number who have not responded and a number of responses with differences. **(5 marks)**

Required:

Describe substantive procedures you would perform to obtain sufficient and appropriate audit evidence in relation to the above matters.

Note: The mark allocation is shown against each of the matters above.

(Total: 10 marks)

166 PINEAPPLE BEACH HOTEL *Walk in the footsteps of a top tutor*

Pineapple Beach Hotel Co (Pineapple) operates a hotel providing accommodation, leisure facilities and restaurants. Its year end was 30 April 2012. You are the audit senior of Berry & Co and are currently preparing the audit programmes for the year end audit of Pineapple. You are reviewing the notes of last week's meeting between the audit manager and finance director where two material issues were discussed.

Depreciation

Pineapple incurred significant capital expenditure during the year on updating the leisure facilities for the hotel. The finance director has proposed that the new leisure equipment should be depreciated over 10 years using the straight-line method.

Food poisoning

Pineapple's directors received correspondence in March from a group of customers who attended a wedding at the hotel. They have alleged that they suffered severe food poisoning from food eaten at the hotel and are claiming substantial damages. Pineapple's lawyers have received the claim and believe that the lawsuit against the company is unlikely to be successful.

Required:

Describe substantive procedures to obtain sufficient and appropriate audit evidence in relation to the above two issues.

Note: The total marks will be split equally between each issue.

(Total: 10 marks)

167 TIRROL WALK IN THE FOOTSTEPS OF A TOP TUTOR

ONLINE QUESTION ASSISTANCE

TIMED QUESTION WITH ONLINE TUTOR DEBRIEF

Following a competitive tender, your audit firm Cal & Co has just gained a new audit client Tirrol Co. You are the manager in charge of planning the audit work. Tirrol Co's year end is 30 June 2009 with a scheduled date to complete the audit of 15 August 2009. The date now is 3 June 2009.

Tirrol Co provides repair services to motor vehicles from 25 different locations. All inventory, sales and purchasing systems are computerised, with each location maintaining its own computer system. The software in each location is the same because the programs were written specifically for Tirrol Co by a reputable software house. Data from each location is amalgamated on a monthly basis at Tirrol Co's head office to produce management and financial accounts.

You are currently planning your audit approach for Tirrol Co. One option being considered is to re-write Cal & Co's audit software to interrogate the computerised inventory systems in each location of Tirrol Co (except for head office) as part of inventory valuation testing. However, you have also been informed that any computer testing will have to be on a live basis and you are aware that July is a major holiday period for your audit firm.

Required:

(a) (i) **Explain the benefits of using audit software in the audit of Tirrol Co. (4 marks)**

(ii) **Explain the problems that may be encountered in the audit of Tirrol Co and for each problem, explain how that problem could be overcome. (10 marks)**

(b) Following a discussion with the management at Tirrol Co you now understand that the internal audit department are prepared to assist with the statutory audit. Specifically, the chief internal auditor is prepared to provide you with documentation on the computerised inventory systems at Tirrol Co. The documentation provides details of the software and shows diagrammatically how transactions are processed through the inventory system. This documentation can be used to significantly decrease the time needed to understand the computer systems and enable audit software to be written for this year's audit.

Required:

Explain how you will evaluate the computer systems documentation produced by the internal audit department in order to place reliance on it during your audit. (6 marks)

(Total: 20 marks)

Calculate your allowed time, allocate the time to the separate parts..............

168 CONTROLS

(a) ISA 315 *Identifying and Assessing the Risks of Material Misstatement through Understanding the Entity and Its Environment* requires auditors to understand the entity's internal control. An entity's internal control is made up of several components.

Required:

State the FIVE components of an entity's internal control and give a brief explanation of each component. (5 marks)

(b) Auditors are required to document their understanding of the client's internal controls. There are various options available for recording the internal control system. Two of these options are narrative notes and internal control questionnaires.

Required:

Describe the advantages and disadvantages to the auditor of narrative notes and internal control questionnaires as methods for documenting the system. (5 marks)

(Total: 10 marks)

169 AUDIT PROCEDURES AND EVIDENCE

(a) **(i)** **Define a 'test of control' and provide an example of a test of control in relation to the audit of wages and salaries; and**

(ii) **Define a 'substantive procedure' and provide an example of a substantive procedure in relation to the audit of wages and salaries.**

Note: The total marks will be split equally between each part. **(4 marks)**

(b) ISA 500 *Audit Evidence* requires auditors to obtain sufficient and appropriate audit evidence. Appropriateness is a measure of the quality of audit evidence; that is, its relevance and its reliability.

Required:

Identify and explain THREE factors which influence the reliability of audit evidence. **(3 marks)**

(c) **Describe THREE substantive procedures an auditor should perform to confirm revenue.** **(3 marks)**

(Total: 10 marks)

170 EXPERTS/SAMPLING/ASSERTIONS ***Walk in the footsteps of a top tutor***

(a) ISA 620 *Using the Work of an Auditor's Expert* explains how an auditor may use an expert to obtain audit evidence.

Required:

Explain THREE factors that the external auditor should consider when assessing the competence and objectivity of the expert. **(3 marks)**

(b) **List and explain FOUR methods of selecting a sample of items to test from a population in accordance with ISA 530 *Audit Sampling*.** **(4 marks)**

(c) **List THREE assertions relevant to the audit of tangible non-current assets and state one audit procedure which provides appropriate evidence for each assertion.** **(3 marks)**

(Total: 10 marks)

171 SAMPLING

Required:

(a) **Define the term 'sampling'.** **(2 marks)**

(b) **In the context of ISA 530 *Audit Sampling*, explain and provide examples of the terms 'sampling risk' and 'non-sampling' risk.** **(4 marks)**

(c) **Briefly explain how sampling and non-sampling risk can be controlled by the audit firm.** **(4 marks)**

(Total: 10 marks)

172 RELIABILITY/ASSERTIONS/INTERIM AND FINAL AUDITS

Walk in the footsteps of a top tutor

(a) ISA 500 *Audit Evidence* requires audit evidence to be reliable.

Required:

List THREE factors that influence the reliability of audit evidence. (3 marks)

(b) **List and explain FOUR assertions from ISA 315 *Identifying and Assessing the Risk of Material Misstatement Through Understanding the Entity and its Environment* that relate to the recording of classes of transactions. (4 marks)**

(c) **Explain the difference between the interim audit and the final audit. (3 marks)**

(Total: 10 marks)

173 EXTERNAL CONFIRMATIONS ***Walk in the footsteps of a top tutor***

(a) **Explain the purpose of obtaining external confirmations. (1 mark)**

(b) **Describe the steps to be taken to obtain a bank confirmation letter. (5 marks)**

(c) **Other than a bank confirmation, describe FOUR types of external confirmation that can be obtained by an auditor. (4 marks)**

(Total: 10 marks)

174 AUDIT PROCEDURES – PROVISIONS

(a) Rose Leisure Club has recently announced its plans to reorganise its health and fitness clubs. This will involve closing some locations for refurbishment, retraining some existing staff and disposing of some surplus assets. These plans were agreed at a board meeting in October and announced to their shareholders on 29 October 2013. The company is proposing to make a reorganisation provision in the financial statements for the year ended 31 October 2013.

Required:

Describe the substantive procedures the auditor should perform to obtain sufficient appropriate evidence for the provision. (5 marks)

(b) Chuck Industries has decided to outsource its sales ledger department and as a result it is making 14 employees redundant. A redundancy provision, which is material, will be included in the draft accounts.

Required:

Describe substantive procedures you should perform to confirm the redundancy provision at the year end. (5 marks)

(Total: 10 marks)

175 CAAT'S

(a) In relation to INVENTORY, describe FOUR audit procedures that could be carried out using computer-assisted audit techniques (CAATS). **(4 marks)**

(b) Explain the potential advantages of using CAATs. **(3 marks)**

(c) Explain the potential disadvantages of using CAATs. **(3 marks)**

(Total: 10 marks)

176 AUDIT PROCEDURES – PURCHASES *Walk in the footsteps of a top tutor*

The auditor has a responsibility to design audit procedures to obtain sufficient and appropriate evidence. There are various audit procedures for obtaining evidence, such as external confirmation.

Required:

Apart from external confirmation:

(i) State and explain FIVE procedures for obtaining evidence. **(5 marks)**

(ii) For each procedure, describe an example relevant to the audit of purchases and other expenses. **(5 marks)**

(Total: 10 marks)

ETHICS

177 CINNAMON *Walk in the footsteps of a top tutor*

Salt & Pepper & Co (Salt & Pepper) is a firm of Chartered Certified Accountants which has seen its revenue decline steadily over the past few years. The firm is looking to increase its revenue and client base and so has developed a new advertising strategy where it has guaranteed that its audits will minimise disruption to companies as they will not last longer than two weeks. In addition, Salt & Pepper has offered all new audit clients a free accounts preparation service for the first year of the engagement, as it is believed that time spent on the audit will be reduced if the firm has produced the financial statements.

The firm is seeking to reduce audit costs and has therefore decided not to update the engagement letters of existing clients, on the basis that these letters do not tend to change much on a yearly basis. One of Salt & Pepper's existing clients has proposed that this year's audit fee should be based on a percentage of their final pre-tax profit. The partners are excited about this option as they believe it will increase the overall audit fee.

Salt & Pepper has recently obtained a new audit client, Cinnamon Brothers Co (Cinnamon), whose year end is 31 December. Cinnamon requires their audit to be completed by the end of February; however, this is a very busy time for Salt & Pepper and so it is intended to use more junior staff as they are available. Additionally, in order to save time and cost, Salt & Pepper have not contacted Cinnamon's previous auditors.

Required:

(i) **Identify and explain FIVE ethical risks which arise from the above actions of Salt & Pepper & Co; and**

(ii) **For each ethical risk explain the steps which Salt & Pepper & Co should adopt to reduce the risks arising.**

Note: The total marks will be split equally between each part.

(Total: 10 marks)

178 GOOFY *Walk in the footsteps of a top tutor*

You are an audit manager in NAB & Co, a large audit firm which specialises in the audit of retailers. The firm currently audits Goofy Co, a food retailer, but Goofy Co's main competitor, Mickey Co, has approached the audit firm to act as auditors. Both companies are highly competitive and Goofy Co is concerned that if NAB & Co audits both companies then confidential information could pass across to Mickey Co.

Required:

(a) **Explain the safeguards that your firm should implement to ensure that this conflict of interest is properly managed.** **(4 marks)**

(b) The audit engagement partner for Goofy Co has been in place for approximately six years and her son has just accepted a job offer from Goofy Co as a sales manager; this role would entitle him to shares in Goofy Co as part of his remuneration package. If NAB & Co is appointed as internal as well as external auditors, then Goofy Co has suggested that the external audit fee should be renegotiated with at least 20% of the fee being based on the profit after tax of the company as they feel that this will align the interests of NAB & Co and Goofy Co.

Required:

From the information above, explain the ethical threats which may affect the independence of NAB & Co in respect of the audit of Goofy Co, and for each threat explain how it may be reduced. **(6 marks)**

(Total: 10 marks)

179 ORANGE FINANCIALS *Walk in the footsteps of a top tutor*

You are the audit manager of Currant & Co and you are planning the audit of Orange Financials Co (Orange), who specialise in the provision of loans and financial advice to individuals and companies. Currant & Co has audited Orange for many years.

The directors are planning to list Orange on a stock exchange within the next few months and have asked if the engagement partner can attend the meetings with potential investors. In addition, as the finance director of Orange is likely to be quite busy with the listing, he has asked if Currant & Co can produce the financial statements for the current year.

During the year, the assistant finance director of Orange left and joined Currant & Co as a partner. It has been suggested that due to his familiarity with Orange, he should be appointed to provide an independent partner review for the audit.

Once Orange obtains its stock exchange listing it will require several assignments to be undertaken, for example, obtaining advice about corporate governance best practice. Currant & Co is very keen to be appointed to these engagements, however, Orange has implied that in order to gain this work Currant & Co needs to complete the external audit quickly and with minimal questions/issues.

The finance director has informed you that once the stock exchange listing has been completed, he would like the engagement team to attend a weekend away at a luxury hotel with his team, as a thank you for all their hard work. In addition, he has offered a senior member of the engagement team a short-term loan at a significantly reduced interest rate.

Required:

(i) Explain FIVE ethical threats which may affect the independence of Currant & Co's audit of Orange Financials Co; and

(ii) For each threat explain how it might be reduced to an acceptable level. (10 marks)

(Total: 10 marks)

180 LV FONES *Walk in the footsteps of a top tutor*

Online question assistance

You are the audit manager of Jones & Co and you are planning the audit of LV Fones Co, which has been an audit client for four years and specialises in manufacturing luxury mobile phones.

During the planning stage of the audit you have obtained the following information. The employees of LV Fones Co are entitled to purchase mobile phones at a discount of 10%. The audit team has in previous years been offered the same level of staff discount.

During the year the financial controller of LV Fones was ill and hence unable to work. The company had no spare staff able to fulfil the role and hence a qualified audit senior of Jones & Co was seconded to the client for three months. The audit partner has recommended that the audit senior work on the audit as he has good knowledge of the client. The fee income derived from LV Fones was boosted by this engagement and along with the audit and tax fee, now accounts for 16% of the firm's total fees.

From a review of the correspondence files you note that the partner and the finance director have known each other socially for many years and in fact went on holiday together last summer with their families. As a result of this friendship the partner has not yet spoken to the client about the fee for last year's audit, 20% of which is still outstanding.

Required:

(i) Explain the ethical threats which may affect the independence of Jones & Co's audit of LV Fones Co. (5 marks)

(ii) For each threat explain how it might be avoided. (5 marks)

(Total: 10 marks)

181 ETHICS

(a) **Identify and explain each of the FIVE fundamental principles contained within ACCA's Code *of Ethics and Conduct.*** **(5 marks)**

(b) **Explain FIVE safeguards which can be applied to reduce ethical threats to an acceptable level.** **(5 marks)**

(Total: 10 marks)

182 ETHICAL THREATS

(i) **Explain the FIVE threats contained within ACCA's Code of Ethics and Conduct** **(5 marks)**

(ii) **For each threat list ONE example of a circumstance that may create the threat and an appropriate safeguard.** **(5 marks)**

(Total: 10 marks)

183 CONFIDENTIALITY *Walk in the footsteps of a top tutor*

(a) **Explain the situations where an auditor may disclose confidential information about a client.** **(6 marks)**

(b) **Explain what is meant by confidential information and why it is important for the auditor to not disclose confidential information without proper reason.** **(4 marks)**

(Total: 10 marks)

CORPORATE GOVERNANCE AND INTERNAL AUDIT

184 BLUEBIRD ENTERPRISES *Walk in the footsteps of a top tutor*

Bluebird Enterprises Co (Bluebird) is a retail company planning to list on a stock exchange within the next six months, and management has been advised by the company's auditors about the need for compliance with corporate governance provisions. In particular, the finance director is looking to recruit non-executive directors as he understands that Bluebird will need to establish an audit committee.

The finance director has two potential non-executive directors whom he is considering approaching to join the board of Bluebird. Antony Goldfinch is currently an executive sales director of a listed multi-national banking company; he sits on an audit committee of another company as a non-executive director and is agreeable to being paid a fixed fee which is not related to profits. Jacob Mallard is currently a finance director of a small retail company, which does not compete with Bluebird; he has expressed an interest in a fixed seven year contract and he is the brother of Bluebird's chief executive.

Required

(a) Explain the benefits to Bluebird Enterprises Co of establishing an audit committee. (4 marks)

(b) Discuss the advantages and disadvantages of appointing:

(i) Anthony Goldfinch; and

(ii) Jacob Mallard

as non-executive directors of Bluebird Enterprises Co.

Note: The total marks will be split equally between each part. (6 marks)

(Total: 10 marks)

Homework

185 SAXOPHONE ENTERPRISES *Walk in the footsteps of a top tutor*

Saxophone Enterprises Co (Saxophone) has been trading for 15 years selling insurance and has recently become a listed company. In accordance with corporate governance principles Saxophone maintains a small internal audit department. The directors feel that the team needs to increase in size and specialist skills are required, but they are unsure whether to recruit more internal auditors, or to outsource the whole function to their external auditors, Cello & Co.

Saxophone is required to comply with corporate governance principles in order to maintain its listed status; hence the finance director has undertaken a review of whether or not the company complies.

Bill Bassoon is the chairman of Saxophone, until last year he was the chief executive. Bill is unsure if Saxophone needs more non-executive directors as there are currently three non-executive directors out of the eight board members. He is considering appointing one of his close friends, who is a retired chief executive of a manufacturing company, as a non-executive director.

The finance director, Jessie Oboe, decides on the amount of remuneration each director is paid. Currently all remuneration is in the form of an annual bonus based on profits. Jessie is considering setting up an audit committee, but has not undertaken this task yet as she is very busy. A new sales director was appointed nine months ago. He has yet to undertake his board training as this is normally provided by the chief executive and this role is currently vacant.

There are a large number of shareholders and therefore the directors believe that it is impractical and too costly to hold an annual general meeting of shareholders. Instead, the board has suggested sending out the financial statements and any voting resolutions by email; shareholders can then vote on the resolutions via email.

Required:

(a) Explain the advantages and disadvantages for each of Saxophone Enterprises Co AND Cello & Co of outsourcing the internal audit department.

Note: The total marks will be split as follows:

Saxophone Enterprises Co (8 marks)

Cello & Co (2 marks) (10 marks)

(b) In respect of the corporate governance of Saxophone Enterprises Co:

(i) Identify and explain FIVE corporate governance weaknesses; and

(ii) Provide a recommendation to address each weakness.

Note: The total marks will be split equally between each part. (10 marks)

(Total: 20 marks)

186 BUSH-BABY HOTELS

Bush-Baby Hotels Co operates a chain of 18 hotels located across the country. Each hotel has bedrooms, a restaurant and leisure club facilities. Most visitors to the restaurant and leisure club are hotel guests; however, these facilities are open to the public as well. Hotel guests generally charge any costs to their room but other visitors must make payment directly to the hotel staff.

During the year, senior management noticed an increased level of cash discrepancies and inventory discrepancies, and they suspect that some employees have been stealing cash and goods from the hotels. They are keen to prevent this from reoccurring and are considering establishing an internal audit department to undertake a fraud investigation.

Required:

(a) Explain how the new internal audit department of Bush-Baby Hotels Co could assist the directors in preventing and detecting fraud and error. (3 marks)

(b) Describe the limitations of Bush-Baby Hotels Co establishing and maintaining an internal audit department. (2 marks)

The directors would like the internal audit department to have as broad a role as possible, as this will make the decision to recruit an internal audit department more cost effective.

Required:

(c) Describe additional functions, other than fraud investigations, the directors of Bush-Baby Hotels Co could ask the internal audit department to undertake. (5 marks)

(Total: 10 marks)

187 CONOY *Walk in the footsteps of a top tutor*

Timed question with Online tutor debrief

Conoy Co designs and manufactures luxury motor vehicles. The company employs 2,500 staff and consistently makes a net profit of between 10% and 15% of sales. Conoy Co is not listed; its shares are held by 15 individuals, most of them from the same family. The maximum shareholding is 15% of the share capital.

The executive directors are drawn mainly from the shareholders. There are no non-executive directors because the company legislation in Conoy Co's jurisdiction does not require any. The executive directors are very successful in running Conoy Co, partly from their training in production and management techniques, and partly from their 'hands-on' approach providing motivation to employees.

The board are considering a significant expansion of the company. However, the company's bankers are concerned with the standard of financial reporting as the financial director (FD) has recently left Conoy Co. The board are delaying provision of additional financial information until a new FD is appointed.

Conoy Co does have an internal audit department, although the chief internal auditor frequently comments that the board of Conoy Co do not understand his reports or provide sufficient support for his department or the internal control systems within Conoy Co. The board of Conoy Co concur with this view. Anders & Co, the external auditors have also expressed concern in this area and the fact that the internal audit department focuses work on control systems, not financial reporting. Anders & Co are appointed by and report to the board of Conoy Co.

The board of Conoy Co are considering a proposal from the chief internal auditor to establish an audit committee. The committee would consist of one executive director, the chief internal auditor as well as three new appointees. One appointee would have a non-executive seat on the board of directors.

Required:

Discuss the benefits to Conoy Co of forming an audit committee. **(10 marks)**

(Total: 10 marks)

Calculate your allowed time, allocate the time to the separate parts..............

188 MONTEHODGE

MonteHodge Co has a sales income of $253 million and employs 1,200 people in 15 different locations. MonteHodge Co provides various financial services from pension and investment advice to individuals, to maintaining cash books and cash forecasting in small to medium-sized companies. The company is owned by six shareholders, who belong to the same family; it is not listed on any stock-exchange and the shareholders have no intention of applying for a listing. However, an annual audit is required by statute and additional regulation of the financial services sector is expected in the near future.

Most employees are provided with on-line, real-time computer systems, which present financial and stock market information to enable the employees to provide up-to-date advice to their clients. Accounting systems record income, which is based on fees generated from investment advice. Expenditure is mainly fixed, being salaries, office rent, lighting and heating, etc. Internal control systems are limited; the directors tending to trust staff and being more concerned with making profits than implementing detailed controls.

Four of the shareholders are board members, with one member being the chairman and chief executive officer. The financial accountant is not qualified, although has many years experience in preparing financial statements.

Required:

Discuss the reasons for and against having an internal audit department in MonteHodge Co. **(10 marks)**

(Total: 10 marks)

189 INTERNAL AUDIT

(a) Explain the factors to be taken into account when assessing the need for internal audit. (5 marks)

(b) Describe additional assignments that an internal audit department can be asked to perform by those charged with governance. (5 marks)

(Total: 10 marks)

COMPLETION AND REPORTING

190 BULLFINCH *Walk in the footsteps of a top tutor*

(a) ISA 700 *Forming an Opinion and Reporting on Financial Statements* requires auditors to produce an audit report. This report should contain a number of consistent elements so that users are able to understand what the audit report means.

Required:

Describe FOUR elements of an unmodified auditor's report and for each explain why they are included. (4 marks)

(b) Bullfinch.com is a website design company whose year end was 31 October 2014. The audit is almost complete and the financial statements are due to be signed shortly. Revenue for the year is $11.2 million and profit before tax is $3.8 million. A key customer, with a receivables balance at the year end of $283,000, has just notified Bullfinch.com that they are experiencing cash flow difficulties and so are unable to make any payments for the foreseeable future. The finance director has notified the auditor that he will write this balance off as an irrecoverable debt in the 2015 financial statements.

Required:

(i) Explain whether or not the 2014 financial statements require amendment; and

(ii) Describe audit procedures which should be performed in order to form a conclusion on any required amendment.

Note: The total marks will be split equally between each part. (6 marks)

(Total: 10 marks)

191 CLARINET *Walk in the footsteps of a top tutor*

Clarinet Co (Clarinet) is a computer hardware specialist and has been trading for over five years. The company is funded partly through overdrafts and loans and also by several large shareholders; the year end is 30 April.

Clarinet has experienced significant growth in previous years; however, in the current year a new competitor, Drums Design Co (Drums), has entered the market and through competitive pricing has gained considerable market share from Clarinet. One of Clarinet's larger customers has stopped trading with them and has moved its business to Drums. In addition, a number of Clarinet's specialist developers have left the company and joined Drums. Clarinet has found it difficult to replace these employees due to the level of their skills and knowledge. Clarinet has just received notification that its main supplier who provides the company with specialist electrical equipment has ceased to trade.

Clarinet is looking to develop new products to differentiate itself from the rest of its competitors. It has approached its shareholders to finance this development; however, they declined to invest further in Clarinet. Clarinet's loan is long term and it has met all repayments on time. The overdraft has increased significantly over the year and the directors have informed you that the overdraft facility is due for renewal next month, and they are confident it will be renewed.

The directors have produced a cash flow forecast which shows a significantly worsening position over the coming 12 months. The auditors have been informed that Clarinet's bankers will not make a decision on the overdraft facility until after the audit report is completed. The directors have now agreed to include some going concern disclosures.

Required:

(a) Explain SIX potential indicators that Clarinet Co is not a going concern. (6 marks)

(b) Describe the impact on the audit report of Clarinet Co if the auditor believes the company is a going concern but that this is subject to a material uncertainty. (4 marks)

(Total: 10 marks)

192 PAPRIKA *Walk in the footsteps of a top tutor*

You are an audit manager in Brown & Co and you are nearing completion of the audit of Paprika & Co (Paprika). The audit senior has produced extracts below from the draft audit report for Paprika.

Auditor's responsibility

(1) Our responsibility is to express an opinion on all pages of the financial statements based on our audit. We conducted our audit in accordance with most of the International Standards on Auditing.

(2) Those standards require that we comply with ethical requirements and plan and perform the audit to obtain maximum assurance as to whether the financial statements are free from all misstatements whether caused by fraud or error.

(3) We have a responsibility to prevent and detect fraud and error and to prepare the financial statements in accordance with International Financial Reporting Standards.

(4) An audit involves performing procedures to obtain evidence about the amounts and disclosures in the financial statements. The procedures selected depend on the availability and experience of audit team members. We considered internal controls relevant to the entity; and express an opinion on the effectiveness of these internal controls.

(5) We did not evaluate the overall presentation of the financial statements, as this is management's responsibility. We considered the reasonableness of any new accounting estimates made by management. We did not review the appropriateness of accounting policies as these are the same as last year. In order to confirm raw material inventory quantities, we relied on the work undertaken by an independent expert.

The extracts are numbered to help you refer to them in your answer.

Required:

For the above audit report extracts, identify and explain FIVE elements of this report which require amendment.

Note: Redrafted audit report extracts are not required. **(10 marks)**

(Total: 10 marks)

193 PANDA *Walk in the footsteps of a top tutor*

(a) Panda Co manufactures chemicals and has a factory and four offsite storage locations for finished goods. Panda Co's year end was 30 April 2013. The final audit is almost complete and the financial statements and audit report are due to be signed next week. Revenue for the year is $55 million and profit before taxation is $5.6 million.

The following event has occurred subsequent to the year end. No amendments or disclosures have been made in the financial statements.

Explosion

An explosion occurred at the smallest of the four offsite storage locations on 20 May 2013. This resulted in some damage to inventory and property, plant and equipment. Panda Co's management have investigated the cause of the explosion and believe that they are unlikely to be able to claim on their insurance. Management of Panda Co has estimated that the value of damaged inventory and property, plant and equipment was $0.9 million and it now has no scrap value.

Required:

(i) Explain whether the financial statements require amendment; and

(ii) Describe audit procedures that should be performed in order to form a conclusion on any required amendment. **(6 marks)**

(b) The directors do not wish to make any amendments or disclosures to the financial statements for the explosion.

Required:

Explain the impact on the audit report should this issue remain unresolved. **(4 marks)**

(Total: 10 marks)

194 VIOLET & CO *Walk in the footsteps of a top tutor*

You are the audit manager of Violet & Co and you are currently reviewing the audit files for several of your clients for which the audit fieldwork is complete. The audit seniors have raised the following issues:

Daisy Designs Co (Daisy)

Daisy's year end is 30 September, however, subsequent to the year end the company's sales ledger has been corrupted by a computer virus. Daisy's finance director was able to produce the financial statements prior to this occurring; however, the audit team has been unable to access the sales ledger to undertake detailed testing of revenue or year-end receivables. All other accounting records are unaffected and there are no backups available for the sales ledger. Daisy's revenue is $15.6m, its receivables are $3.4m and profit before tax is $2m.

Fuchsia Enterprises Co (Fuchsia)

Fuchsia has experienced difficult trading conditions and as a result it has lost significant market share. The cash flow forecast has been reviewed during the audit fieldwork and it shows a significant net cash outflow. Management are confident that further funding can be obtained and so have prepared the financial statements on a going concern basis with no additional disclosures; the audit senior is highly skeptical about this. The prior year financial statements showed a profit before tax of $1.2m; however, the current year loss before tax is $4.4m and the forecast net cash outflow for the next 12 months is $3.2m.

Required:

For each of the two issues:

(i) Discuss the issue, including an assessment of whether it is material

(ii) Recommend a procedure the audit team should undertake at the completion stage to try to resolve the issue; and

(iii) Describe the impact on the audit report if the issue remains unresolved.

Notes: 1 The total marks will be split equally between each issue.

2 Audit report extracts are NOT required. **(10 marks)**

(Total: 10 marks)

195 STRAWBERRY KITCHEN DESIGNS *Walk in the footsteps of a top tutor*

You are the audit manager of Kiwi & Co and you have been provided with financial statements extracts and the following information about your client, Strawberry Kitchen Designs Co (Strawberry), who is a kitchen manufacturer. The company's year end is 30 April 2012.

Strawberry has recently been experiencing trading difficulties, as its major customer who owes $0·6m to Strawberry has ceased trading, and it is unlikely any of this will be received. However the balance is included within the financial statements extracts below. The sales director has recently left Strawberry and has yet to be replaced.

The monthly cash flow has shown a net cash outflow for the last two months of the financial year and is forecast as negative for the forthcoming financial year. As a result of this, the company has been slow in paying its suppliers and some are threatening legal action to recover the sums owing.

Due to its financial difficulties, Strawberry missed a loan repayment and, as a result of this breach in the loan covenants, the bank has asked that the loan of $4·8m be repaid in full within six months. The directors have decided that in order to conserve cash, no final dividend will be paid in 2012.

Required:

(a) **Describe the audit procedures that you should perform in assessing whether or not the company is a going concern. (5 marks)**

(b) Having performed the going concern audit procedures, you have serious concerns in relation to the going concern status of Strawberry. The finance director has informed you that as the cash flow issues are short term he does not propose to make any amendments to the financial statements.

Required:

(i) **State Kiwi & Co's responsibility for reporting on going concern to the directors of Strawberry Kitchen Designs Co; and (2 marks)**

(ii) **If the directors refuse to amend the financial statements, describe the impact on the audit report. (3 marks)**

(Total: 10 marks)

196 HUMPHRIES *Walk in the footsteps of a top tutor*

Humphries Co operates a chain of food wholesalers across the country and its year end was 30 September 2011. The final audit is nearly complete and it is proposed that the financial statements and audit report will be signed on 13 December. Revenue for the year is $78 million and profit before taxation is $7.5 million. The following events have occurred subsequent to the year end.

Receivable

A customer of Humphries Co has been experiencing cash flow problems and its year-end balance is $0.3 million. The company has just become aware that its customer is experiencing significant going concern difficulties. Humphries believe that as the company has been trading for many years, they will receive some, if not full, payment from the customer; hence they have not adjusted the receivable balance.

Lawsuit

A key supplier of Humphries Co is suing them for breach of contract. The lawsuit was filed prior to the year end, and the sum claimed by them is $1 million. This has been disclosed as a contingent liability in the notes to the financial statements; however correspondence has just arrived from the supplier indicating that they are willing to settle the case for a payment by Humphries Co of $0.6 million. It is likely that the company will agree to this.

Required:

For each of the events above:

(i) **discuss whether the financial statements require amendment**

(ii) **describe audit procedures that should be performed in order to form a conclusion on the amendment; and**

(iii) **explain the impact on the audit report should the issue remain unresolved.**

Note: The total marks will be split equally between each event.

(10 marks)

(Total: 10 marks)

197 MINNIE *Walk in the footsteps of a top tutor*

You are the audit manager of Daffy & Co. The following additional issues have arisen during the course of the audit of Minnie Co. Profit before tax is $10m.

(i) Minnie Co's computerised wages program is backed up daily, however for a period of two months the wages records and the back-ups have been corrupted, and therefore cannot be accessed. Wages and salaries for these two months are $1.1m. **(5 marks)**

(ii) Minnie Co's main competitor has filed a lawsuit for $5m against them alleging a breach of copyright; this case is ongoing and will not be resolved prior to the audit report being signed. The matter is correctly disclosed as a contingent liability. **(5 marks)**

Required:

Discuss each of these issues and describe the impact on the audit report if the above issues remain unresolved.

Note: The mark allocation is shown against each of the issues above. Audit report extracts are NOT required.

(Total: 10 marks)

198 MICKEY *Walk in the footsteps of a top tutor*

You are the audit manager of Disney & Co and you are briefing your team on the approach to adopt in undertaking the review and finalisation stage of the audit. In particular, your audit senior is unsure about the steps to take in relation to uncorrected misstatements.

Required:

(a) **Explain the term 'misstatement' and describe the auditor's responsibility in relation to misstatements.** **(5 marks)**

(b) During the audit of Mickey Co, you identify that depreciation has been calculated on the total of land and buildings. In previous years it has only been charged on buildings. Total depreciation is $2.5m and the element charged to land only is $0.7m. Profit before tax is $10m.

Required:

Discuss the issue and describe the impact on the audit report if this issue remains unresolved. **(5 marks)**

(Total: 10 marks)

199 GREENFIELDS *Walk in the footsteps of a top tutor*

Online question assistance

Greenfields Co specialises in manufacturing equipment which can help to reduce toxic emissions in the production of chemicals. The company has grown rapidly over the past eight years and this is due partly to the warranties that the company gives to its customers. It guarantees its products for five years and if problems arise in this period it undertakes to fix them, or provide a replacement product.

You are the manager responsible for the audit of Greenfields and you are performing the final review stage of the audit and have come across the following two issues.

Receivable balance owing from Yellowmix Co

Greenfields has a material receivable balance owing from its customer, Yellowmix Co. During the year-end audit, your team reviewed the ageing of this balance and found that no payments had been received from Yellowmix for over six months, and Greenfields would not allow this balance to be circularised. Instead management has assured your team that they will provide a written representation confirming that the balance is recoverable.

Warranty provision

The warranty provision included within the statement of financial position is material. The audit team has performed testing over the calculations and assumptions which are consistent with prior years. The team has requested a written representation from management confirming the basis and amount of the provision are reasonable. Management has yet to confirm acceptance of this representation.

Required:

(a) Discuss the appropriateness of written representations as a form of audit evidence for each of the two issues above. **(4 marks)**

Note: The total marks will be split equally between each issue.

(b) The directors of Greenfields have decided not to provide the audit firm with the written representation for the warranty provision as they feel that it is unnecessary.

Required:

Explain the steps the auditor of Greenfields Co should now take and the impact on the audit report in relation to the refusal to provide the written representation. **(6 marks)**

(Total: 10 marks)

200 GOING CONCERN *Walk in the footsteps of a top tutor*

(a) **Explain the audit procedures that the auditor should perform in assessing whether or not a company is a going concern. (6 marks)**

(b) The auditors of Kennedy Co have been informed that the client's bankers will not make a decision on an overdraft facility until after the audit report is completed. The directors have agreed to include going concern disclosures.

Required:

Describe the impact on the audit report of Kennedy Co if the auditor believes the company is a going concern but a material uncertainty exists. (4 marks)

(Total: 10 marks)

201 REPORTING

(a) **Explain why it is important that auditors communicate throughout the audit with those charged with governance. (2 marks)**

(b) **Explain THREE examples of matters that might be communicated to those charged with governance by the auditor. (3 marks)**

(c) **Explain the meaning of the term 'pervasive' in the context of the audit report. (2 marks)**

(d) **List the three types of modified opinions and give an example of a circumstance when each would be used. (3 marks)**

(Total: 10 marks)

AUDIT FRAMEWORK

202 TRUE & FAIR/ISAS/RIGHTS *Walk in the footsteps of a top tutor*

(a) **Explain the concept of TRUE and FAIR presentation.** **(4 marks)**

(b) **Explain the status of International Standards on Auditing.** **(2 marks)**

(c) **State THREE rights of an auditor, excluding those related to resignation and removal.** **(4 marks)**

(Total: 10 marks)

203 AUDIT & ASSURANCE

(a) **Explain the term limited assurance and explain how this differs from the assurance provided by a statutory audit.** **(5 marks)**

(b) **Explain the purpose of an external audit and its role in the audit of large companies.** **(2 marks)**

(c) **Describe THREE limitations of external audits.** **(3 marks)**

(Total: 10 marks)

204 CHANGE OF AUDITOR

(a) **Explain the steps involved when an auditor is removed or resigns.** **(5 marks)**

(b) **Explain the steps involved to obtain professional clearance.** **(5 marks)**

Total: 10 marks)

Section 3

ANSWERS TO MULTIPLE CHOICE QUESTIONS

PLANNING AND RISK ASSESSMENT

1 B

Results of previous audits and the need to maintain professional scepticism should be included in an audit strategy as opposed to an audit engagement letter.

2 B

Increasing supervision and increasing sample sizes would decrease detection risk.

3 C

Auditors do not have a responsibility to formally report on the going concern status. ISA 570 *Going Concern* requires auditors to obtain sufficient appropriate audit evidence about the appropriateness of management's use of the going concern assumption in the preparation of the financial statements and to conclude whether there is a material uncertainty about the entity's ability to continue as a going concern.

4 B

Audit risk is made up of two components being risk of material misstatement; inherent risk and control risk and also the risk that the auditor will not detect material misstatements being detection risk.

5 A

There is a risk of obsolescence of inventory, leading to inappropriate valuation. B and C give rise to control risks.

6 C

There is a risk that control procedures are not followed due to the unfamiliarity of staff with the requirements of those procedures. A increases inherent risk. B increases detection risk.

7 B

ISA 210 Agreeing the Terms of Audit Engagements requires the contents of an engagement letter to include the objective and scope of the audit, the responsibilities of the auditor and of management, the identification of an applicable financial reporting framework and a reference to the expected form and content of any reports to be issued.

8 B

The risk arises due to the lack of knowledge of the client – in order to address this, the auditor must spend time obtaining that knowledge. This will include, but is not restricted to, documenting their understanding of the internal controls in place.

9 B

Obtaining an understanding of the entity is performed at the planning stage which usually takes place before the year end. Therefore subsequent events cannot be considered at this point in time.

10 D

Analytical procedures are an optional substantive procedure but are required as one of the risk assessment procedures at the planning stage.

11 C

A, B and C are purposes of planning an audit.

12 B

1. Is not material being only 0.25% of assets. 2. Is not material being only 1% of PBT. Disclosures are material as they provide additional information relevant to the understanding of the user. 3. Is material by nature as disclosures are required to aid the understandability of the FS. 4. Is material and pervasive as the basis of preparation is incorrect which will affect whole of the financial statements.

13 B

A. Is the definition of detection risk. C. Is not a risk.

14 D

A, B and C are all business risks. B would be an audit risk if the customer owed money to the client which had not been written off. However, there is no indication of that from the information given.

15 C

C. Compliance with laws and regulations is a business risk. The audit risk would be potential unrecorded liabilities as a result of non-compliance.

16 A

The auditor has to consider the risk of material misstatement in the financial statements. Non-compliance may lead to unrecorded liabilities which may have a material effect on the financial statements.

17 A

Ratio analysis is one type of analytical procedure. An analytical procedure requires evaluation of plausible relationships between financial and non-financial information. Enquiry and recalculation are different types of auditing techniques.

18 A

The audit strategy is one of the first stages of the audit process and looks at the characteristics of the audit with a view to design an appropriate audit plan. Substantive procedures will not have been performed at this stage therefore will not appear in the audit strategy.

19 B

A, C and D are all business risks. An audit risk must be either a detection risk or a risk of material misstatement in the FS. A bad debt is a business risk. The associated audit risk would be overstated receivables if the debt has not been written off. If there was a product recall, the associated audit risk would be misstatement of inventory and liabilities if the affected inventory had not been written down or if the costs of the recall have not been provided for.

20 B

Receivables days are calculated as receivables/revenue × 365.

121,000/1,267,000 × 365 = 35 days

21 D

Higher receivables days indicate overstatement or receivables. Higher payables days would indicate overstatement of payables or would be used to assess the need for going concern disclosure due to cash flow issues. Higher inventory days would indicate overvaluation of closing inventory which would decrease cost of sales and therefore lead to understatement of cost of sales.

22 C

Prevention of fraud is solely the responsibility of management. Both management and auditors have some responsibility to detect fraud. However, auditors are mainly concerned with material misstatements. Auditors are not required to detect all fraud.

23 D

Audit files should be retained for at least five years after the date of the audit report. Every aspect of the audit need not be documented, only those aspects which support the basis of opinion. Audit files can only be destroyed after the minimum retention period has lapsed.

INTERNAL CONTROLS AND AUDIT EVIDENCE

24 D

Entering dummy data into the company's own computer system is a test data technique as it involves the use of the company's system rather than the auditor's own computer programs.

25 A

Internal control questionnaires can sometimes contain a large number of irrelevant controls; hence this is a disadvantage. B relates to disadvantages of using narrative notes and C is incorrect as questionnaires are quick to prepare.

26 C

Substantive procedure 1 provides evidence over the assertion of completeness as the direction of the test is from source documents to accounting records. Substantive procedure 4 provides evidence over valuation and allocation rather than existence.

27 B

Procedures 2 and 3 are substantive procedures rather than tests of control.

28 C

C is an example of the use of test data in the application of computer assisted audit techniques.

29 A

B is systematic sampling and C is haphazard sampling.

30 B

The auditor can never eliminate the need for substantive procedures entirely because there are inherent limitations to the reliance that can be placed on internal controls.

31 B

A is the definition of statistical sampling, where each item has an equal chance of selection. C could mean that every item was tested which would not represent sampling.

32 C

Narrative notes are the auditor's description of a system. Internal Control Questionnaires list possible controls, and the client simply confirms which controls are applicable to their system.

33 B

The control environment includes the attitude, actions and awareness of those charged with governance and management, not all personnel. Segregation of duties is a control activity.

34 A

B and C are elements of an internal control system, but are not a control activity.

35 A

B and C verify the cost of inventory.

36 A

The auditor may be able to place a high degree of reliance on the reports produced by the service organisation because of their independence and their specialist skills.

37 D

A verifies existence; B verifies rights and obligations; C verifies valuation.

38 C

A verifies completeness. B verifies cut-off. D verifies existence and completeness.

39 D

Third party evidence is the most reliable followed by auditor generated, company documentation and the least reliable is verbal evidence.

40 A

A verifies rights and obligations and existence. B verifies completeness and valuation. C verifies completeness and existence. D verifies existence.

41 A

Valuation relates to account balances and presentation and disclosure. Existence relates to account balances only.

42 D

Inventory is an account balance therefore completeness, existence, valuation and allocation and rights and obligations are the relevant assertions. However, inventory is also deducted from cost of sales on the income statement. Therefore cut-off is also a relevant assertion.

43 B

Statement A describes a limitation of inspection of documentation. C describes limitation of inspection of tangible assets. D describes a limitation of recalculation and analytical procedures.

44 C

Any approach to sampling that does not have both these characteristics is considered to be non-statistical sampling.

45 B

3 and 4 are application controls.

46 B

2 is an objective of the purchase cycle. 4 is an objective of the payroll cycle.

47 D

1 and 2 are objectives of the purchase cycle.

48 A

The goods received should be agreed to the purchase order before signing the delivery note to ensure that Coastal Co does not accept goods not required

49 D

Pre-printed payroll sheets ensure that only genuine employees are paid. Quarterly reviews of standing data ensure that unauthorised amendments are identified and resolved.

50 B

The sales invoice should be raised from the goods despatch note to ensure that only goods despatched are invoiced.

51 B

1 prevents stock-outs/manufacturing delays. 4 prevents unnecessary goods being ordered.

52 B

2 ensures requisitions can be traced. 3 gives assurance about the quality of goods and reliability of supply.

53 A

Testing completeness tests for understatement.

54 C

As a reconciling item on the bank reconciliation, the outstanding lodgements need to be traced through to post year end bank statements to ensure they have cleared.

55 B

Inspection of credit checks is a test of control, not a substantive procedure.

56 C

All risks given are relevant to NFP organisations.

57 D

NFP's are likely to have a finance person in charge of the finances. Some NFP's are required by law to have an audit such as government bodies. Charities are required to be audited if they are of a certain size. Although ISA's are written for audits of companies, they should still be followed in an audit of an NFP. Additional standards may be applicable specific to the audit of an NFP.

58 D

Due diligence is usually performed when a company is acquiring another company therefore is not a typical reporting requirement relevant for NFP's.

59 A

Computer assisted auditing techniques.

60 C

A is a benefit of using CAAT's. B does not test the programmed controls of the system therefore does not constitute test data. An assumption would be made that if the output was consistent with the input the internal controls will have worked properly, however, this has not been directly tested. Scrutinising source code is a more specialised type of CAAT.

61 B

CAAT's are usually expensive to set up but become more cost effective over time.

62 B

The auditor must not make reference to the fact they have used someone else's work. They cannot delegate responsibility for any aspect of their audit report. The auditor must consider whether it is appropriate to rely on the work of others before placing reliance. If it is not appropriate they should find alternative evidence.

63 C

A is true under ISA 610 revised. B is true. C is false as the external auditor must always evaluate the work before relying on it to ensure it is relevant and reliable for external audit purposes. The presence of an audit committee does not guarantee this.

64 A

B is a control, not a test of control. C is a substantive procedure. D is an analytical procedure.

65 B

B is a substantive procedure as it is testing one of the financial statement assertions. A test of control is performed to verify that a control is in place and working effectively. Evidence of reconciliations being performed, quotations being received and asset tagging are all tests of controls.

66 D

The fact that a company has no overdue debts does not confirm that a credit check was performed. The company may be fortunate to have customers who pay on time. Enquiry of management is not the most reliable method of testing the control. It is possible that credit checks are supposed to be performed but are not being performed and management may not be aware of this. Credit limits may be set by the client without reference to a credit report. The best procedure to confirm the credit check takes place is to view the credit report.

67 B

Insignificant deficiencies are not required to be communicated. Communication of significant deficiencies must be in writing.

68 A

If management do not scrutinise transactions and keep control of the organisation, significant deficiencies can occur.

69 C

C is a test on the payables balance not the purchases figure.

70 D

Recalculation is not an analytical procedure. An analytical procedure looks at relationships between data. Expectations are formed by the auditor and then compared with actual figures to assess whether they are in line with expectation.

71 B

The external auditor must evaluate the internal audit function before evaluating the work. If the function is not deemed reliable the work will not be reviewed.

72 D

Valuation is an assertion relevant to balances. Purchases are a transaction and as such are tested for the assertion of accuracy.

73 A

Cut-off testing must be performed every year. All lines must have been counted at least once during the year.

74 C

An analytical procedure is a type of substantive procedure. All material balances must substantively tested but there is no requirement for substantive tests of detail to be performed. Analytical procedures may be sufficient.

75 C

Board minutes, written representation and calculations of the financial controller are internally generated. Evidence from solicitors provided a more reliable source of evidence in respect of a legal provision.

76 A

True.

77 B

A service organisation is likely to be more proficient at payroll processing as they are specialists, therefore the risk of material misstatement of payroll is reduced. However, evidence may be more difficult to obtain if the service organisation or their auditors are not cooperative.

ETHICS

78 D

In the case of situations 1 and 4, the auditor has an obligation to disclose details of their clients' affairs to third parties. Situations 2 and 3 are ones where voluntary disclosure should be made.

79 B

Members of an assurance team should not disclose any information to anyone outside of the engagement team, whether or not they work for the audit firm.

80 C

Members should not disclose client information to third parties. The fact that they did not know their friend held shares in the company is not an excuse.

81 D

The member has a professional right to disclose confidential client information to protect their own interests, such as at a disciplinary hearing.

82 A

The audit team may be too trusting of or too sympathetic to the financial controller because of their previous relationship with him (familiarity threat). A self-review threat would apply if the financial controller was now employed as an auditor and assigned to the audit of the previous employer.

83 C

1 is a safeguard to manage conflicts of interest. 3 is a safeguard to manage a familiarity threat, self-interest threat or intimidation threat.

84 C

This is a conflict of interest. There is a risk that confidential information may be passed between the clients. The audit firm may put their own interests first in order to obtain the fees from both clients which may be contrary to the interests of the client's.

85 A

The firm cannot audit a client in which they own shares – no safeguards can reduce this threat to an acceptable level. With client permission, a conflict of interest can be managed with the implementation of appropriate safeguards (information barriers for example).

86 A

Self-interest (and also intimidation and familiarity) threat will arise as the auditor will want to ensure they get the job.

87 D

The Code of Ethics describes a presumption of fee dependency when fees for all work provided to public interest/listed clients will exceed 15% for two consecutive years.

88 C

The conceptual framework provides guidelines with the objective that the auditor chooses the most appropriate course of action in the circumstances. This allows flexibility to deal with all possible situations. The guidelines followed are professional guidance but are not legal requirements.

CORPORATE GOVERNANCE AND INTERNAL AUDIT

89 A

Costs may reduce if the internal audit function is outsourced; however, this would not always be the case as redundancies of the company's existing internal audit function may increase the overall costs.

90 B

Statement 1 is not correct as internal audit (IA) should not report to the finance director as this would impact on their independence. Some of the internal controls and functions IA review are the responsibility of the finance director and they may not act on any recommendations which appear to criticise their department. Statement 2 is correct as companies are not required to implement and maintain an IA function. Corporate governance principles recommend that listed companies maintain an IA function and annually consider the need for such a function; however, they do not require it.

91 A

B relates only to publicly traded companies, but corporate governance relates to all companies. C describes corporate social responsibility.

92 C

Economy is minimising cost. Efficiency is maximum output with minimum use of resources. Value for money is obtaining the best possible combination of services for the least resources. VFM is a typical assignment of the internal audit function.

93 C

1 is incorrect since internal audit would not retain their independence if they reviewed an area for which they had operational responsibility. 3 is incorrect since internal audit would not retain their independence if they implemented controls; their role is to review the controls once implemented. 2 is correct as ISA 610 allows the auditors to obtain direct assistance from internal auditors under supervision of the audit firm.

94 B

Listed companies are not normally required to have an internal audit function. Listed companies must however consider the need for internal audit as part of their annual monitoring of the effectiveness of the internal control system. They must have an audit committee to comply with corporate governance regulations.

95 A

Audit, remuneration and nomination committees are recommended by corporate governance regulations.

96 B

Control risk will be lower as the control environment is stronger. Inherent risk is unaffected. There is no effect on the likelihood of external auditor reappointment.

97 A

Internal auditors report to the audit committee or the board of directors. External audit reports are prescribed by ISA 700.

98 C

An outsourced firm is likely to have less awareness of the client's risks. Flexibility is reduced as the internal auditor is not an employee and cannot be controlled in the same way.

99 D

Finance staff should not be involved with internal audit work. To ensure errors are identified, someone other than the preparer should review the work.

100 B

The audit opinion on the financial statements can only be expressed by an independent external auditor.

REVIEW AND REPORTING

101 C

When the accounting records are unavailable, it is not acceptable to obtain a written representation as this represents an inability to obtain sufficient and appropriate audit evidence and if material would result in a modified audit report.

102 D

If management are unwilling to make their assessment of going concern this would result in a modified opinion with a qualified or disclaimer opinion. If the going concern basis is not appropriate, then an adverse opinion should be provided rather than a qualified opinion as the matter is material and pervasive.

103 C

Written representations cannot be a substitute for more reliable information that should be available. The auditor should have sought, and been provided with, evidence from the third party, i.e. the inventory count records, to verify the quantity of inventory held by them.

104 C

Subsequent events are those occurring after the date of the financial statements (the period end) up to the date of the auditor's report and facts that become known after the date of the auditor's report.

105 A

1 indicates an inability to meet debts as they fall due. 2: lack of access to cash may make it difficult for a company to manage its operating cycle.

106 C

A basis for opinion paragraph is included in all audit reports when the auditor modifies the opinion, immediately before the opinion paragraph, to provide a description of the matter giving rise to the modification.

107 D

Statement 1 would require an other matter paragraph. Statement 2 would require an emphasis of matter paragraph.

108 C

A, B and D describe a matter that is material and pervasive – in these circumstances the auditor must give an adverse or disclaimer of opinion. If the matter is material but not pervasive, a qualified opinion must be given.

109 B

A is incorrect as an other matter paragraph is used to draw attention to a matter that does not affect the financial statements or the users' understanding of them. C is incorrect as an other matter paragraph results in the report being modified but the opinion is unmodified. D is incorrect as the auditor cannot use an other matter (or emphasis of matter) paragraphs as a substitute for a qualified opinion.

110 C

The omission or inadequacy of a disclosure note is material by nature. The financial statements are therefore not fairly presented and so A is not correct. The matter is unlikely to be pervasive therefore D is not correct. B is incorrect because an emphasis of matter paragraph is used to draw the users' attention to a matter appropriately presented or disclosed in the financial statements.

111 B

An emphasis of matter paragraph is only required if there is a fundamental matter affecting the financial statements to draw the users' attention to, and would not appear in an unmodified audit report, therefore option 1 is incorrect. The audit report would name the auditor's location but not provide any other contact details, therefore option 4 is incorrect.

112 A

Statement B is the wording used for an unmodified opinion in a limited assurance engagement. Statement C is a phrase included in the objective of an audit, but not the audit opinion.

113 A

The introductory paragraph states that an audit has been carried out and specifies the subject matter of the audit. The auditor's opinion does not include any additional information other than the audit opinion itself.

114 C

The introductory paragraph states that an audit has been carried out and specifies the subject matter of the audit.

115 C

When the auditor has not been able to obtain sufficient appropriate evidence to provide a basis for the audit opinion, they provide a disclaimer of opinion, i.e. they do not express an opinion on the financial statements.

116 D

A is not correct as the event is an adjusting event so the financial statements must be adjusted if the effect is material. EOM is not appropriate here as the financial statements are materially misstated so the opinion must be modified. As the adjustment required of $40,000 represents 5% of PBT the matter is material but not pervasive, therefore an adverse opinion is not correct.

Tutorial note: The inventory should be valued at the lower of cost and net realisable value. Cost is $400,000. NRV is $410,000 less $50,000 = $360,000. An adjustment of $40,000 is required.

117 D

The report would be modified with an emphasis of matter paragraph. The opinion would not be modified as the auditor is satisfied that the client has dealt with the material uncertainty appropriately in the financial statements.

118 B

Inspection of board minutes would be performed prior to the overall review. The overall review is one of the final stages of the audit before issuing the opinion.

119 A

True.

120 C

An unmodified opinion can be issued if the uncorrected misstatements are immaterial. All uncorrected misstatements must be communicated and requested to be adjusted, not just the material ones. Shareholders are not informed of all uncorrected misstatements. If the uncorrected misstatements are material the opinion will be modified and therefore the shareholders will be made aware of the material misstatements via the audit report.

121 B

An inability to obtain sufficient appropriate evidence is not the same as a material uncertainty. Where there is an uncertainty the evidence does not exist yet as it is dependent on future events. A lack of sufficient appropriate evidence arises when evidence that the auditor would expect to obtain has not been obtained.

122 A

ISA 580 suggests that a disclaimer of opinion should be issued where a written representation is not obtained. The matters included in the representation are likely to be pervasive in aggregate and therefore the auditor will not express an opinion on the financial statements.

AUDIT FRAMEWORK

123 B

The responsible party prepares the subject matter; the practitioner gives the assurance opinion. In order to give that opinion, they must evaluate the subject matter against criteria.

124 A

True.

125 B

ISAs can be applied to the audit of other historical financial information but are not relevant to limited assurance engagements such as examination of prospective financial information.

126 D

If the directors lack the necessary skills or knowledge, they must engage an accountant to help them prepare the financial statements before they are reviewed (therefore A is incorrect). Small, privately owned companies are often exempt (therefore B is incorrect). Accounting profit is normally adjusted for tax purposes and therefore an audit of the financial statements will not ensure that the correct tax is calculated or paid (therefore C is incorrect).

127 C

There are five elements of an assurance engagement:

The three parties involved (the practitioner, the intended users, the responsible party); an appropriate subject matter; suitable criteria; sufficient appropriate evidence; a written assurance report in an appropriate form. The intended users are not always the shareholders. The practitioner need not be a registered auditor if it is not an audit.

128 A

An audit is designed to give reasonable assurance that the financial statements are free from material misstatement whether caused by fraud or error. However, there is an unavoidable risk that some material misstatements may not be detected. The risks in respect of fraud are higher than those for error because fraud may involve sophisticated and carefully organised schemes designed to conceal it. The auditor may highlight deficiencies in the internal control system, but it is the directors' responsibility to safeguard a company's assets including designing and implementing an adequate internal control system in order to prevent and detect fraud.

The auditor has a duty of confidentiality and will not report any fraud detected without client permission, unless it is in the public interest to do so.

129 C

All of the other answers relate to a reasonable assurance engagement.

130 D

If a misstatement has been identified, this will affect the practitioner's ability to give assurance, but does not change the level of assurance or type of engagement. The practitioner must gather sufficient appropriate evidence in both types of engagements, although the level of assurance will affect what the practitioner determines to be sufficient and appropriate. The practitioner could only be liable if they did not perform the audit with professional competence and due care – the level of assurance has no bearing on that liability.

131 B

2 and 4 are factually correct. 1 and 3 are factually incorrect, and are examples of the expectations gap.

132 A

Any country may implement International Standards on Auditing (ISAs), or they can set their own auditing standards. There is no requirement for all countries to implement ISAs. National standard setters (including EU member states) may modify ISAs to suit national requirements.

133 B

1 and 4 are duties of the auditor not rights.

134 C

The 3 parties in an assurance engagement are the responsible party, practitioner and intended user.

135 B

Reasonable conclusions.

136 B

A moderate level of assurance is provided for a limited assurance engagement.

137 A

Credibility of financial information is likely to be increased and risk of management fraud is likely to be decreased as they are aware that an independent expert review of the financial information being performed. The cost of financial reporting is unlikely to be impacted by the audit process.

138 D

The Auditor is required to present a statement of circumstances when they vacate office, irrespective of the circumstances.

139 B

False. Companies which are under the audit threshold do not need to have an external audit.

140 B

Where there is a conflict between national and international regulations, national regulations take precedence.

Section 4

ANSWERS TO PRACTICE QUESTIONS

PLANNING AND RISK ASSESSMENT

141 SEAGULL *Walk in the footsteps of a top tutor*

Top tutor tips

Audit risks and responses should be expected on every exam paper. To answer well you need to explain how the factors in the scenario could lead to a material misstatement in the financial statements or increase detection risk. Do not give business risks.

The auditor's response should explain how the auditor will obtain evidence over this risk. Do not give suggestions to the client on how they can mitigate the risk. This is not what the question has asked for and will not score you marks. Read the question carefully to ensure you answer from the correct perspective. Also, make sure your response links with the specific risk. For example, if there is a risk associated with valuation of receivables, the response must obtain evidence with regard to valuation and not existence or completeness.

Audit risks and responses

Audit risk	**Auditors response**
Eagle Heating Co (Eagle) has decreased the selling price of products significantly since September and there are increased levels of inventory expected at the year end. It is possible that the selling price may have fallen so that the net realisable value (NRV) of inventory is below cost. IAS 2 Inventory requires inventory to be stated at the lower of cost and NRV. Hence it is possible that inventory is overvalued.	The auditor should undertake detailed cost and NRV testing to assess whether inventory is overvalued and requires write down.

Audit risk	Auditors response
A key customer of Eagle has been experiencing financial difficulties and Eagle has agreed a six-month payment break; however, the finance director does not believe an allowance is required. If the customer is experiencing difficulties, there is an increased risk that the receivable is not recoverable and hence is overvalued.	If the six-months payment break has now ended, review after date cash receipts for this customer to assess whether any payments have been made. Discuss with the finance director why he feels an allowance is not required. Review whether any general allowance for uncollectable accounts is sufficient to cover the amount of this receivable.
In light of the increased competition, reduction in selling price and financial difficulties of a key customer, there is an increased risk that Eagle is facing going concern difficulties.	The auditor should undertake detailed going concern testing. They should review the cash flow forecast for the foreseeable future to assess whether the going concern basis is appropriate or whether additional going concern disclosures are required in the financial statements.
The financial controller of Eagle was dismissed in October and is threatening to sue the company for unfair dismissal. If it is probable that Eagle will make payment to the financial controller, a provision for unfair dismissal is required. If the payment is possible rather than probable, a contingent liability disclosure would be necessary. If Eagle has not done this, there is a risk over the completeness of any provisions or contingent liabilities.	The audit team should write to the company's lawyers to enquire of the existence and likelihood of success of any claim from the former financial controller.
The financial controller has been dismissed and his tasks have been allocated between the finance department team, this has increased their workload. This increases the inherent and control risk within Eagle as errors may have been made within the accounting records by the overworked finance team members and there is no one working in a supervisory capacity.	The team should remain alert throughout the audit for additional errors within the finance department. In addition, discuss with the finance director whether he will be able to provide the team with assistance for any audit issues as there is no financial controller available.
The purchase ledger supervisor left in August and no reconciliations of supplier statements and purchase ledger control account have been performed. There is an increased risk of errors within trade payables and the year-end payable may be under or overstated.	The audit team should increase their testing on trade payables at the year end, with a particular focus on completeness of payables. A detailed review of the year-end purchase ledger control account reconciliation should be performed with a focus on any unusual reconciling items.

Audit risk	**Auditors response**
Preliminary analytical review of the draft statement of profit or loss has identified a significant fall in administration expenses. Administration expenses tend to be fixed costs and hence would be unlikely to fluctuate significantly with changes in sales volumes. Hence there is a risk that administration expenses are understated.	Update the analytical review with the full year results and if significant fluctuations on prior year remain, discuss these with management. Obtain supporting evidence to verify management explanations.

ACCA marking scheme	
	Marks
Up to 1 mark per well explained risk and up to 1 mark for each well explained response. Overall max of 5 marks for risks and 5 marks for responses. – Inventory valuation – Receivable valuation – Going concern – Unfair dismissal of financial controller – Increased inherent risk of errors in finance department due to loss of financial controller – Under or overstated trade payables – Completeness of administration expenses	
Total	**10**

142 RECORDER COMMUNICATIONS *Walk in the footsteps of a top tutor*

Top Tutor Tips

Audit risks need to relate to either a risk of material misstatement or a detection risk. For risk of material misstatement, identify a balance in the scenario that is at risk of misstatement and explain why you believe it could be misstated. This is usually because the client has failed to apply the relevant IFRS correctly. The IFRS's examinable for ACCA paper F3 are examinable for paper F8.

Detection risks are the risks the auditor does not detect material misstatements in the financial statements e.g. when it is a new audit client or if there is a tight reporting deadline.

For the response, make sure it relates to the risk, not the balance in general. Try and be as specific as possible, simply saying more testing is required will not be sufficient. State the nature of the tests that should be performed.

A 2 column table should be used to keep the risks in line with the responses and to make sure you address both parts of the requirement.

Audit risks and responses

Audit risk	**Auditor's response**
Recorder Communications Co (Recorder) is a new client for Piano & Co. As the team is not so familiar with the accounting policies, transactions and balances of Recorder, there will be an increased detection risk on the audit.	Piano & Co should ensure they have a suitably experienced team. Also, adequate time should be allocated for team members to obtain an understanding of the company and the risks of material misstatement.
Recorder purchases their goods from South Asia and the goods are in transit for two weeks. At the year end there is a risk that the cut-off of inventory, purchases and payables may not be accurate. The company correctly accounts for goods when they receive them. Therefore at the year end only goods which have been received into the warehouse should be included in the inventory balance and a respective payables balance recognised.	The audit team should undertake detailed cut-off testing of goods in transit from the suppliers in South Asia to ensure that the cut-off is complete and accurate.
The company undertakes continuous (perpetual) inventory counts at its central warehouse. Under such a system all inventory must be counted at least once a year with adjustments made to the inventory records. Inventory could be under or overstated if the continuous (perpetual) inventory counts are not complete and the inventory records accurately updated for adjustments.	The completeness of the continuous (perpetual) inventory counts should be reviewed. In addition, the level of adjustments made to inventory should be considered to assess whether reliance on the inventory records at the year end will be acceptable.
A sales-related bonus scheme has been introduced in the year; this may lead to sales cut-off errors with employees aiming to maximise their current year bonus.	Increased sales cut-off testing will be performed along with a review of any post year-end cancellations of contracts as they may indicate cut-off errors.
Receivables are considerably higher than the prior year and there are concerns about the creditworthiness of some customers. There is a risk that some receivables may be overvalued as they are not recoverable.	Extended post year-end cash receipts testing and a review of the aged receivables ledger to be performed to assess valuation. Also consider the adequacy of any allowance for receivables.
In addition, receivables could be overstated as a result of the bonus scheme; some of the customers signed up for contracts may not actually exist.	External confirmation of receivables to confirm that customers exist and represent valid amounts due.

Audit risk	**Auditor's response**
Recorder has a policy of revaluing its land and buildings and these valuations have been updated during the year. Property, plant and equipment could be under or overvalued if the recent valuation has not been carried out in accordance with IAS 16 *Property, Plant and Equipment* and adequate disclosures may not have been made in the financial statements.	Discuss with management the process adopted for undertaking the valuation, including whether the whole class of assets was revalued and if the valuation was undertaken by an expert. This process should be reviewed for compliance with IAS 16. Review the disclosures of the revaluation in the financial statements for compliance with IAS 16.
The directors have each been paid a significant bonus and separate disclosure of this in the financial statements is required by local legislation. The directors' remuneration disclosure will not be complete and accurate if the bonus paid is not disclosed in accordance with the relevant local legislation.	Discuss this matter with management and review the disclosure in the financial statements to ensure compliance with local legislation.

ACCA marking scheme	
	Marks
Up to 1 mark per well described risk and up to 1 mark for each well explained response. Overall maximum of 5 marks for risks and 5 marks for responses.	
New client leading to increased detection risk	
Cut-off of goods in transit	
Continuous (perpetual) inventory counts	
Sales cut-off	
Overstatement of receivables	
Valuation of land and buildings	
Directors' bonus remuneration	
Maximum	**10**
Total	**10**

Examiner's comments

This question was based on a mobile phone company Recorder Communications Co (Recorder). The question tested the areas of audit risks and responses and required identification and description of five audit risks from the scenario and the auditor's response for each. Performance on this question was mixed, and unfortunately not as good as in December 2013 when audit risk was last tested. The scenario contained significantly more than five risks and so candidates were able to easily identify enough risks, and strong answers went on to describe how the point identified from the scenario was an audit risk by referring to the assertion and the account balance impacted. As in previous diets, some candidates tended to only identify facts from the scenario such as 'Recorder purchases goods from a supplier in South Asia and the goods are in transit for two weeks' but failed to describe how this could impact audit risk; this would only have scored ½ marks. To gain 1 mark the point needed to be developed to also explain that this could result in issues over the completeness of inventory. More so than in previous diets, candidates disappointingly provided business risks rather than audit risks with answers such as stock outs due to the two week transit period and possible damage to inventory during transit. As a result these candidates then provided responses related to how management should address these business risks rather than how the auditor should respond. This meant that out of a potential 2 marks per point, candidates would only score ½ marks for the identification of the issue from the scenario. Some candidates also identified irrelevant risks such as Recorder undertaking continuous inventory counts. While an audit risk was present around inventory in relation to the effectiveness of the perpetual inventory system, very few candidates explained the risk in this manner instead focussing on the lack of a full year-end count. This demonstrated a lack of understanding of continuous inventory counts. Additionally, many candidates performed poorly with regards to the auditor's responses. Many candidates gave business advice, such as changing the salesmen's bonus structure or provided vague responses such as perform detailed substantive testing or maintain professional scepticism. Responses which start with 'ensure that……' are unlikely to score marks as they usually fail to explain exactly how the auditor will address the audit risk.

Audit responses need to be practical and should relate to the approach (i.e. what testing) the auditor will adopt to assess whether the balance is materially misstated or not. Most candidates presented their answers well, adopting a two column approach with audit risk in one column and the related response next to it. This helps candidates to ensure that for every risk identified there is a related response and candidates are encouraged to continue to use this approach where appropriate.

143 MINTY COLA *Walk in the footsteps of a top tutor*

Top Tutor Tips

Audit risks need to relate to either a risk of material misstatement or a detection risk. For risk of material misstatement, identify a balance in the scenario that is at risk of misstatement and explain why you believe it could be misstated. Detection risks are the risks the auditor does not detect material misstatements in the financial statements e.g. when it is a new audit client or if there is a tight reporting deadline.

For the response, make sure it relates to the risk, not the balance in general. Try and be as specific as possible, simply saying more testing is required will not be sufficient. State the nature of the tests that should be performed.

A 2 column table should be used to keep the risks in line with the responses and to make sure you address both parts of the requirement.

(a) **Audit risks and responses**

Audit risk	*Auditor response*
Minty has incurred $5m on updating, repairing and replacing a significant amount of the production process machinery. If this expenditure is of a capital nature, it should be capitalised as part of property, plant and equipment (PPE) in line with IAS 16 *Property, Plant and Equipment*. However, if it relates more to repairs, then it should be expensed to the statement of profit or loss. If the expenditure is not correctly classified, profit and PPE could be under or overstated.	The auditor should review a breakdown of these costs to ascertain the split of capital and revenue expenditure, and further testing should be undertaken to ensure that the classification in the financial statements is correct.
At the year end there will be inventory counts undertaken in all 15 warehouses. It is unlikely that the auditor will be able to attend all 15 inventory counts and therefore they need to ensure that they obtain sufficient evidence over the inventory counting controls, and completeness and existence of inventory for any warehouses not visited.	The auditor should assess which of the inventory sites they will attend the counts for. This will be any with material inventory or which have a history of significant errors. For those not visited, the auditor will need to review the level of exceptions noted during the count and discuss with management any issues which arose during the count.
Inventory is stored within 15 warehouses; some are owned by Minty and some rented from third parties. Only warehouses owned by Minty should be included within PPE. There is a risk of overstatement of PPE and understatement of rental expenses if Minty has capitalised all 15 warehouses.	The auditor should review supporting documentation for all warehouses included within PPE to confirm ownership by Minty and to ensure non-current assets are not overstated.
A new accounting general ledger system has been introduced at the beginning of the year and the old system was run in parallel for two months. There is a risk of opening balances being misstated and loss of data if they have not been transferred from the old system correctly. In addition, the new general ledger system will require documenting and the controls over this will need to be tested.	The auditor should undertake detailed testing to confirm that all opening balances have been correctly recorded in the new general ledger system. They should document and test the new system. They should review any management reports run comparing the old and new system during the parallel run to identify any issues with the processing of accounting information.
The finance director of Minty has decided to release the opening provision of $1.5 million for allowance for receivables as	Extended post year-end cash receipts testing and a review of the aged receivables ledger to be performed to

Audit risk	*Auditor response*
he feels it is unnecessary. There is a risk that receivables will be overvalued, as despite having a credit controller, some balances will be irrecoverable and so will be overstated if not provided against. In addition, due to the damaged inventory there is an increased risk of customers refusing to make payments in full.	assess valuation and the need for an allowance for receivables.
Minty has incurred expenditure of $4.5 million on developing a new brand of fizzy drink. This expenditure is research and development under IAS 38 *Intangible Assets*. The standard requires research costs to be expensed and development costs to be capitalised as an intangible asset. If Minty has incorrectly classified research costs as development expenditure, there is a risk the intangible asset could be overstated and expenses understated.	Obtain a breakdown of the expenditure and undertake testing to determine whether the costs relate to the research or development stage. Discuss the accounting treatment with the finance director and ensure it is in accordance with IAS 38.
A large batch of cola products has been damaged in the production process and will be in inventory at the year end. No adjustment has been made by management. The valuation of inventory as per IAS 2 *Inventories* should be at the lower of cost and net realisable value. Hence it is likely that this inventory is overvalued.	Detailed cost and net realisable value testing to be performed to assess how much the inventory requires writing down by.
Due to the damaged cola products, a number of customers have complained. It is likely that for any of the damaged goods sold, Minty will need to refund these customers. Revenue is possibly overstated if the sales returns are not completely and accurately recorded.	Review the breakdown of sales of damaged goods, and ensure that they have been accurately removed from revenue.
The management of Minty receives a significant annual bonus based on the value of year end total assets. There is a risk that management might feel under pressure to overstate the value of assets through the judgements taken or through the use of releasing provisions.	Throughout the audit the team will need to be alert to this risk. They will need to maintain professional scepticism and carefully review judgemental decisions and compare treatment against prior years.

(b) **Audit strategy document**

The audit strategy sets out the scope, timing and direction of the audit and helps the development of the audit plan. It should consider the following main areas.

It should identify the main characteristics of the engagement which define its scope. For Minty it should consider the following:

- Whether the financial information to be audited has been prepared in accordance with IFRS.
- To what extent audit evidence obtained in previous audits for Minty will be utilised.
- Whether computer-assisted audit techniques will be used and the effect of IT on audit procedures.
- The availability of key personnel at Minty.

It should ascertain the reporting objectives of the engagement to plan the timing of the audit and the nature of the communications required, such as:

- The audit timetable for reporting and whether there will be an interim as well as final audit.
- Organisation of meetings with Minty's management to discuss any audit issues arising.
- Location of the 15 inventory counts.
- Any discussions with management regarding the reports to be issued.
- The timings of the audit team meetings and review of work performed.
- If there are any expected communications with third parties.

The strategy should consider the factors that, in the auditor's professional judgement, are significant in directing Minty's audit team's efforts, such as:

- The determination of materiality for the audit.
- The need to maintain a questioning mind and to exercise professional scepticism in gathering and evaluating audit evidence.

It should consider the results of preliminary audit planning activities and, where applicable, whether knowledge gained on other engagements for Minty is relevant, such as:

- Results of previous audits and the results of any tests over the effectiveness of internal controls.
- Evidence of management's commitment to the design, implementation and maintenance of sound internal control.
- Volume of transactions, which may determine whether it is more efficient for the audit team to rely on internal control.
- Significant business developments affecting Minty, such as the change in the accounting system and the significant expenditure on an overhaul of the factory.

The audit strategy should ascertain the nature, timing and extent of resources necessary to perform the audit, such as:

- The selection of the audit team with experience of this type of industry.
- Assignment of audit work to the team members.
- Setting the audit budget.

Tutorial note

The answer is longer than required for four marks but represents a teaching aid.

(c) **Substantive procedures**

Top Tutor Tips

Audit procedures should be specific. They should be clear instructions to an audit team member. For this question the procedures are required over specific matters, not just balances in general e.g. the 'release of the allowance for receivables' not audit procedures over receivables. Take care to answer the question set.

(i) **Release of $1.5 million allowance for receivables**

- Discuss with the finance director his rationale for not providing against any receivables.
- Review the aged receivable ledger to identify any slow moving or old receivable balances, discuss the status of these balances with the credit controller to assess whether they are likely to pay.
- Review whether there are any after date cash receipts for slow moving/old receivable balances.
- Review customer correspondence to identify any balances which are in dispute or unlikely to be paid.
- Review board minutes to identify whether there are any significant concerns in relation to payments by customers.
- Calculate the potential level of receivables which are not recoverable and assess whether this is material or not and discuss with management.

(ii) **Damaged inventory**

- Obtain a schedule of the $1 million damaged cola products and cast to ensure accuracy.
- During the inventory count identify the quantity of the damaged goods and agree to the schedule.
- Discuss with management their plans for disposing of these goods, whether they believe these goods have a net realisable value (NRV) at all or if they will need to be scrapped.
- If any of the goods have been sold post year end, agree to the sales invoice to assess NRV.
- Agree the cost of the inventory to supporting documentation to confirm the raw material cost, labour cost and any overheads attributed to the cost.
- Quantify the level of adjustment required to value inventory at the lower of cost and NRV and discuss with management.

ACCA marking scheme

		Marks
(a)	Up to 1 mark per well described risk and up to 1 mark for each well explained response. Overall max of 6 marks for risks and 6 marks for responses. – $5 million expenditure on production process – Inventory counts at 15 warehouses at year end – Treatment of owned v third party warehouses – New general ledger system introduced at the beginning of the year – Release of opening provision for allowance for receivables – Research and development expenditure – Damaged inventory – Sales returns – Management bonus based on asset values	
	Max	**12**
(b)	½ mark for identifying an area of the audit strategy document and ½ mark for an example for each area relevant to Minty. – Main characteristics of the audit – Reporting objectives of the audit and nature of communications required – Factors that are significant in directing the audit team's efforts – Results of preliminary engagement activities and whether knowledge gained on other engagements is relevant – Nature, timing and extent of resources necessary to perform the audit	
	Max	**4**
(c)	Up to 1 mark per well described substantive procedure, overall maximum of 2 marks per issue. (i) Release of $1.5 million allowance for receivables – Discuss with the finance director rationale for not providing against any receivables – Review aged receivable ledger to identify any slow moving or old receivable balances, discuss with the credit controller – Review after date cash receipts for slow moving/old receivable balances – Review customer correspondence to identify any balances in dispute or unlikely to be paid – Review board minutes to identify any significant concerns in relation to payments by customers – Calculate the potential level of receivables which are not recoverable and assess if material or not (ii) Damaged inventory – Obtain a schedule of the $1 million damaged cola products and cast – During the inventory count identify the damaged goods and agree to the schedule – Discuss with management whether these goods have a net realisable value (NRV) – If any goods sold post year end, agree to sales invoice to assess NRV – Agree the cost of the inventory to supporting documentation to verify the raw material cost, labour cost and any overheads attributed to the cost – Quantify the level of adjustment required to value inventory at the lower of cost and NRV and discuss with management	
	Max	**4**
Total		**20**

Examiner's comments

This question was based on a fizzy drinks manufacturer, Minty Cola Co (Minty), and tested candidates' knowledge of audit risks and responses, audit strategy documents and substantive procedures for three specific areas.

Part (a) required an identification and description of audit risks from the scenario and the auditor's response for each. Performance on this question was mixed.

The scenario contained significantly more risks than required and so many candidates were able to easily identify enough risks, they then went on to describe how the point identified from the scenario was an audit risk by referring to the assertion and the account balance impacted.

As in previous diets, some candidates tended to only identify facts from the scenario such as 'Minty's finance director does not see the need for an allowance for receivables and so has released the opening balance' but failed to describe how this could impact audit risk; this would only have scored 1⁄2 marks. To gain 1 mark they needed to refer to the risk of receivables being overvalued. Where candidates did attempt to cover the assertion it was often vague and non-committal; for example stating that 'receivables may be misstated', this is not sufficient to gain the 1⁄2 mark available.

Also it was disappointing to see that rather than consider audit risks, some candidates continued to focus on business risks and hence provided responses related to how management should address these business risks. For example, the scenario stated that 'the company has expanded the number of warehouses it uses to store inventory'. Some candidates focused on how management should look to control all of these warehouses, rather than focus on the auditor's increased detection risk as inventory counts were taking place at all the sites simultaneously.

Some candidates also identified irrelevant risks such as going concern and litigation risks surrounding the batch of damaged cola. It is highly unlikely that $1 million of damaged inventory will cause the company with revenue of $85 million to experience going concern problems. Candidates are clearly learning a list of generic risks and providing them for every audit risk question; this is not the correct approach to take.

Additionally, some candidates performed poorly with regards to the auditor's responses. Some candidates gave business advice, other responses focused more on repeating what the appropriate accounting treatment should be, therefore for the risk of inventory valuation due to the damaged cola, the response given was 'inventory should be valued at the lower of cost and NRV', this is not a valid audit response.

Responses which start with 'ensure that......' are unlikely to score marks as they usually fail to explain exactly how the auditor will address the audit risk. Also some responses were weak such as 'discuss with the directors' without making it clear what would be discussed and how this would gather evidence re the risk. Audit responses need to be practical and should relate to the approach the auditor will adopt to assess whether the balance is materially misstated or not.

Most candidates presented their answers well as they adopted a two column approach with audit risk in one column and the related response next to it.

Part (b) required an identification of the main areas to be included within Minty's audit strategy document and an example for each area.

This question, where attempted, was poorly answered by most candidates. Most candidates did not answer both parts of the requirement; failing to identify the areas of an audit strategy. This is a knowledge area and demonstrated a gap in candidates' technical knowledge. Where candidates did score marks this was for providing examples, the most common answers given were around materiality, timetable and staff resources.

Those candidates who did not score well tended to repeat points made on audit risks, despite the question requirement clearly stating 'other than audit risks' or they listed out lots of audit tests.

Part (c) required substantive procedures the auditor should perform on two areas; the release of the opening allowance for receivables and the damaged inventory. Performance on this question was disappointing.

Candidates were unable to tailor their knowledge of general substantive procedures to the specific issues in the scenario. Many identified the account balances being audited of receivables and inventory and proceeded to list all possible tests for these areas. This is not what was required and hence did not score well. The scenario was provided so that candidates could apply their knowledge; however it seems that many did not take any notice of the scenario at all.

As addressed in other examiners reports candidates must strive to understand substantive procedures. Learning a generic list of tests will not translate to exam success as they must be applied to the scenario. For example on the release of the allowance for receivables, the scenario clearly stated that there was no longer an allowance, yet many candidates provided tests on 'recalculating the allowance', or 'comparing it to last year' these scored no marks. In addition the damaged inventory had a different taste due to an error in the mixing process; many candidates suggested 'inspecting the damaged inventory to assess the level of damage' this is impossible as the problem was the taste of the cola not the physical condition.

Common mistakes made by candidates were:

- Giving objectives rather than procedures 'ensure that inventory is valued at the lower of cost and NRV', this is not a substantive procedure and so would not score any marks.
- Believing that 'obtaining a management representation' is a valid answer for all substantive procedure questions.
- Providing controls tests rather than substantive procedures.
- Not providing enough tests, candidates should assume 1 mark per valid procedure. The requirement verb was to 'describe' therefore sufficient detail was required to score the 1 mark available per test. Candidates are reminded yet again that substantive procedures are a core topic area and they must be able to produce relevant detailed procedures.

144 KANGAROO CONSTRUCTION *Walk in the footsteps of a top tutor*

Top Tutor Tips

Audit risks need to relate to either a risk of material misstatement or a detection risk. For risk of material misstatement, identify a balance in the scenario that is at risk of misstatement and explain why you believe it could be misstated. Detection risks are the risks the auditor does not detect material misstatements in the financial statements e.g. when it is a new audit client or if there is a tight reporting deadline.

For the response, make sure it relates to the risk, not the balance in general. Try and be as specific as possible, simply saying more testing is required will not be sufficient. State the nature of the tests that should be performed.

A 2 column table should be used to keep the risks in line with the responses and to make sure you address both parts of the requirement.

(a) **Materiality and performance materiality**

Materiality and performance materiality are dealt with under ISA 320 *Materiality in Planning and Performing an Audit*. Auditors need to establish the materiality level for the financial statements as a whole, as well as assess performance materiality levels, which are lower than the overall materiality.

Materiality is defined in ISA 320 as follows:

'Misstatements, including omissions, are considered to be material if they, individually or in the aggregate, could reasonably be expected to influence the economic decisions of users taken on the basis of the financial statements.'

In assessing the level of materiality, there are a number of areas that should be considered. First the auditor must consider both the amount (quantity) and the nature (quality) of any misstatements, or a combination of both. The quantity of the misstatement refers to the relative size of it and the quality refers to an amount that might be low in value but due to its prominence could influence the user's decision, for example, directors' transactions.

As per ISA 320, materiality is often calculated using benchmarks such as 5% of profit before tax or 1% of total revenue or total expenses. These values are useful as a starting point for assessing materiality.

The assessment of what is material is ultimately a matter of the auditor's professional judgement, and it is affected by the auditor's perception of the financial information needs of users of the financial statements and the perceived level of risk; the higher the risk, the lower the level of overall materiality.

In assessing materiality, the auditor must consider that a number of errors each with a low value may, when aggregated, amount to a material misstatement.

In calculating materiality, the auditor should also set the performance materiality level. Performance materiality is normally set at a level lower than overall materiality. It is used for testing individual transactions, account balances and disclosures. The aim of performance materiality is to reduce the risk that the total of errors in balances, transactions and disclosures does not in total exceed overall materiality.

Tutorial note

Award marks for ISA 320 definition of performance materiality below:

'Performance materiality means the amount or amounts set by the auditor at less than materiality for the financial statements as a whole to reduce to an appropriately low level the probability that the aggregate of uncorrected and undetected misstatements exceeds materiality for the financial statements as a whole. If applicable, performance materiality also refers to the amount or amounts set by the auditor at less than the materiality level or levels for particular classes of transactions, account balances or disclosures.'

(b) (i) **Ratios**

Top Tutor Tips

Ratios are relationships between different numbers in the financial statements. Percentage movements year to year are trends. The question asks for ratios therefore there will be no marks for calculating the percentage decrease in revenue/cost of sales.

Ratios to assist the audit supervisor in planning the audit:

	2013	*2012*
Gross margin	5.5/12.5 = 44%	7/15 = 46.7%
Operating margin	0.5/12.5 = 4%	1.9/15 = 12.7%
Inventory days	1.9/7 * 365 = 99 days	1.4/8 * 365 = 64 days
Inventory turnover	7/1.9 = 3.7	8/1.4 = 5.7
Receivable days	3.1/12.5 * 365 = 91 days	2.0/15 * 365 = 49 days
Payable days	1.6/7 * 365 = 83 days	1.2/8 * 365 = 55 days
Current ratio	5.8/2.6 = 2.2	5.3/1.2 = 4.4
Quick ratio	(5.8 – 1.9)/2.6 = 1.5	(5.3 – 1.4)/1.2 = 3.3

(ii) **Audit risks and responses**

Audit risk	**Audit response**
Receivable days have increased from 49 to 91 days and management has significantly extended the credit terms given to customers. This leads to an increased risk of recoverability of receivables as they may be overvalued.	Extended post year-end cash receipts testing and a review of the aged receivables ledger to be performed to assess valuation.
Due to the fall in demand for Kangaroo Construction Co's (Kangaroo) houses, there are some houses where the selling price may be below cost. IAS 2 *Inventories* requires that inventory should be stated at the lower of cost and NRV.	Detailed cost and net realisable value (NVR) testing to be performed and the aged inventory report to be reviewed to assess whether inventory requires writing down.

Audit risk	Audit response
In addition, inventory days have increased from 64 to 99 days and inventory turnover has fallen from 5.7 in 2012 to 3.7 in the current year. There is a risk that inventory is overvalued.	
The directors have extended the useful lives of plant and machinery from three to five years, resulting in the depreciation charge reducing. Under IAS 16 *Property, Plant and Equipment*, useful lives are to be reviewed annually, and if asset lives have genuinely increased, then this change is reasonable. However, there is a risk that this reduction has occurred in order to achieve profit targets. If this is the case, then plant and machinery is overvalued and profit overstated.	Discuss with the directors the rationale for extending the useful lives. Also, the five year life should be compared to how often these assets are replaced, as this provides evidence of the useful life of assets.
The directors need to reach a profit level of $0.5 million in order to receive their annual bonus. There is a risk that they might feel under pressure to manipulate the results through the judgements taken or through the use of provisions.	Throughout the audit, the team will need to be alert to this risk and maintain professional scepticism. They will need to carefully review judgemental decisions and compare treatment against prior years. In addition, a written representation should be obtained from management confirming the basis of any significant judgements.
Due to a change in material supplier, the quality of products used has deteriorated and this has led to customers claiming on their five-year building warranty. If the overall number of people claiming on the warranty is likely to increase, then the warranty provision should possibly be higher. If the directors have not increased the level of the provision, then there is a risk the provision is understated.	Review the level of the warranty provision in light of the increased level of claims to confirm completeness of the provision.
Kangaroo has borrowed $1.0m from the bank via a short-term loan. This loan needs to be repaid in 2013 and so should be disclosed as a current liability.	During the audit, the team would need to check that the $1.0m loan finance was received. In addition, the disclosures for this loan should be reviewed in detail to ensure compliance with relevant accounting standards and legislation.

Audit risk	**Audit response**
In addition, Kangaroo may have given the bank a charge over its assets as security for the loan. There is a risk that the disclosure of any security given is not complete.	The loan correspondence should be reviewed to ascertain whether any security has been given, and this bank should be circularised as part of the bank confirmation process.
The current and quick ratios have decreased from 4.4 to 2.2 and 3.3 to 1.5 respectively. In addition, the cash balances have decreased over the year, there is a fall in demand and Kangaroo have taken out a short-term loan of $1 million, which needs to be repaid in 2013. Although all ratios are above the minimum levels, this is still a significant decrease and along with the fall in both operating and gross profit margins, as well as the significant increase in payable days could be evidence of going concern difficulties.	Detailed going concern testing to be performed during the audit and discussed with the directors to ensure that the going concern basis is reasonable. The team should discuss with the directors how the short-term loan of $1.0 million will be repaid later in 2013.

Tutorial note

It has been assumed that customers do not pay in advance for houses and hence the company has receivable balances.

ACCA marking scheme

		Marks
(a)	Up to 1 mark per well explained point: • Materiality for financial statements as a whole and also performance materiality levels • Definition of materiality • Amount or nature of misstatements, or both • 5% profit before tax or 1% revenue or total expenses Judgement, needs of users and level of risk Small errors aggregated Performance materiality	
	Max	5

(b)	(i)	½ mark per ratio calculation per year. Gross margin Operating margin Inventory days Inventory turnover Receivable days Payable days Current ratio Quick ratio		
			Max	**5**
	(ii)	Up to 1 mark per well described audit risk and up to 1 mark per well explained audit response Receivables valuation Inventory valuation Depreciation of plant and machinery Management manipulation of profit to reach bonus targets Completeness of warranty provision Disclosure of bank loan of $1 million Going concern risk		
			Max	**10**
Total				**20**

Examiner's comments

Part (a) for 5 marks required an explanation of the concepts of materiality and performance materiality. Candidates' performed well on this question. The vast majority of candidates were able to score marks on the definition of materiality, provision of some benchmarks for the calculations and a reference to performance materiality being at a lower level. These points would have achieved a pass for this part of the question. An adequate level of detail was provided for this 'explain' requirement by the majority of candidates. Some candidates just gave a definition of materiality and nothing else; this would have gained a maximum of 1 mark.

Part (b) (i) for 5 marks required candidates to calculate ratios for 2012 and 2013 to assist in planning the audit. This question was answered very well by the vast majority of candidates with many scoring full marks.

Some candidates attempted to calculate ratios despite there being inadequate data available, namely return on capital employed and gearing. Candidates need to think about the information provided in the scenario prior to calculating ratios.

In order to gain the 1⁄2 mark available for each year a relevant ratio had to be calculated. Some candidates did not bring a calculator into the exam and hence were unable to calculate the final ratios; these candidates would not be able to score the 5 available marks. Future candidates are reminded, once again, to bring a calculator into the F8 exam as they are often required.

Part (b) (ii) for 10 marks required a description of five audit risks from the scenario and ratios calculated and the auditor's response for each. Performance on this question was once again unsatisfactory.

The scenario contained more than five risks and so candidates were able to easily identify enough risks, they then went on to describe how the point identified from the scenario or movement in a ratio was an audit risk by referring to the assertion and the account balances impacted. The improvement in this area noted in December 12 has been reversed and the proportion of candidates who described the audit risk adequately has declined in this session.

Some candidates tended to only identify facts from the scenario such as 'Kangaroo has completed houses in inventory where selling price may be below cost' but failed to explain how this could impact audit risk; this would only have scored ½ marks. To gain a full 1 mark they needed to refer to the risk of the inventory being overvalued. Where candidates did attempt to cover the assertion it was often vague; for example stating that 'inventory may be misstated', this is not sufficient to gain the ½ mark available.

Additionally, many candidates used the ratios calculated in part (bi) and then gave a detailed analytical review of the ratio movements, commenting on ratio increases and decreases, but with no link at all to the audit risks. It was not uncommon to see very lengthy answers with no audit risks; this just puts the candidate under time pressure.

Many candidates focused on business risks rather than audit risks and hence provided responses related to how management should address these business risks. For example, the scenario stated that 'Kangaroo had changed their main supplier to a cheaper alternative and as a result warranty claims had increased'. Some candidates answered 'this would lead to the company's reputation suffering as the quality of their buildings would decline'. The suggested auditor's response was 'to change back to a more expensive supplier'. Neither the risk nor the response has been related to the financial statements and hence would only gain a ½mark being the identification of the fact from the scenario.

Additionally, candidates performed inadequately with regards to the auditor's responses. As detailed above some candidates gave business advice, other responses focused more on repeating what the appropriate accounting treatment should be, therefore for the risk of inventory valuation due to number of houses where selling price was below cost, the response given was 'inventory should be valued at the lower of cost and NRV', this is not a valid audit response.

Responses which start with 'ensure that......' are unlikely to score marks as they usually fail to explain exactly how the auditor will address the audit risk. Also some responses were weak such as 'discuss with the directors' without making it clear what would be discussed and how this would gather evidence. Audit responses need to be practical and should relate to the approach the auditor will adopt to assess whether the balance is materially misstated or not.

Most candidates presented their answers well as they adopted a two column approach with audit risk in one column and the related auditor's response next to it.

145 SUNFLOWER STORES *Walk in the footsteps of a top tutor*

(a) **Understanding an entity**

> ***Top Tutor Tips***
>
> *The question asks for sources of information and the information you would expect to obtain to gain an understanding of Sunflower Stores. Make sure you suggest information that would help you gain an understanding and not substantively test the financial statements. Think about what information you would require at the planning stage of the audit specifically. Suggesting information such as bank letters and receivables circularisations will not score marks as these are obtained at the substantive testing stage not the planning stage. The source is 'where' the information will come from.*

Source of information	*Information expect to obtain*
Prior year audit file	Identification of issues that arose in the prior year audit and how these were resolved. Also whether any points brought forward were noted for consideration for this year's audit.
Prior year financial statements	Provides information in relation to the size of the entity as well as the key accounting policies and disclosure notes.
Accounting systems notes	Provides information on how each of the key accounting systems operates.
Discussions with management	Provides information in relation to any important issues which have arisen or changes to the company during the year.
Current year budgets and management accounts of Sunflower Stores Co (Sunflower)	Provides relevant financial information for the year to date. Will help the auditor to identify whether Sunflower has changed materially since last year. In addition, this will be useful for preliminary analytical review and risk identification.
Permanent audit file	Provides information in relation to matters of continuing importance for the company and the audit team, such as statutory books information or important agreements.
Sunflower's website	Recent press releases from the company may provide background on changes to the business during the year as this could lead to additional audit risks.

Prior year report to management	Provides information on the internal control deficiencies noted in the prior year; if these have not been rectified by management then they could arise in the current year audit as well.
Financial statements of competitors	This will provide information about Sunflower's competitors, in relation to their financial results and their accounting policies. This will be important in assessing Sunflower's performance in the year and also when undertaking the going concern review.

(b) **Audit risks and auditor responses**

Top Tutor Tips

Audit risks need to relate to either a risk of material misstatement or a detection risk. For risk of material misstatement, identify a balance in the scenario that is at risk of misstatement and explain why you believe it could be misstated. Detection risks are the risks the auditor does not detect material misstatements in the financial statements e.g. when it is a new audit client or if there is a tight reporting deadline.

For the response, make sure it relates to the risk, not the balance in general. Try and be as specific as possible, simply saying more testing is required will not be sufficient. State the nature of the tests that should be performed.

A 2 column table should be used to keep the risks in line with the responses and to make sure you address both parts of the requirement.

Audit risk	*Auditor response*
Sunflower has spent $1.6m on refurbishing its 25 food supermarkets. This expenditure needs to be reviewed to assess whether it is of a capital nature and should be included within non-current assets or expensed as repairs.	Review a breakdown of the costs and agree to invoices to assess the nature of the expenditure and, if capital, agree to inclusion within the asset register and, if repairs, agree to the statement of profit or loss.
During the year a small warehouse has been disposed of at a profit. The asset needs to have been correctly removed from property plant and equipment to ensure the non-current asset register is not overstated, and the profit on disposal should be included within the statement of profit or loss.	Review the non-current asset register to ensure that the asset has been removed. Also confirm the disposal proceeds as well as recalculating the profit on disposal. Consideration should be given as to whether the profit on disposal is significant enough to warrant separate disclosure within the statement of profit or loss.

Audit risk	*Auditor response*
Sunflower has borrowed $1.5m from the bank via a five year loan. This loan needs to be correctly split between current and non-current liabilities.	During the audit the team would need to confirm that the $1.5m loan finance was received. In addition, the split between current and non-current liabilities and the disclosures for this loan should be reviewed in detail to ensure compliance with relevant accounting standards.
In addition, Sunflower may have given the bank a charge over its assets as security for the loan. There is a risk that the disclosure of any security given is not complete.	The loan agreement should be reviewed to ascertain whether any security has been given, and this bank should be circularised as part of the bank confirmation process.
Sunflower will be undertaking a number of simultaneous inventory counts on 31 December including the warehouse and all 25 supermarkets. It is not practical for the auditor to attend all of these counts; hence it may not be possible to gain sufficient appropriate audit evidence over inventory counts.	The team should select a sample of sites to visit. It is likely that the warehouse contains most goods and therefore should be selected. In relation to the 25 supermarkets, the team should visit those with material inventory balances and/or those with a history of inventory count issues.
Sunflower's inventory valuation policy is selling price less average profit margin. Inventory should be valued at the lower of cost and net realisable value (NRV) and if this is not the case, then inventory could be under or overvalued.	Testing should be undertaken to confirm cost and NRV of inventory and that on a line-by-line basis the goods are valued correctly.
IAS 2 *Inventories* allows this as an inventory valuation method as long as it is a close approximation to cost. If this is not the case, then inventory could be under or overvalued.	In addition, valuation testing should focus on comparing the cost of inventory to the selling price less margin to confirm whether this method is actually a close approximation to cost.
The opening balances for each supermarket have been transferred into the head office's accounting records at the beginning of the year. There is a risk that if this transfer has not been performed completely and accurately, the opening balances may not be correct.	Discuss with management the process undertaken to transfer the data and the testing performed to confirm the transfer was complete and accurate. Computer-assisted audit techniques could be utilised by the team to sample test the transfer of data from each supermarket to head office to identify any errors.
There has been an increased workload for the finance department, the financial controller has left and his replacement will only start in late December.	The team should remain alert throughout the audit for additional errors within the finance department.

Audit risk	*Auditor response*
This increases the inherent risk within Sunflower as errors may have been made within the accounting records by the overworked finance team members. The new financial controller may not be sufficiently experienced to produce the financial statements and resolve any audit issues.	In addition, discuss with the finance director whether he will be able to provide the team with assistance for any audit issues the new financial controller is unable to resolve.

(c) **Internal audit department**

Prior to establishing an internal audit (IA) department, the finance director of Sunflower should consider the following:

(i) The costs of establishing an IA department will be significant, therefore prior to committing to these costs and management time, a cost benefit analysis should be performed.

(ii) The size and complexity of Sunflower should be considered. The larger, more complex and diverse a company is, then the greater the need for an IA department. At Sunflower there are 25 supermarkets and a head office and therefore it would seem that the company is diverse enough to gain benefit from an IA department.

(iii) The role of any IA department should be considered. The finance director should consider what tasks he would envisage IA performing. He should consider whether he wishes them to undertake inventory counts at the stores, or whether he would want them to undertake such roles as internal controls reviews.

(iv) Having identified the role of any IA department, the finance director should consider whether there are existing managers or employees who could perform these tasks, therefore reducing the need to establish a separate IA department.

(v) The finance director should assess the current control environment and determine whether there are departments or stores with a history of control deficiencies. If this is the case, then it increases the need for an IA department.

(vi) If the possibility of fraud is high, then the greater the need for an IA department to act as both a deterrent and also to possibly undertake fraud investigations. As Sunflower operates 25 food supermarkets, it will have a significant risk of fraud of both inventory and cash.

ACCA marking scheme		
		Marks
(a)	½ mark for source of documentation and ½ mark for information expect to obtain, max of 2½ marks for sources and 2½ marks for information expect – Prior year audit file – Prior year financial statements – Accounting systems notes – Discussions with management – Permanent audit file – Current year budgets and management accounts – Sunflower's website – Prior year report to management – Financial statements of competitors	
	Max	**5**
(b)	Up to 1 mark per well described risk and up to 1 mark for each well explained response. Overall max of 5 marks for risks and 5 marks for responses. Treatment of $1.6m refurbishment expenditure Disposal of warehouse Bank loan of $1.5m Attendance at year-end inventory counts Inventory valuation Transfer of opening balances from supermarkets to head office Increased inherent risk of errors in finance department and new financial controller	
	Max	**10**
(c)	Up to 1 mark per well described point Costs versus benefits of establishing an internal audit (IA) department Size and complexity of Sunflower should be considered The role of any IA department should be considered Whether existing managers/employees can undertake the roles required Whether the control environment has a history of control deficiencies Whether the possibility of fraud is high	
	Max	**5**
Total		**20**

Examiner's comments

Part (a) for 5 marks required a list of five sources of information for gaining an understanding of Sunflower and what each source would be used for. Candidates' performance on this question was unsatisfactory.

A significant proportion of candidates did not seem to understand what was required from them for this question. They did not seem to understand what a 'source of information' was and so failed to list where they would obtain information from such as prior year financial statements or last year's audit file. Some were able to explain what they would want to gain knowledge on e.g. audit risks or accounting policies but did not tie this into the source of information.

In addition the question requirement related to gaining an understanding of Sunflower, this is part of the planning process, however a significant proportion of candidates gave sources of information relevant to carrying out the audit fieldwork, such as bank letters, written representations or receivables circularisation.

Most candidates' confused requirements a and b and so gave sources of information relevant to auditing the risks from requirement b. These points were not relevant to gaining an understanding of Sunflower and hence scored no marks.

Part (b) for 10 marks required a description of five audit risks from the scenario and the auditor's response for each. Performance on this question was mixed, although slightly better than December 2011 when audit risk was last tested.

The scenario contained many more than five risks and so many candidates were able to easily identify enough risks, they then went on to describe how the point identified from the scenario was an audit risk by referring to the assertion and the account balance impacted. There seemed to be a higher proportion of candidates this session who described the audit risk adequately.

Some candidates tended to only identify facts from the scenario such as 'Sunflower has spent $1.6 million in refurbishing all of its supermarkets' but failed to explain how this could impact audit risk; this would only have scored ½ marks. To gain 1 mark they needed to refer to the risk of the expenditure not being correctly classified between capital and repairs resulting in misstated expenses or non-current assets. Additionally, candidates were able to identify the fact from the question but then focused on categorising this into an element of the audit risk model such as inherent or control risk. The problem with this approach is that just because they have stated an issue could increase control risk does not mean that they have described the audit risk and so this does not tend to score well.

The area where most candidates performed inadequately is with regards to the auditor's responses. Some candidates gave business advice such as, for the risk of the finance director (FD) leaving early, that 'the auditor should ask management to replace the FD quicker' this is not a valid audit response. Other responses focused more on repeating what the appropriate accounting treatment should be, therefore for the risk of inventory valuation due to the policy of valuing at selling price less margin, the response given was 'inventory should be valued at the lower of cost and NRV', again this is not a valid audit response.

Responses which start with 'ensure that......' are unlikely to score marks as they usually fail to explain exactly how the auditor will address the audit risk. Also some responses were too vague such as 'increase substantive testing' without making it clear how, or in what area, this would be addressed. Audit responses need to be practical and should relate to the approach the auditor will adopt to assess whether the balance is materially misstated or not.

A significant minority of candidates misread the scenario and where it stated that it was the first year on this audit for the senior, candidates seemed to think that it was the first year for the firm as a whole and so identified an audit risk of Sunflower being a new client with higher detection risk. This scored no marks as it was not the first year of the audit, candidates must read the scenario more carefully.

Most candidates presented their answers well as they adopted a two column approach with audit risk in one column and the related response next to it.

Part (c) for 5 marks required candidates to describe factors the finance director should consider before establishing an internal audit (IA) department. Performance was unsatisfactory on this part of the question.

Many candidates were able to gain a few marks with points on considering cost and benefits of the IA department and whether it should be outsourced or run in house. However, this seemed to be the limit of most candidates' knowledge in this area. Unfortunately many candidates strayed into the area of who IA should report to and the qualifications and independence of the department; these are factors to consider when running IA as opposed to whether or not to establish an IA department. Once again, candidates must answer the question set and not the one they wish had been asked.

146 ABRAHAMS *Walk in the footsteps of a top tutor*

(a) **Components of audit risk**

Inherent risk

The susceptibility of an assertion about a class of transaction, account balance or disclosure to a misstatement that could be material, either individually or when aggregated with other misstatements, before consideration of any related controls.

Inherent risk is affected by the nature of an entity and factors which can result in an increase include:

- Changes in the industry it operates in.
- Operations that are subject to a high degree of regulation.
- Going concern and liquidity issues including loss of significant customers.
- Developing or offering new products or services, or moving into new lines of business. – Expanding into new locations.
- Application of new accounting standards.
- Accounting measurements that involve complex processes.
- Events or transactions that involve significant accounting estimates.
- Pending litigation and contingent liabilities.

Control risk

The risk that a misstatement that could occur in an assertion about a class of transaction, account balance or disclosure and that could be material, either individually or when aggregated with other misstatements, will not be prevented, or detected and corrected, on a timely basis by the entity's internal control.

The following factors can result in an increase in control risk:

- Lack of personnel with appropriate accounting and financial reporting skills.
- Changes in key personnel including departure of key management.
- Deficiencies in internal control, especially those not addressed by management.
- Changes in the information technology (IT) environment.
- Installation of significant new IT systems related to financial reporting.

Detection risk

The risk that the procedures performed by the auditor to reduce audit risk to an acceptably low level will not detect misstatement that exists and that could be material, either individually or when aggregated with other misstatements.

Detection risk is affected by sampling and non-sampling risk and factors which can result in an increase include:

- Inadequate planning.
- Inappropriate assignment of personnel to the engagement team.

- Failing to apply professional scepticism.
- Inadequate supervision and review of the audit work performed.
- Inappropriate sampling techniques performed.
- Inappropriate sample sizes.

(b) **Audit risks and responses**

Top Tutor Tips

Audit risks need to relate to either a risk of material misstatement or a detection risk. For risk of material misstatement, identify a balance in the scenario that is at risk of misstatement and explain why you believe it could be misstated. Detection risks are the risks the auditor does not detect material misstatements in the financial statements e.g. when it is a new audit client or if there is a tight reporting deadline.

For the response, make sure it relates to the risk, not the balance in general. Try and be as specific as possible, simply saying more testing is required will not be sufficient. State the nature of the tests that should be performed.

A 2 column table should be used to keep the risks in line with the responses and to make sure you address both parts of the requirement.

Audit risk	**Audit response**
The finance director of Abrahams is planning to capitalise the full $2.2 million of development expenditure incurred. However in order to be capitalised it must meet all of the criteria under IAS 38 *Intangible Assets.* There is a risk that some projects may not reach final development stage and hence should be expensed rather than capitalised. Intangible assets could be overstated and this risk is increased due to the loan covenant requirements to maintain a minimum level of assets.	A breakdown of the development expenditure should be reviewed and tested in detail to ensure that only projects which meet the capitalisation criteria are included as an intangible asset, with the balance being expensed.
The inventory valuation method used by Abrahams is standard costing. This method is acceptable under IAS 2 *Inventories;* however, only if standard cost is a close approximation to actual cost. Abrahams has not updated their standard costs from when the product was first developed and hence there is a risk that the standard costs could be out of date, resulting in over or undervalued inventory.	The standard costs used for the inventory valuation should be tested in detail and compared to actual cost. If there are significant variations this should be discussed with management, to ensure that the valuation is appropriate.

Audit risk	Audit response
The work in progress balance at the year end is likely to be material; however there is a risk that due to the nature of the production process the audit team may not be sufficiently qualified to assess the quantity and value of work in progress leading to misstated work in progress.	Consideration should be given as to whether an independent expert is required to value the work in progress. If so this will need to be arranged with consent from management and in time for the year-end count.
Over one-third of the warehouses of Abrahams belong to third parties. Sufficient and appropriate evidence will need to be obtained to confirm the quantities of inventory held in these locations in order to verify completeness and existence.	Additional procedures will be required to ensure that inventory quantities have been confirmed for both third party and company owned locations.
In September Abrahams Co introduced a new accounting system. This is a critical system for the accounts preparation and if there were any errors that occurred during the changeover process, these could impact on the final amounts in the trial balance.	The new system will need to be documented in full and testing should be performed over the transfer of data from the old to the new system.
The new accounting system is bespoke and the IT manager who developed it has left the company already and his replacement is not due to start until just before the year end. The accounting personnel who are using the system may have encountered problems and without the IT manager's support, errors could be occurring in the system due to a lack of knowledge and experience. This could result in significant errors arising in the financial statements.	This issue should be discussed with the finance director to understand how he is addressing this risk of misstatement. In addition, the team should remain alert throughout the audit for evidence of such errors.
Significant finance has been obtained in the year, $1 million of equity finance and $2.5 million of long-term loans. This finance needs to be accounted for correctly, with adequate disclosure made. The equity finance needs to be allocated correctly between share capital and share premium, and the loan should be presented as a non-current liability.	Check that the split of the equity finance is correct and that total financing proceeds of $3.5 million were received. In addition, the disclosures for this finance should be reviewed in detail to ensure compliance with relevant accounting standards.

Audit risk	Audit response
The loan has a number of covenants attached to it. If these are breached then the loan would be instantly repayable and would be classified as a current liability. This could result in the company being in a net current liability position. If the company did not have sufficient cash flow to meet this loan repayment then there could be going concern implications.	Review the covenant calculations prepared by Abrahams Co and identify whether any defaults have occurred; if so then determine the effect on the company. The team should maintain their professional scepticism and be alert to the risk that assets have been overstated to ensure compliance with covenants.
The land and buildings are to be revalued at the year end, it is likely that the revaluation needs to be carried out and recorded in accordance with IAS 16 *Property, Plant and Equipment*; otherwise non-current assets may be incorrectly valued.	Review the reasonableness of the valuation and recalculate the revaluation surplus/deficit to ensure that land and buildings are correctly valued.
The reporting timetable for Abrahams Co is likely to be reduced. The previous timetable was already quite short and any further reductions will increase detection risk and place additional pressure on the team in obtaining sufficient and appropriate evidence.	The timetable should be confirmed with the financial director. If it is to be reduced then consideration should be given to performing an interim audit in late December or early January, this would then reduce the pressure on the final audit.

(c) (i) **Procedures to confirm inventory held at third party locations**

- Send a letter requesting direct confirmation of inventory balances held at year end from the third party warehouse providers used by Abrahams Co regarding quantities and condition.
- Attend the inventory count (if one is to be performed) at the third party warehouses to review the controls in operation to ensure the completeness and existence of inventory.
- Inspect any reports produced by the auditors of the warehouses in relation to the adequacy of controls over inventory.
- Inspect any documentation in respect of third party inventory.

(ii) **Procedures to confirm use of standard costs for inventory valuation**

- Discuss with management of Abrahams Co the basis of the standard costs applied to the inventory valuation, and how often these are reviewed and updated.
- Review the level of variances between standard and actual costs and discuss with management how these are treated.
- Obtain a breakdown of the standard costs and agree a sample of these costs to actual invoices or wage records to assess their reasonableness.

ACCA marking scheme		
		Marks
(a)	Up to 1 mark for each component of audit risk (if just a component is given without an explanation then just give 0.5) and up to 1 mark for each example of factor which increases risk. Inherent risk Control risk Detection risk	
	Max	**6**
(b)	Up to 1 mark per well explained risk and up to 1 mark for each well explained response. Overall max of 5 for risks and 5 for responses. Development expenditure treatment Standard costing for valuation of inventory Expert possibly required in verifying work in progress Third party inventory locations New accounting system introduced in the year Lack of support by IT staff on new system may result in errors in accounting system New finance obtained; loans and equity finance treatment Loan covenants and risk of going concern problems Revaluation of land and buildings Reduced reporting timetable	
	Max	**10**
(c)	1 mark per well explained procedure, maximum of 2 marks for each of (i) and (ii) (i) Third party locations Letter requesting direct confirmation Attend inventory count Review other auditor reports and documentation	
	Max	**2**
	(ii) Standard costing Discuss with management basis of standard costs Review variances Breakdown of standard costs and agree to actual costs	
	Max	**2**
Total		**20**

147 REDSMITH *Walk in the footsteps of a top tutor*

> ***Top Tutor Tips***
>
> *Part (a) is a purely knowledge based requirement covering part of ISA 210 Agreeing the Terms of Audit Engagements. It is a difficult requirement – you either know the answer or you don't. A common sense approach will not help you here. If you don't have the knowledge, move on and try to compensate by scoring well on other requirements.*
>
> *Part (b) is another purely knowledge based requirement, but a common sense approach will score well here. If you don't know the requirements of ISA 315 Identifying and Assessing Risks of Material Misstatement through Understanding the Entity and its Environment you can still score well by thinking generally about the areas/matters that the auditor should obtain an understanding of.*
>
> *Part (c) is a core topic in the F8 syllabus – audit risk and the auditor's response. The auditor's response should be directly linked to the audit risks explained and therefore a columnar approach is appropriate. This is a skills based question – the answers must relate to the issues presented in the scenario. Each sufficiently explained audit risk will be awarded 1 mark and each appropriate response a further mark. You therefore need to explain five audit risks for 10 marks.*
>
> *The highlighted words are key phases that markers are looking for.*

(a) ISA 210 *Agreeing the Terms of Audit Engagements* provides guidance to auditors on the steps they should take in accepting a new audit or continuing on an existing audit engagement. It sets out a number of processes that the auditor should perform including agreeing whether the preconditions are present, agreement of audit terms in an engagement letter, recurring audits and changes in engagement terms.

To assess whether the preconditions for an audit are present the auditor must determine whether the financial reporting framework to be applied in the preparation of the financial statements is acceptable. In considering this the auditor should assess the nature of the entity, the nature and purpose of the financial statements and whether law or regulations prescribes the applicable reporting framework.

In addition they must obtain the agreement of management that it acknowledges and understands its responsibility for the following:

- Preparation of the financial statements in accordance with the applicable financial reporting framework, including where relevant their fair presentation
- For such internal control as management determines is necessary to enable the preparation of financial statements that are free from material misstatement, whether due to fraud or error; and
- To provide the auditor with access to all relevant information for the preparation of the financial statements, any additional information that the auditor may request from management and unrestricted access to persons within the entity from whom the auditor determines it necessary to obtain audit evidence.

If the preconditions for an audit are not present, the auditor shall discuss the matter with management. Unless required by law or regulation to do so, the auditor shall not accept the proposed audit engagement:

- If the auditor has determined that the financial reporting framework to be applied in the preparation of the financial statements is unacceptable; or
- If management agreement of their responsibilities has not been obtained.

(b) **Matters to consider in obtaining an understanding of the entity:**

- The market and its competition
- Legislation and regulation
- Regulatory framework
- Ownership of the entity
- Nature of products/services and markets
- Location of production facilities and factories
- Key customers and suppliers
- Capital investment activities
- Accounting policies and industry specific guidance
- Financing structure
- Significant changes in the entity on prior years.

Top tutor tips

Note the requirement asks for matters to consider in obtaining an understanding of the entity. Procedures that the auditor should perform or sources from which they would obtain this understanding will not score any marks. Also note the verb requirement 'list' and the number of marks available. With a 'list' requirement, each appropriate matter listed will be awarded ½ mark. The length of points provided in the model answer is appropriate for ½ mark.

(c) (i) **Ratios to assist the audit supervisor in planning the audit:**

	2010	*2009*
Gross margin	12/23 = 52.2%	8/18 = 44.4%
Operating margin	45/23 = 19.6%	4/18 = 22.2%
Inventory days	21/11 * 365 = 70 days	16/10 * 365 = 58 days
Receivable days	45/23 * 365 = 71 days	30/18 * 365 = 61 days
Payable days	16/11 * 365 = 53 days	12/10 * 365 = 44 days
Current ratio	66/25 = 2.6	69/12 = 5.8
Quick ratio	(66 – 21)/25 = 1.8	(69 – 16)/12 = 4.4

Top tutor tips

Be sure to calculate ratios *and not* trends *in order to score well in part (i). Simple % increases will not be awarded marks. The auditor will calculate ratios as part of the analytical review required at the planning stage. You should expect to be examined on the practical application of skills required during the audit process.*

(ii)

Audit risk	**Response to risk**
Management were disappointed with 2009 results and hence undertook strategies to improve the 2010 trading results. There is a risk that management might feel under pressure to manipulate the results through the judgements taken or through the use of provisions.	Throughout the audit the team will need to be alert to this risk. They will need to carefully review judgemental decisions and compare treatment against prior years.
A generous sales-related bonus scheme has been introduced in the year, this may lead to sales cut-off errors with employees aiming to maximise their current year bonus.	Increased sales cut-off testing will be performed along with a review of post year-end sales returns as they may indicate cut-off errors.
Revenue has grown by 28% in the year however, cost of sales has only increased by 10%. This increase in sales may be due to the bonus scheme and the advertising however, this does not explain the increase in gross margin. There is a risk that sales may be overstated.	During the audit a detailed breakdown of sales will be obtained, discussed with management and tested in order to understand the sales increase.
Gross margin has increased from 44.4% to 52.2%. Operating margin has decreased from 22.2% to 19.6%. This movement in gross margin is significant and there is a risk that costs may have been omitted or included in operating expenses rather than cost of sales. There has been a significant increase in operating expenses which may be due to the bonus and the advertising campaign but could be related to the misclassification of costs.	The classification of costs between cost of sales and operating expenses will be compared with the prior year to ensure consistency.

The finance director has made a change to the inventory valuation in the year with additional overheads being included. In addition inventory days have increased from 58 to 70 days. There is a risk that inventory is overvalued.	The change in the inventory policy will be discussed with management and a review of the additional overheads included performed to ensure that these are of a production nature. Detailed cost and net realisable value testing to be performed and the aged inventory report to be reviewed to assess whether inventory requires writing down.
Receivable days have increased from 61 to 71 days and management have extended the credit period given to customers. This leads to an increased risk of recoverability of receivables.	Extended post year-end cash receipts testing and a review of the aged receivables ledger to be performed to assess valuation.
The current and quick ratios have decreased from 5.8 to 2.6 and 4.4 to 1.8 respectively. In addition the cash balances have decreased significantly over the year. Although all ratios are above the minimum levels, this is still a significant decrease and along with the increase of sales could be evidence of overtrading which could result in going concern difficulties.	Detailed going concern testing to be performed during the audit and discussed with management to ensure that the going concern basis is reasonable.

Top tutor tips

Take care to describe audit risks in part (c) and not business risks or interpretations of the ratios. Audit risk is the risk of giving an inappropriate opinion – you should describe the potential for misstatement in the financial statements or explain how detection risk is increased – be specific. Link the ratios you calculate in part (i) to the information given about the entity described when explaining the audit risk. The auditor's response must directly relate to the risk described – describe a procedure that would help the auditor detect any misstatement that may exist.

ACCA marking scheme			
			Marks
(a)		Up to 1 mark per valid point – ISA 210 provides guidance – Determination of acceptable framework – Agreement of management responsibilities – Preparation of financial statements with applicable framework – Internal controls – Provide auditor with relevant information and access – If preconditions are not present discuss with management – Decline if framework unacceptable – Decline if agreement of responsibilities not obtained	
		Max	**3**
(b)		½ mark per example of matter to consider in obtaining an understanding of the nature of an entity.	
		Max	**2**
(c)	(i)	½ mark per ratio calculation per year. – Gross margin – Operating margin – Inventory days – Receivable days – Payable days – Current ratio – Quick ratio	
		Max	**5**
	(ii)	Up to 1 mark per well explained audit risk and up to 1 mark per audit response – Management manipulation of results – Sales cut-off – Revenue growth – Misclassification of costs between cost of sales and operating – Inventory valuation – Receivables valuation – Going concern risk	
		Max	**10**
Total			**20**

148 SPECS4YOU *Walk in the footsteps of a top tutor*

Top Tutor Tips

Parts (a) and (b) are book knowledge. Part (c) expects you to apply that knowledge to identify deficiencies in a working paper, illustrating that memorising without understanding is insufficient.

(a) **The purposes of audit working papers include:**

- To assist with the planning and performance of the audit.
- To assist in the supervision and review of audit work.
- To record the audit evidence resulting from the audit work performed to support the auditor's opinion.

(b) **Familiarisation**

Documentation	**Information obtained**
Memorandum and articles of association	Details of the objectives of Specs4You, its permitted capital structure and the internal constitution of the company.
Most recent published financial statements	Provide detail on the size of the company, profitability, etc. as well as any unusual factors such as loans due for repayment.
Most recent management accounts/budgets/cash flow information	Determine the current status of the company including ongoing profitability, ability to meet budget, etc. as well as identifying any potential going concern problems.
Organisation chart of Specs4You	To identify the key managers and employees in the company and other people to contact during the audit.
Industry data on spectacle sales	To find out how Specs4You is performing compared to the industry standards. This will help to highlight any areas of concern, for example higher than expected cost of sales, for investigation on the audit.
Financial statements of similar entities	To compare the accounting policies of Specs4You and obtain additional information on industry standards.
Prior year audit file	To establish what problems were encountered in last year's audit, how those problems were resolved and identify any areas of concern for this year's audit.
Search of Internet news sites	To find out whether the company has any significant news stories (good or bad) which may affect the audit approach.

(c) The audit working paper does not meet the standards normally expected in a working paper because:

- The page reference is unclear making it very difficult to either file the working paper in the audit file or locate the working paper should there be queries on it.
- It is not clear what the client year-end date is – the year is missing. The working paper could easily be filed in the wrong year's audit file.
- There is no signature of the person who prepared the working paper. This means it is unclear who to address queries to regarding the preparation or contents of the working paper.

- There is evidence of a reviewer's signature. However, given that the reviewer did not query the lack of preparer's signature or other omissions noted below, the effectiveness of the review must be put in question.
- The test 'objective' is vague – it is not clear what 'correct' means for example, it would be better to state the objective in terms of assertions such as completeness or accuracy.
- The test objective is also stated as an audit assertion. This is not the case as no audit assertions are actually listed here.
- It is not clear how the number for testing was determined. This means it will be very difficult to determine whether sufficient audit evidence was obtained for this test.
- Stating that details of testing can be found on another working paper is insufficient – time will be wasted finding the working paper, if it has, in fact, been included in the audit working paper file.
- Information on the results of the test is unclear – the working paper should clearly state the results of the test without bias. The preparer appears to have used personal judgement which is not appropriate as the opinion should be based on the facts available, not speculation.
- The conclusion provided does not appear to be consistent with the results of the test. Five errors were found therefore it is likely that there are some systems deficiencies.

ACCA marking scheme

			Marks
(a)	1 mark for each purpose		
	– Assist planning and performance of audit		
	– Assist supervision and review		
	– Support audit opinion		
		Max	**3**
(b)	½ per item of documentation and ½ for the information it provides		
	– Memorandum and articles of association		
	– Published FS		
	– Management accounts		
	– Budgets/forecasts		
	– Organisation chart		
	– Industry data		
	– Competitor FS		
	– Prior year audit file		
	– Internet/press articles		
		Max	**8**
(c)	Up to 1 mark per point		
	– Page reference		
	– Year end		
	– Name of preparer		
	– Objective/assertion		
	– Justification of sample size		
	– No reference of other working paper		
	– Results of the test unclear		
	– Conclusion inconsistent		
	– Results of the test unclear		
		Max	**9**
Total			**20**

149 DOCUMENTATION/PLANNING

(a) **Benefits of documenting audit work**

- Provides evidence of the auditor's basis for a conclusion about the achievement of the overall objective of the audit.
- Provides evidence that the audit was planned and performed in accordance with ISAs and applicable legal and regulatory requirements.
- Assists the engagement team to plan and perform the audit.
- Assists members of the engagement team responsible for supervision to direct, supervise and review the audit work.
- Enables the engagement team to be accountable for its work.
- Retains a record of matters of continuing significance to future audits.

(b) **Working papers**

- Name of client – identifies the client being audited.
- Year-end date – identifies the year end to which the audit working papers relate.
- Subject – identifies the area of the financial statements that is being audited, the topic area of the working paper, such as receivables circularisation.
- Working paper reference – provides a clear reference to identify the number of the working paper, for example, R12 being the 12th working paper in the audit of receivables.
- Preparer – identifies the name of the audit team member who prepared the working paper, so any queries can be directed to the relevant person.
- Date prepared – the date that the audit work was performed by the team member; this helps to identify what was known at the time and what issues may have occurred subsequently.
- Reviewer – the name of the audit team member who reviewed the working paper; this provides evidence that the audit work was reviewed by an appropriate member of the team.
- Date of review – the date the audit work was reviewed by the senior member of the team; this should be prior to the date that the audit report was signed.
- Objective of work/test – the aim of the work being performed, could be the related financial statement assertion; this provides the context for why the audit procedure is being performed.
- Details of work performed – the audit tests performed along with sufficient detail of items selected for testing.
- Results of work performed – whether any exceptions arose in the audit work and if any further work is required.
- Conclusion – the overall conclusion on the audit work performed, whether the area is true and fair.

(c) **Planning documents**

Audit strategy sets the scope, timing and direction of the audit. It includes the characteristics of the engagement, reporting objectives, results of preliminary engagement activities, and enables the auditor to determine the nature, timing and extent of any resources necessary to perform the audit.

Audit plan contains the nature, timing and extent of risk assessment procedures, and further audit procedures necessary to comply with ISA's.

The audit strategy is used to guide the development of the audit plan. For example, further audit procedures will be included in the audit plan in response to risk assessment and preliminary engagement activities.

ACCA marking scheme

		Marks
(a)	Up to 1 mark per valid point Evidence of conclusions Evidence of compliance with ISAs Helps team to plan and perform audit Helps supervision Team is accountable Record of matters of continuing significance	
	Max	**3**
(b)	Up to 1 mark per well explained point, ½ mark only if just identifies item to be included, max of 4 points. Name of client Year-end date Subject Working paper reference Preparer Date prepared Reviewer Date of review Objective of work/test Details of work performed Results of work performed Conclusion	
	Max	**4**
(c)	Up to 1 mark per valid point. – Audit strategy – Audit plan – Relationship between the strategy and plan	
	Max	**3**
Total		**10**

Examiner's comments

Part (a) required benefits of documenting audit work. This question was answered well by most candidates. In addition the verb of 'state' was addressed by most candidates and answers were generally succinct. Where candidates did not score full marks this tended to be because they repeated points or because they gave points which related to the benefits of audit planning rather than the benefits of documenting audit work.

Part (b) for 4 marks required an explanation of four items that would be included on every working paper prepared by the audit team. This was answered unsatisfactorily. Many candidates seemed completely confused by what was required and instead of focusing on contents of a working paper provided answers in relation to contents of an audit report, or contents of a permanent and current audit file. Answers giving examples such as engagement letter, management letter, risk assessments, representation letter, etc. were common. It is not clear why candidates failed to understand this question as the requirement was clear. Where candidates did provide examples of items to be included in working papers, they often failed to explain their purpose and so this reduced their available marks.

150 AUDITOR RESPONSIBILITIES *Walk in the footsteps of a top tutor*

(a) **Fraud**

Top Tutor Tips

The question asks for the external auditor's responsibilities in relation to fraud and error. Make sure you don't just talk about general responsibilities. Relate it to fraud and error.

An auditor conducting an audit in accordance with ISA 240 *The Auditor's Responsibilities Relating to Fraud in an Audit of Financial Statements is* responsible for obtaining reasonable assurance that the financial statements taken as a whole are free from material misstatement, whether caused by fraud or error.

In order to fulfil this responsibility auditors are required to identify and assess the risks of material misstatement of the financial statements due to fraud.

The auditor will need to obtain sufficient appropriate audit evidence regarding the assessed risks of material misstatement due to fraud, through designing and implementing appropriate responses.

In addition, the auditor must respond appropriately to fraud or suspected fraud identified during the audit.

When obtaining reasonable assurance, the auditor is responsible for maintaining professional scepticism throughout the audit, considering the potential for management override of controls and recognising the fact that audit procedures that are effective in detecting error may not be effective in detecting fraud.

To ensure that the whole engagement team is aware of the risks and responsibilities for fraud and error, ISAs require that a discussion is held within the team. For members not present at the meeting the engagement partner should determine which matters are to be communicated to them.

To be able to make such an assessment auditors must identify, through enquiry, how management assesses and responds to the risk of fraud. The auditor must also enquire of management, internal auditors and those charged with governance if they are aware of any actual or suspected fraudulent activity.

If the auditor identifies a fraud they should communicate the matter on a timely basis to the appropriate level of management (i.e. those with the primary responsibility for prevention and detection of fraud). If the suspected fraud involves management the auditor shall communicate such matters to those charged with governance. If the auditor has doubts about the integrity of those charged with governance they should seek legal advice regarding an appropriate course of action.

In addition to these responsibilities the auditor must also consider whether they have a responsibility to report the occurrence of a suspicion to a party outside the entity. Whilst the auditor does have an ethical duty to maintain confidentiality, it is likely that any legal responsibility will take precedent.

In these circumstances it is advisable to seek legal advice.

(b) **Laws and Regulations**

Noncompliance with laws and regulations can impact the financial statements because companies in breach of the law may need to make provisions for future legal costs and fines. In the worst case scenario this could affect the ability of the company to continue as a going concern.

In addition the auditor may need to report identified noncompliance with laws and regulations either to management or to a regulatory body, if the issue requires such action. An example of the latter would be when the client is in breach of money laundering regulations.

The auditor must obtain sufficient, appropriate evidence regarding compliance with those laws and regulations generally recognised to have a direct effect on the determination of material amounts and disclosures in the financial statements.

The auditor must also perform specified audit procedures to help identify instances of noncompliance with those laws and regulations that may have a material impact on the financial statements. If noncompliance is identified (or suspected) the auditor must then respond appropriately.

ISA 250 *Consideration of Laws and Regulations in an Audit of Financial Statements* requires an auditor to perform the following procedures:

- obtaining a general understanding of the client's legal and regulatory environment
- inspecting correspondence with relevant licensing and regulatory authorities
- enquiring of management and those charged with governance as to whether the entity is compliant with laws and regulations
- remaining alert to possible instances of noncompliance; and
- obtaining written representations that the directors have disclosed all instances of known and possible noncompliance to the auditor.

ACCA marking scheme		
		Marks
(a)	Up to 1 mark per well explained point Per ISA 240 – obtain reasonable assurance that the financial statements are free from material misstatement, whether caused by fraud or error Identify and assess the risks of material misstatement due to fraud Obtain sufficient appropriate audit evidence Respond appropriately to fraud or suspected fraud Maintain professional scepticism throughout the audit Discussion within the engagement team	
	Max	**5**
(b)	Up to 1 mark per well explained point Non-compliance could result in material misstatement May be a responsibility to report non-compliance Obtain sufficient appropriate evidence regarding compliance Perform procedures to identify non-compliance ISA 250 procedures	
	Max	**5**
Total		**10**

Examiner's comments

Part (a) required an explanation of auditors' responsibilities in relation to prevention and detection of fraud and error. This question was answered unsatisfactorily.

The focus of the question was what the auditors' responsibilities were; it did not require an explanation of directors' responsibilities, however many candidates did provide this and there were no marks available for this. Candidates also wanted to focus on what was not the auditors responsibility, namely to prevent fraud and error. In addition some answers strayed onto providing procedures for detecting fraud and error rather than just addressing responsibilities.

A majority of candidates were able to gain marks for reporting any frauds to management or those charged with governance, for the auditors' general responsibility to detect material misstatements caused by fraud or error and that the auditors are not responsible for preventing fraud or error.

151 ENGAGEMENT LETTERS/PLANNING

(a) Benefits of audit planning

Audit planning is addressed by ISA 300 *Planning an Audit of Financial Statements.* It states that adequate planning benefits the audit of financial statements in several ways:

- Helping the auditor to devote appropriate attention to important areas of the audit.
- Helping the auditor to identify and resolve potential problems on a timely basis.
- Helping the auditor to properly organise and manage the audit engagement so that it is performed in an effective and efficient manner.

- Assisting in the selection of engagement team members with appropriate levels of capabilities and competence to respond to anticipated risks and the proper assignment of work to them.
- Facilitating the direction and supervision of engagement team members and the review of their work.
- Assisting, where applicable, in coordination of work done by experts.

(b) (i) **Purpose of an engagement letter**

An engagement letter provides a written agreement of the terms of the audit engagement between the auditor and management or those charged with governance.

Confirming that there is a common understanding between the auditor and management, or those charged with governance, of the terms of the audit engagement helps to avoid misunderstandings with respect to the audit.

(ii) Matters to be included in an audit engagement letter:

- The objective and scope of the audit
- The responsibilities of the auditor
- The responsibilities of management
- Identification of the financial reporting framework for the preparation of the financial statements
- Expected form and content of any reports to be issued
- Elaboration of the scope of the audit with reference to legislation
- The form of any other communication of results of the audit engagement
- The fact that some material misstatements may not be detected
- Arrangements regarding the planning and performance of the audit, including the composition of the audit team
- The expectation that management will provide written representations
- The basis on which fees are computed and any billing arrangements
- A request for management to acknowledge receipt of the audit engagement letter and to agree to the terms of the engagement
- Arrangements concerning the involvement of internal auditors and other staff of the entity
- Any obligations to provide audit working papers to other parties
- Any restriction on the auditor's liability
- Arrangements to make available draft financial statements and any other information
- Arrangements to inform the auditor of facts that might affect the financial statements, of which management may become aware during the period from the date of the auditor's report to the date the financial statements are issued.

ACCA marking scheme				
				Marks
(a)	Up to 1 mark per well explained point			
	Important areas of the audit			
	Potential problems			
	Effective and efficient audit			
	Selection of engagement team members and assignment of work			
	Direction, supervision and review			
	Coordination of work			
			Max	**5**
(b)	(i)	Up to 1 mark per valid point		
		Written agreement of terms of engagement		
		Avoid misunderstandings		
			Max	**2**
	(ii)	½ mark per valid point		
		– Objective/scope		
		– Responsibilities of auditor		
		– Responsibilities of management		
		– Identification of framework for financial statements		
		– Form/content reports		
		– Elaboration of scope		
		– Form of communications		
		– Some misstatements may be missed		
		– Arrangement for audit		
		– Written representations required		
		– Fees/billing		
		– Management acknowledge letter		
		– Internal auditor arrangements		
		– Obligations to provide working papers to others		
		– Restriction on auditor's liability		
		– Arrangements to make draft financial statements available		
		– Arrangements to inform auditors of subsequent events		
			Max	**3**
Total				**10**

152 ACCEPTANCE *Walk in the footsteps of a top tutor*

Top Tutor Tips

This question requires steps prior to accepting the audit. These are the considerations that would affect the auditor's decision to accept. A common sense approach can be taken to this question if you don't know the knowledge. Think about what would make you decline the engagement. Remember that ISA's require the audit firm to only accept clients and engagements of an acceptable level of risk.

(a) (i) **Steps prior to accepting an audit**

ISA 210 *Agreeing the Terms of Audit Engagements* provides guidance to auditors on the steps they should take in accepting a new audit client. It sets out a number of processes that the auditor should perform prior to accepting a new engagement, in addition to considering whether preconditions for the audit are in place.

Consider any issues which might arise which could threaten compliance with ACCA's *Code of Ethics and Conduct* or any local legislation, including conflict of interest with existing clients. If issues arise, then their significance must be considered.

In addition, they should consider whether they are competent to perform the work and whether they would have appropriate resources available, as well as any specialist skills or knowledge required for the audit.

Consider what they already know about the directors of the prospective client; they need to consider the reputation and integrity of the directors. If necessary, the firm may want to obtain references if they do not formally know the directors.

Consider the level of risk attached to the audit and whether this is acceptable to the firm. As part of this, they should consider whether the expected audit fee is adequate in relation to the risk.

Communicate with the outgoing auditor to assess if there are any ethical or professional reasons why they should not accept appointment. They should obtain permission from management to contact the existing auditor; if this is not given, then the engagement should be refused.

If given permission to respond, the auditors should carefully review the response for any issues that could affect acceptance.

(ii) **Preconditions for the audit**

> ***Top Tutor Tips***
>
> *This is a purely knowledge based requirement covering part of ISA 210 Agreeing the Terms of Audit Engagements. It is a difficult requirement – you either know the answer or you don't. A common sense approach will not help you here. If you don't have the knowledge, move on and try to compensate by scoring well on other requirements.*

ISA 210 *Agreeing the Terms of Audit Engagements* requires auditors to only accept a new audit engagement when it has been confirmed that the preconditions for an audit are present.

To assess whether the preconditions for an audit are present, the auditor must determine whether the financial reporting framework to be applied in the preparation of the financial statements is acceptable. In considering this, the auditor should assess the nature of the entity, the nature and purpose of the financial statements and whether law or regulations prescribes the applicable reporting framework.

In addition, they must obtain the agreement of management that it acknowledges and understands its responsibility for the following:

- Preparation of the financial statements in accordance with the applicable financial reporting framework, including where relevant their fair presentation
- For such internal control as management determines is necessary to enable the preparation of financial statements which are free from material misstatement, whether due to fraud or error; and
- To provide the auditor with access to all relevant information for the preparation of the financial statements, any additional information that the auditor may request from management and unrestricted access to persons within the company from whom the auditor determines it necessary to obtain audit evidence.

If the preconditions for an audit are not present, the auditor shall discuss the matter with management.

Unless required by law or regulation to do so, the auditor shall not accept the proposed audit engagement:

- If the auditor has determined that the financial reporting framework to be applied in the preparation of the financial statements is unacceptable; or
- If management agreement of their responsibilities has not been obtained.

(b) **Engagement letters**

Top Tutor Tips

This is a purely knowledge based requirement covering part of ISA 210 Agreeing the Terms of Audit Engagements. The engagement letter is used to minimise misunderstandings during the audit so think of matters that could lead to misunderstandings to generate ideas.

Matters to be included in an audit engagement letter:

- The objective and scope of the audit
- The responsibilities of the auditor
- The responsibilities of management
- Identification of the financial reporting framework for the preparation of the financial statements
- Expected form and content of any reports to be issued
- Elaboration of the scope of the audit with reference to legislation
- The form of any other communication of results of the audit engagement
- The fact that some material misstatements may not be detected
- Arrangements regarding the planning and performance of the audit, including the composition of the audit team
- The expectation that management will provide written representations

- The basis on which fees are computed and any billing arrangements
- A request for management to acknowledge receipt of the audit engagement letter and to agree to the terms of the engagement
- Arrangements concerning the involvement of internal auditors and other staff of the entity
- Any obligations to provide audit working papers to other parties
- Any restriction on the auditor's liability; and
- Arrangements to make available draft financial statements and any other information.

ACCA marking scheme				
				Marks
(a)	(i)	Up to 1 mark per well described point. Compliance with ACCA's Code of Ethics and Conduct Competent Reputation and integrity of directors Level of risk Fee adequate to compensate for risk Write to outgoing auditor after obtaining permission to contact Review response for any issues		
			Max	**5**
	(ii)	Up to 1 mark per valid point. Determination of acceptable framework Agreement of management responsibilities Preparation of financial statements with applicable framework Internal controls Provide auditor with relevant information and access If preconditions are not present discuss with management Decline if framework unacceptable Decline if agreement of responsibilities not obtained		
			Max	**3**
(b)	½ mark per valid point. Objective/scope Responsibilities of auditor Responsibilities of management Identification of framework for financial statements Form/content reports Elaboration of scope Form of communications Some misstatements may be missed Arrangement for audit Written representations required Fees/billing Management acknowledge letter Internal auditor arrangements Obligations to provide working papers to others Restriction on auditor's liability Arrangements to make draft financial statements available			
			Max	**2**
Total				**10**

Examiner's comments

Part (a) (i) for 5 marks required a description of the steps the firm should take prior to accepting a new audit client. Candidates performed satisfactorily on this part of the question. Many candidates were able to identify a good range of points including ensuring the firm had adequate resources to complete this audit, identifying if any ethical threats arise, understanding the entity and contacting the previous auditors.

However some candidates focused solely on obtaining professional clearance from the previous auditors and it was not uncommon to see a whole page on the detailed steps to be taken. The question requirement was steps prior to accepting an audit; it was not the process for obtaining professional clearance. Those that focused solely on this area would not have scored enough marks to pass this part of the question. Candidates are reminded to answer the question actually asked as opposed to the one they wish had been asked.

In addition, some candidates provided answers which focused on the engagement letter; this was incorrect as an engagement letter is only produced once an engagement has been accepted as opposed to prior to acceptance.

Part (a) (ii) for 3 marks required the steps the firm should take to confirm whether the preconditions for the audit were in place. Where it was answered, candidates performed unsatisfactorily on this question. Answers tended to be in two camps, those who had studied preconditions and were able to score all three marks and those who had not studied it and so failed to score any marks. This is a knowledge area and has been tested in a previous diet. Candidates must practice past exam questions and ensure they study the breadth of the syllabus.

Those candidates who did not score well, tended to repeat points that had been made in part (a) (i) of the question or they included points that should have been in their answer for (a) (i). Some chose to combine their answers for (a) (i) and (a) (ii) together, this tended to produce unfocused answers.

Part (b) for 2 marks required four matters to be included within an engagement letter. This was knowledge based and unrelated to the scenario. Candidates performed well on this question with many scoring full marks.

Where candidates did not score full marks this tended to be because they focused on generic items which would appear in any letter such as, the date, signature and addressee, none of these points scored marks.

153 SWANDIVE *Walk in the footsteps of a top tutor*

Top Tutor Tips

*Part (a) is a straightforward knowledge question. Notice that the question asks for the **importance** of planning. Answers which just state what activities are performed at the planning stage will not score marks. As planning is the most important part of the process, students should be aware of the reasons why it is important to plan the audit.*

Part (b) is a tricky question as this requirement has not been seen before. The question focuses on what the auditor should do now they know there is an increased risk of fraud. Procedures to be performed in respect of payroll in general will not score marks. Think about the effect the increased risk will have on the audit.

(a) **Importance of audit planning**

- It helps the auditor to devote appropriate attention to important areas of the audit.
- It helps the auditor to identify and resolve potential problems on a timely basis.
- It helps the auditor to properly organise and manage the audit engagement so that it is performed in an effective and efficient manner.
- It assists in the selection of engagement team members with appropriate levels of capabilities and competence to respond to anticipated risks and the proper assignment of work to them.
- It facilitates the direction and supervision of engagement team members and the review of their work.
- It assists, where applicable, in the coordination of work done by experts.

(b) **Procedures due to increased risk of fraud**

The audit senior should consider undertaking the following procedures as a result of the increased risk of the payroll fraud.

- Discuss with management and those charged with governance as to whether they are aware of any other payroll frauds or potential frauds.
- Review board minutes for evidence of management discussion of the materiality of the payroll fraud and to the existence of any additional frauds or suspected frauds.
- Discuss with the payroll manager the nature of the payroll fraud, how it occurred and the financial impact of amounts incorrectly paid into the payroll clerk's bank account.
- Review the supporting documentation to confirm the total of the fraudulent payments made and assess the materiality of this misstatement.
- Review and test the internal controls surrounding setting up of and payments to new joiners to assess whether further frauds may have occurred.

- Consider whether other information obtained by the audit team indicates risks of additional material misstatements with regards to payroll fraud.
- Obtain a written representation from management acknowledging that they have disclosed to the auditors all knowledge of actual and suspected payroll frauds.

ACCA marking scheme		
		Marks
(a)	Up to 1 mark per well explained point. – Important areas of the audit – Potential problems – Effective and efficient audit – Selection of engagement team members and assignment of work – Direction, supervision and review – Coordination of work	
	Maximum	5
(b)	Up to 1 mark per well described procedure. – Discuss with management as to whether they are aware of any additional payroll frauds – Review board minutes – Discuss with the payroll manager the nature of the payroll fraud, how it occurred and the impact – Review supporting documentation to confirm the total of the fraudulent payments made – Review and test the internal controls surrounding setting up of and the payments to new joiners – Consider if other information obtained indicates risks of material misstatement due to payroll fraud – Obtain a written representation from management	
	Maximum	5
Total		**10**

INTERNAL CONTROLS AND AUDIT EVIDENCE

154 HUMMINGBIRD *Walk in the footsteps of a top tutor*

Top Tutor Tips

Part (a) requires the control deficiencies within the sales cycle to be identified. Use the specific information in scenario rather than giving deficiencies that could be present in any sales system. There are always more deficiencies than you need so choose the ones you can write well about. Suggest controls the client can implement to address the control deficiency. Be specific about which member of client staff should be responsible for the control and how frequently they should perform the control.

Note the requirement to produce a covering letter for 2 marks. These are easy marks and should not be overlooked. To obtain the marks you need to include an address, an appropriate greeting, a disclaimer and appropriate sign off.

Part (b) asks for substantive procedures to be performed over the revenue figure. A substantive procedure is used to detect material misstatement in the figure. Tests of controls will not score marks. The requirement relates to revenue within the statement of profit or loss. Do not give procedures over receivables as this is not what the question asks for.

(a) **Board of directors**
Hummingbird Co
23 Buzzard Lane
Peregrine City
Hawk Country

4 December 2014

Dear Sirs,

Audit of Hummingbird Scents Co (Hummingbird) for the year ended 30 September 2014

Please find enclosed the report to management on deficiencies in internal controls identified during the audit for the year ended 30 September 2014. The appendix to this report considers deficiencies in the sales system and recommendations to address those deficiencies.

Please note that this report only addresses the deficiencies identified during the audit and if further testing had been performed, then more deficiencies may have been reported.

This report is solely for the use of management and if you have any further questions, then please do not hesitate to contact us.

Yours faithfully

An audit firm

APPENDIX

Deficiency	**Control**
Brenda the sales clerk receives customer orders, raises sales invoices and processes payments for hotel customers. This is a lack of segregation of duties and could lead to a risk of fraudulent transactions or errors, as no one checks the work undertaken by this clerk.	Another sales ledger clerk should be involved in the processing of hotel customer transactions so that no one individual undertakes all elements of the sales cycle. The work could be split so that one clerk raises orders and invoices but a second clerk processes the payments.
Hotel customers have contracted sales prices; however, as online trade prices are automatically loaded into the sales invoices, Brenda has to manually amend the invoices. This significantly increases the risk of error, as if Brenda incorrectly increases the sales prices, then this can lead to a loss of customer goodwill and if they are too low, this results in a loss of revenue for Hummingbird.	As hotel customers account for 40% of revenue, consideration should be given to amending the sales system so that each customer's agreed prices are pre-loaded, therefore no manual amendment of invoices would be required. If this is not feasible, then all sales invoices for hotel customers should be double checked by another member of the finance department prior to being sent out.
Credit limits are determined by the finance director when a new trade customer is set up in the system. However, these limits could be out of date, resulting in limits being too high and sales being made to poor credit risks or too low and Hummingbird losing potential revenue.	Customer credit limits should be regularly reviewed by the finance director and updated based on the level of sales transactions and credit risk.
Customer orders and goods despatched notes (GDN) are given a number based on the customer account number and order number. These numbers are not sequential. Without sequential numbers, it is difficult for Hummingbird to identify missing orders and to monitor if all orders are being despatched in a timely manner, leading to a loss of customer goodwill.	Sales orders and goods despatched notes should be sequentially numbered. On a regular basis, a sequence check of orders should be undertaken to identify any missing orders. Upon despatch, the GDN should be matched to the order; a regular review of unmatched orders should be undertaken to identify any unfulfilled orders.
Hummingbird has changed from a reliable national courier company to a cheaper local courier; as a result some orders have been delivered late. There is a risk that orders may be lost resulting in a loss of revenue for Hummingbird or orders arriving later than normal which would lead to a loss of customer goodwill.	The courier company should be set targets with regards to timeliness of despatches. A review should be undertaken of target despatch times and actual times taken by the new courier company. If late delays continue, then consideration should be given to changing back to the original courier company.

Deficiency	**Control**
Trade customers' sales invoices are automatically generated by the system at the same time that the online order is placed. However, if goods are not despatched straight away, then customers could be invoiced in advance of receipt of their goods. This is likely to lead to a loss of customer goodwill and the early recognition of revenue in the accounting records.	The system should be amended so that it links into the despatch system. Sales invoices should not be raised until after goods have been despatched.
If Hummingbird makes special offers or discounts sales, the master file data for sales prices is amended by a senior sales ledger clerk. There is a risk that these amendments could be made incorrectly resulting in a loss of sales revenue or overcharging of customers.	When special offers or discounted sales occur, the changes to master file data should be made by a supervisor and each change checked by a responsible official to reduce the risk of errors occurring.
In addition, the sales ledger clerk, although senior, is not senior enough to be given access to changing master file data as this could increase the risk of fraud.	Amendments to master file data should be restricted so that only supervisors and above can make changes.
Monthly statements are not sent to trade customers. If statements are not sent regularly, this increases the likelihood of errors and any disputed invoices not being quickly identified and resolved by Hummingbird.	Hummingbird should produce monthly customer statements for both hotel and trade customers and send them out promptly.
The sales ledger control account is only reconciled at the end of September in order to verify the year-end balance. If the sales ledger is only reconciled annually, there is a risk that errors will not be spotted promptly.	The sales ledger control account should be reconciled on a monthly basis to identify any errors. The reconciliations should be reviewed by a responsible official and they should evidence their review.

(b) **Substantive procedures for revenue**

- Compare the overall level of revenue against prior years and budget and investigate any significant fluctuations.
- Obtain a schedule of sales for the year broken down into the two categories of hotel and trade customers and compare this to the prior year breakdown and for any unusual movements discuss with management.
- Calculate the gross profit margin for Hummingbird and compare this to the prior year and investigate any significant fluctuations.
- Select a sample of sales invoices for hotel customers and agree the sales prices back to the contracted rates to ensure the accuracy of invoices.
- Select a sample of credit notes raised, trace through to the original invoice and ensure invoice correctly removed from sales.

ACCA marking scheme		
		Marks
(a)	Up to 1 mark each per well explained deficiency and recommendation. If not well explained, then just give ½ marks for each. Overall maximum of 7 marks each for deficiencies and recommendations. 2 marks for presentation: 1 mark for address and intro and 1 mark for conclusion. – Lack of segregation of duties for sales ledger clerk processing hotel customer transactions – Manual override of sales invoices for hotel customers – Credit limits set up when trade customer established, limits not regularly reviewed – Sales orders and goods despatch notes not sequentially numbered – Change to a cheaper courier company to despatch goods increases risk of customer complaints – Trade customers' sales invoices generated on order date, goods may not have been despatched at this stage – Senior sales clerk amends master data file for special offers and discount sales – Monthly statements not sent to trade customers – Sales ledger control account only reconciled at the year end	
	Maximum	16
(b)	Up to 1 mark per well explained procedure. – Analytical review over revenue compared to budget and prior year – Analytical review of two categories of sales compared to prior year – Gross margin review – Agree sales prices for hotel customers to contracted rates – Review credit notes – Follow trade online orders to goods despatched note to sales invoice to sales ledger – Sales cut-off	
	Maximum	4
Total		**20**

155 TROMBONE *Walk in the footsteps of a top tutor*

Top Tutor Tips

Part (a) requires the control deficiencies within the payroll cycle to be identified. Use the specific information in scenario rather than giving deficiencies that could be present in any payroll system. There are always more deficiencies than you need so choose the ones you can write well about. Suggest controls the client can implement to address the control deficiency. Be specific about which member of client staff should be responsible for the control and how frequently they should perform the control. Tests of controls are the audit procedures the auditor will perform to obtain evidence to prove the control suggested is in place and working effectively. Be specific about how they would do this.

Part (b) asks for substantive procedures to be performed over the payroll figure. A substantive procedure is used to detect material misstatement in the figure. Tests of controls will not score marks in part b.

(a) **Trombone Co's payroll system deficiencies, controls and test of controls**

Deficiencies	**Controls**	**Test of controls**
The wages calculations are generated by the payroll system and there are no checks performed. Therefore, if system errors occur during the payroll processing, this would not be identified. This could result in wages being over or under calculated, leading to an additional payroll cost or loss of employee goodwill.	A senior member of the payroll team should recalculate the gross to net pay workings for a sample of employees and compare their results to the output from the payroll system. These calculations should be signed as approved before payments are made.	Review a sample of the gross to net pay calculations for evidence that they are undertaken and signed as approved.
Annual wages increases are updated in the payroll system standing data by clerks.	Payroll clerks should not have access to standing data changes within the system.	Ask a clerk to attempt to make a change to payroll standing data; the system should reject this attempt.
Payroll clerks are not senior enough to be making changes to standing data as they could make mistakes leading to incorrect payment of wages. In addition, if they can access standing data, they could make unauthorised changes.	The annual wages increase should be performed by a senior member of the payroll department and this should be checked by another responsible official for errors.	Review the log of standing data amendments to identify whether the wage rate increases were changed by a senior member of payroll.
Overtime worked by employees is not all authorised by the relevant department head, as only overtime in excess of 30% of standard hours requires authorisation. This increases the risk that employees will claim for overtime even though they did not work these additional hours resulting in additional payroll costs for Trombone.	All overtime hours worked should be authorised by the relevant department head. This should be evidenced by signature on the employees' weekly overtime sheets.	Review a sample of employee weekly overtime sheets for evidence of signature by relevant department head.

Deficiencies	Controls	Test of controls
Time taken off as payment for overtime worked should be agreed by payroll clerks to the overtime worked report; however, this has not always occurred. Employees could be taking unauthorised leave if they take time off but have not worked the required overtime.	Payroll clerks should be reminded of the procedures to be undertaken when processing the overtime sheets. They should sign as evidence on the overtime sheets that they have agreed any time taken off to the relevant overtime report.	Select a sample of overtime sheets with time taken off and confirm that there is evidence of a check by the payroll clerk to the overtime worked report.
The overtime worked report is emailed to the department heads and they report by exception if there are any errors. If department heads are busy or do not receive the email and do not report to payroll on time, then it will be assumed that the overtime report is correct even though there may be errors. This could result in the payroll department making incorrect overtime payments.	All department heads should report to the payroll department on whether or not the overtime report is correct. The payroll department should follow up on any non-replies and not make payments until agreed by the department head.	For a sample of overtime reports emailed to department heads confirm that a response has been received from each head by reviewing all responses.
Department heads are meant to arrange for annual leave cover so that overtime sheets are authorised on a timely basis; however, this has not always happened. If overtime sheets are authorised late, then this can lead to employee dissatisfaction as it will delay payment of the overtime worked.	Department heads should be reminded of the procedures with regards to annual leave and arrangement of suitable cover. During annual leave periods, payroll clerks should monitor that overtime sheets are being submitted by department heads on a timely basis and follow up any late sheets.	Discuss with payroll clerks the process they follow for obtaining authorisation of overtime sheets, in particular during periods of annual leave. Compare this to the process which they should adopt to identify any control exceptions.

Deficiencies	Controls	Test of controls
The finance director reviews the total list of bank transfers with the total to be paid per the payroll records. There could be employees omitted along with fictitious employees added to the payment listing, so that although the total payments list agrees to payroll totals, there could be fraudulent payments being made.	The finance director when authorising the payments should on a sample basis perform checks from payroll records to payment list and vice versa to confirm that payments are complete and only made to *bona fide* employees. The finance director should sign the payments list as evidence that he has undertaken these checks.	Obtain a sample of payments list and review for signature by the finance director as evidence that the control is operating correctly.

(b) **Payroll substantive procedures**

- Agree the total wages and salaries expense per the payroll system to the trial balance, investigate any differences.
- Cast a sample of payroll records to confirm completeness and accuracy of the payroll expense.
- For a sample of employees, recalculate the gross and net pay and agree to the payroll records to confirm accuracy.
- Recalculate the statutory deductions to confirm whether correct deductions for this year have been made in the payroll.
- Compare the total payroll expense to the prior year and investigate any significant differences.
- Review monthly payroll charges, compare this to the prior year and budgets and discuss with management for any significant variances.
- Perform a proof in total of total wages and salaries, incorporating joiners and leavers and the annual pay increase. Compare this to the actual wages and salaries in the financial statements and investigate any significant differences.
- Select a sample of joiners and leavers, agree their start/leaving date to supporting documentation, recalculate that their first/last pay packet was accurately calculated and recorded.
- Agree the total net pay per the payroll records to the bank transfer listing of payments and to the cashbook.
- Agree the individual wages and salaries per the payroll to the personnel records for a sample.
- Select a sample of weekly overtime sheets and trace to overtime payment in payroll records to confirm completeness of overtime paid.

ACCA marking scheme		
		Marks
(a)	Up to 1 mark per well explained deficiency, up to 1 mark for each well explained recommendation and up to 1 mark for each well described test of control. Overall maximum of 5 marks each for deficiencies, controls and tests of control. Payroll calculations not checked Payroll clerks update standing data for wages increases Authorisation of overtime sheets only undertaken if overtime exceeds 30% of standard hours Time off as payment for overtime not checked to overtime worked report Review of overtime worked reports by department heads Authorisation of overtime sheets when department heads on annual leave Finance director only reviews totals of payroll records and payments list	
	Maximum	**15**
(b)	Up to 1 mark per well described substantive procedure. Agree wages and salaries per payroll to trial balance Cast payroll records Recalculate gross and net pay Recalculate statutory deductions Compare total payroll to prior year Review monthly payroll to prior year and budget Proof in total of payroll and agree to the financial statements Verify joiners/leavers and recalculate first/last pay Agree wages and salaries paid per payroll to bank transfer list and cashbook Agree the individual wages and salaries as per the payroll to the personnel records Agree sample of weekly overtime sheets to overtime payment in payroll records	
	Maximum	**5**
Total		**20**

Examiner's comments

This question was based on a hotel chain, Trombone Co (Trombone), and tested candidates' knowledge of the payroll system including tests of controls and substantive procedures for the payroll expense.

Part (a) for 15 marks required candidates to identify and explain five deficiencies in the payroll system, recommend controls to address these deficiencies, and a test of control for each of these recommendations that could be used to assess if it was operating effectively if implemented. The first two parts of this questions were answered satisfactorily by candidates, however the tests of controls proved challenging for many.

Candidates were able to comfortably identify five deficiencies from the scenario, although a minority of candidates identified deficiencies which were generic to payroll systems rather than specific to the question, such as references to 'clock cards', which were not a component of the system under review. Also some candidates identified points which were not valid deficiencies, such as employees being able to complete their own overtime sheets, being allowed a choice between days off or payment of overtime and overtime sheets being entered by payroll clerks. Although sufficient deficiencies were identified by many candidates, they did not always adequately explain what the deficiency meant to Trombone. For example, candidates identified the deficiency that 'the overtime worked reports are not always checked,' however some failed to explain the implication of this in that it could lead to employees taking days off when they had not worked the overtime hours required. The requirement to provide controls was answered satisfactorily. Most candidates were able to provide good recommendations to address the deficiencies; however in some instances these recommendations were too brief. Candidates have a tendency to state control objectives rather than valid procedures which can be implemented by the client. In addition some recommendations failed to address the deficiency identified, for example where department heads failed to assign a deputy to authorise overtime whilst on annual leave, many candidates simply recommended that this control already existing control be put in place, rather than addressing how the control should be amended to ensure it was followed at all times.

The requirement for tests of controls was answered unsatisfactorily. Many candidates are still confusing substantive procedures and test of controls. A significant number of candidates suggested substantive procedures such as 'recalculating gross and net pay calculations', rather than a test of control which might be to 'review evidence of the recalculation of payroll'. Candidates need to review their understanding of these different types of audit procedures and ensure that they appreciate that substantive tests focus on the number within the financial statements whereas test of controls are verifying if client procedures are operating. In many instances candidates focused on re-performing the control rather than testing it had operated. Observation of a control was commonly suggested by candidates, however in many cases this is not an effective way of testing that a control has operated throughout the year. Most candidates presented their answers well, adopting a three column approach with deficiency, the control recommendation and the test of control in separate columns. This approach ensured that all elements of the question were addressed and it was easier to see which recommendations and tests related to which deficiencies.

Part (b) required substantive procedures to confirm the completeness and accuracy of the payroll expense. On the whole candidates performed well in this area. A good proportion of candidates were able to suggest practical payroll procedures such as analytical review of prior year and current year charges or undertaking a proof in total calculation. Other common answers included recalculation of a sample of payroll calculations or statutory deductions.

Common mistakes made by candidates were:

-Giving objectives rather than procedures 'ensure that the gross and net pay calculations are correct', this is not a detailed substantive procedure and so would not score any marks.

-Lack of detail in tests such as 'check that the payroll calculations are correct', this would not score any marks as it does not explain what should be checked or how this testing would be carried out.

-Providing tests of controls rather than substantive procedures, such as focusing on authorisation of payroll.

The requirement verb was to 'describe' therefore sufficient detail was required to score the 1 mark available per test. Candidates are reminded yet again that substantive procedures are a core topic area and they must be able to produce relevant detailed procedures and to apply their knowledge to different areas of the financial statements.

156 OREGANO *Walk in the footsteps of a top tutor*

(a) **Documenting the sales and despatch system**

> ***Top Tutor Tips***
>
> *Part (a) is quite difficult requirement unless you know the different methods of documenting systems. It isn't a requirement you can blag. Therefore if you don't know it, don't waste time in the exam trying to think of something. Move onto the next part of the question and come back to it when you have finished everything you can do on the paper.*

There are several methods which can be used by the internal audit department of Oregano Co (Oregano) to document their system.

Narrative notes

Narrative notes consist of a written description of the system; they would detail what occurs in the system at each stage and would include any controls which operate at each stage.

Advantages of this method include:

- They are simple to record; after discussion with staff members of Oregano, these discussions are easily written up as notes.
- They can facilitate understanding by all members of the internal audit team, especially more junior members who might find alternative methods too complex.

Disadvantages of this method include:

- Narrative notes may prove to be too cumbersome, especially if the sales and distribution system is complex.
- This method can make it more difficult to identify missing internal controls as the notes record the detail but do not identify control exceptions clearly.

Questionnaires

Internal control questionnaires (ICQ) or internal control evaluation questionnaires (ICEQ) contain a list of questions; ICQs are used to assess whether controls exist whereas ICEQs test the effectiveness of the controls.

Advantages of this method include:

- Questionnaires are quick to prepare, which means they are a timely method for recording the system.
- They ensure that all controls present within the system are considered and recorded; hence missing controls or deficiencies are clearly highlighted by the internal audit team.

Disadvantages of this method include:

- It can be easy for the staff members of Oregano to overstate the level of the controls present as they are asked a series of questions relating to potential controls.
- A standard list of questions may miss out unusual controls of Oregano.

Flowcharts

Flowcharts are a graphic illustration of the internal control system for the sales and despatch system. Lines usually demonstrate the sequence of events and standard symbols are used to signify controls or documents.

Advantages of this method include:

- It is easy to view the sales system in its entirety as it is all presented together in one diagram.
- Due to the use of standard symbols for controls, they are easy to spot as are any missing controls.

Disadvantages of this method include:

- They can sometimes be difficult to amend, as any amendments may require the whole flowchart to be redrawn.
- There is still the need for narrative notes to accompany the flowchart and hence it can be a time consuming method.

Note: Full marks will be awarded for describing TWO methods for documenting the sales and despatch system and explaining ONE advantage and ONE disadvantage for each method.

(b) **Control objectives for sales and despatch system**

> ***Top Tutor Tips***
>
> *Control objectives are the reasons why controls are put in place. They address the risks that could happen in the system. Be careful not to suggest that a control objective is to ensure a control is in place. You need to say the reason why the control should be in place.*

- To ensure that orders are only accepted if goods are available to be processed for customers.
- To ensure that all orders are recorded completely and accurately.
- To ensure that goods are not supplied to poor credit risks.
- To ensure that goods are despatched for all orders on a timely basis.
- To ensure that goods are despatched correctly to customers and that they are of an adequate quality.
- To ensure that all goods despatched are correctly invoiced.
- To ensure completeness of income for goods despatched.
- To ensure that sales discounts are only provided to valid customers.

(c) **Deficiencies and controls for Oregano Co's sales and despatch system**

Top Tutor Tips

Controls deficiencies and recommendations questions are usually quite straightforward, however, you must explain the deficiencies and controls in sufficient detail to score marks. If you are too brief you will only score ½ marks.

Deficiency	*Control*
Inventory availability for telephone orders is not checked at the time the order is placed. The order clerks manually check the availability later and only then inform customers if there is insufficient inventory available. There is the risk that where goods are not available, order clerks could forget to contact the customers, leading to unfulfilled orders. This could lead to customer dissatisfaction, and would impact Oregano's reputation.	When telephone orders are placed, the order clerk should check the inventory system whilst the customer is on the phone; they can then give an accurate assessment of the availability of goods and there is no risk of forgetting to inform customers.
Telephone orders are not recorded immediately on the three part pre-printed order forms; these are completed after the telephone call. There is a risk that incorrect or insufficient details may be recorded by the clerk and this could result in incorrect orders being despatched or orders failing to be despatched at all, resulting in a loss of customer goodwill.	All telephone orders should be recorded immediately on the three part pre-printed order forms. The clerk should also double check all the details taken with the customer over the telephone to ensure the accuracy of the order recorded.
Telephone orders are not sequentially numbered. Therefore if orders are misplaced whilst in transit to the despatch department, these orders will not be fulfilled, resulting in dissatisfied customers.	The three part pre-printed orders forms should be sequentially numbered and on a regular basis the despatch department should run a sequence check of orders received. Where there are gaps in the sequence, they should be investigated to identify any missing orders.

Customers are able to place online orders which will exceed their agreed credit limit by 10%. This increases the risk of accepting orders from bad credit risks.	Customer credit limits should be reviewed more regularly by a responsible official and should reflect the current spending pattern of customers. If some customers have increased the level of their purchases and are making payments on time, then these customers' credit limits could be increased. The online ordering system should be amended to not allow any orders to be processed which will exceed the customer's credit limit.
A daily pick list is used by the despatch department when sending out customer orders. However, it does not appear that the goods are checked back to the original order; this could result in incorrect goods being sent out.	In addition to the pick list, copies of all the related orders should be printed on a daily basis. When the goods have been picked ready to be despatched, they should be cross checked back to the original order. They should check correct quantities and product descriptions, as well as checking the quality of goods being despatched to ensure they are not damaged.
Additional staff have been drafted in to help the two sales clerks produce the sales invoices. As the extra staff will not be as experienced as the sales clerks, there is an increased risk of mistakes being made in the sales invoices. This could result in customers being under or overcharged.	Only the sales clerks should be able to raise sales invoices. As Oregano is expanding, consideration should be given to recruiting and training more permanent sales clerks who can produce sales invoices.
Discounts given to customers are manually entered onto the sales invoices by sales clerks. This could result in unauthorised sales discounts being given as there does not seem to be any authorisation required. In addition, a clerk could forget to manually enter the discount or enter an incorrect level of discount for a customer, leading to the sales invoice being overstated and a loss of customer goodwill.	For customers who are due to receive a discount, the authorised discount levels should be updated to the customer master file. When the sales invoices for these customers are raised, their discounts should automatically appear on the invoice. The invoicing system should be amended to prevent sales clerks from being able to manually enter sales discounts onto invoices.

ACCA marking scheme			
			Marks
(a)	Up to 1 mark each for a description of a method, up to 1 mark each for an advantage, up to 1 mark each for a disadvantage. Overall max of 2 marks each for methods, advantages and disadvantages. – Narrative notes – Questionnaires – Flowcharts		
		Max	**6**
(b)	1 mark for each control objective, overall maximum of 2 points. – To ensure orders are only accepted if goods are available to be processed for customers – To ensure all orders are recorded completely and accurately – To ensure goods are not supplied to poor credit risks – To ensure goods are despatched for all orders on a timely basis – To ensure goods are despatched correctly to customers and are of an adequate quality – To ensure all goods despatched are correctly invoiced – To ensure completeness of income for goods despatched – To ensure sales discounts are only provided to valid customers		
		Max	**2**
(c)	Up to 1 mark per well explained deficiency and up to 1 mark for each control. Overall max of 6 marks for deficiencies and 6 marks for controls. – Inventory not checked when order taken – Orders not completed on pre-printed order forms – Order forms not sequentially numbered – Credit limits being exceeded – Goods despatched not agreed to order to check quantity and quality – Sales invoices being raised by inexperienced staff – Sales discounts manually entered by sales clerks		
		Max	**12**
Total			**20**

Examiner's comments

Part (a) for 6 marks required a description of two methods for documenting the sales and despatch system along with an advantage and disadvantage for each method.

Candidates' performance was unsatisfactory on this question, with a number of candidates not even attempting it. A significant proportion of candidates did not understand the question requirement fully, and so instead of suggesting methods such as flowcharts, narrative notes or questionnaires they considered manual and automated/electronic methods for a system. In addition some candidates considered online versus telephone methods for recording sales transactions and others interpreted the question as requiring the documents of a sales system and so considered sales invoices and despatch notes. The question requirement was clear, candidates either did not read it carefully or they lacked the technical knowledge on documentation methods.

Those candidates who did correctly interpret the requirement often failed to maximise their marks as they identified the methods but did not describe them. In addition, candidates advantages and disadvantages were far too brief, a describe requirement needs more than a few words and 'easy to understand' is not detailed enough to score the 1 mark available.

Part (b) for 2 marks required two controls objectives for the sales and despatch system. Candidates could have used the scenario to help or answered this question using their technical knowledge, however overall performance was unsatisfactory. A significant proportion of candidates provided controls rather than control objectives, this was not what was required and so would not have scored any marks. This indicates a lack of knowledge as to what a control is rather than a control objective. Objectives have been tested in previous diets, and candidates should endeavour to practice past exam questions when preparing for this exam.

Part (c) for 12 marks required an identification and explanation of six deficiencies and a recommendation for each of these deficiencies.

This part of the question was answered very well and candidates were able to confidently identify six deficiencies from the scenario. However, candidates did not always adequately explain what the deficiency meant to Oregano. For example, candidates easily identified the deficiency that credit limits were being exceeded by 10% for online orders; however some failed to explain that this could lead to an increase in bad debts.

The requirement to provide controls was, on the whole, well answered. Most candidates were able to provide good recommendations to address the deficiencies; however some of these recommendations were too brief. In addition some recommendations failed to address the deficiency, for example for the credit limits being exceeded some candidates suggested 'a review of credit limits by a responsible official', this would not prevent orders from exceeding the limits. The main recommendation where candidates failed to maximise their marks was for sequentially numbered orders. Simply recommending 'that sales orders should be sequentially numbered' only scored 1/2 marks, as the control is to undertake sequence checks, for which the orders need to be sequential. This demonstrated a lack of understanding of this type of control.

157 FOX INDUSTRIES *Walk in the footsteps of a top tutor*

(a) **Report to management**

Top Tutor Tips

When asked for a covering letter, don't ignore this as there are usually format marks available. Remember to keep your answer anonymous, don't use your own name in the letter, make up a name. Don't forget to include the point that the letter is solely for the use of management and don't forget to sign off the letter appropriately.

Controls deficiencies and recommendations questions are usually quite straightforward, however, you must be explain the deficiencies and controls in sufficient detail to score marks. If you are too brief you will only score ½ marks.

Board of directors
Fox Industries Co
15 Dog Street
Cat Town
X Country

6 June 2013

Dear Sirs,

Audit of Fox Industries Co (Fox) for the year ended 30 April 2013

Please find enclosed the report to management on deficiencies in internal controls identified during the audit for the year ended 30 April 2013. The appendix to this report considers deficiencies in the purchasing and payments system, the implications of those deficiencies and recommendations to address those deficiencies.

Please note that this report only addresses the deficiencies identified during the audit and if further testing had been performed, then more deficiencies may have been reported.

This report is solely for the use of management and if you have any further questions, then please do not hesitate to contact us.

Yours faithfully

An audit firm

APPENDIX

Deficiency	*Implication*	*Recommendation*
When raising purchase orders, the clerks choose whichever supplier can despatch the goods the fastest.	This could result in Fox ordering goods at a much higher price or a lower quality than they would like, as the only factor considered was speed of delivery. It is important that goods are despatched promptly, but this is just one of many criteria that should be used in deciding which supplier to use.	An approved supplier list should be compiled; this should take into account the price of goods, their quality and also the speed of delivery. Once the list has been produced, all orders should only be placed with suppliers on the approved list.
Purchase orders are not sequentially numbered.	Failing to sequentially number the orders means that Fox's ordering team are unable to monitor if all orders are being fulfilled in a timely manner; this could result in stock outs. If the orders are numbered, then a sequence check can be performed for any	All purchase orders should be sequentially numbered and on a regular basis a sequence check of unfulfilled orders should be performed.

Deficiency	*Implication*	*Recommendation*
	unfulfilled orders.	
Purchase orders below $5,000 are not authorised and are processed solely by an order clerk.	This can result in goods being purchased which are not required by Fox. In addition, there is an increased fraud risk as an order clerk could place orders for personal goods up to the value of $5,000, which is significant.	All purchase orders should be authorised by a responsible official. Authorised signatories should be established with varying levels of purchase order authorisation.
Purchase invoices are input daily by the purchase ledger clerk and due to his experience, he does not utilise any application controls.	Without application controls there is a risk that invoices could be input into the system with inaccuracies or they may be missed out entirely. This could result in suppliers being paid incorrectly or not all, leading to a loss of supplier goodwill.	The purchase ledger clerk should input the invoices in batches and apply application controls, such as control totals, to ensure completeness and accuracy over the input of purchase invoices.
The purchase day book automatically updates with the purchase ledger but this ledger is manually posted to the general ledger.	Manually posting the amounts to the general ledger increases the risk of errors occurring. This could result in the payables balance in the financial statements being under or overstated.	The process should be updated so that on a regular basis the purchase ledger automatically updates the general ledger. A responsible official should then confirm through purchase ledger control account reconciliations that the update has occurred correctly.
Fox's saving (deposit) bank accounts are only reconciled every two months.	If these accounts are only reconciled periodically, there is the risk that errors will not be spotted promptly. Also, this increases the risk of employees committing fraud. If they are aware that these accounts are not regularly reviewed, then they could use these cash sums fraudulently.	All bank accounts should be reconciled on a regular basis, and at least monthly, to identify any unusual or missing items. The reconciliations should be reviewed by a responsible official and they should evidence their review.

Deficiency	*Implication*	*Recommendation*
Fox has a policy of delaying payments to their suppliers for as long as possible.	Whilst this maximises Fox's bank balance, there is the risk that Fox is missing out on early settlement discounts. Also, this can lead to a loss of supplier goodwill as well as the risk that suppliers may refuse to supply goods to Fox.	Fox should undertake cash flow forecasting/budgeting to maximise bank balances. The policy of delaying payment should be reviewed, and suppliers should be paid in a systematic way, such that supplier goodwill is not lost.

(b) **Application controls**

Top Tutor Tips

Make sure you give 'application' controls, i.e. those that you would perform at the time of entering the data to ensure it is complete and accurate. General controls will not score marks.

Document counts – the number of invoices to be input are counted, the invoices are then entered one by one, at the end the number of invoices input is checked against the document count. This helps to ensure completeness of input.

Control totals – here the total of all the invoices, such as the gross value, is manually calculated. The invoices are input, the system aggregates the total of the input invoices' gross value and this is compared to the control total. This helps to ensure completeness and accuracy of input.

One for one checking – the invoices entered into the system are manually agreed back one by one to the original purchase invoices. This helps to ensure completeness and accuracy of input.

Review of output to expected value – an independent assessment is made of the value of purchase invoices to be input, this is the expected value. The invoices are input and the total value of invoices is compared to the expected value. This helps to ensure completeness of input.

Check digits – this control helps to reduce the risk of transposition errors. Mathematical calculations are performed by the system on a particular data field, such as supplier number, a mathematical formula is run by the system, this checks that the data entered into the system is accurate. This helps to ensure accuracy of input.

Range checks – a pre-determined maximum is input into the system for gross invoice value, for example, $10,000; when invoices are input if the amount keyed in is incorrectly entered as being above $10,000, the system will reject the invoice. This helps to ensure accuracy of input.

Existence checks – the system is set up so that certain key data must be entered, such as supplier name, otherwise the invoice is rejected. This helps to ensure accuracy of input.

Tutorial note

Marks will be awarded for any other relevant application controls.

ACCA marking scheme		
		Marks
(a)	Up to 1 mark per well explained deficiency, implication and recommendation. If not well explained then just give ½ mark for each. Overall maximum of 5 marks each for deficiencies, implications and recommendations. 2 marks for presentation: 1 for address and intro and 1 for conclusion. No approved suppliers list Purchase orders not sequentially numbered Orders below $5,000 are not authorised by a responsible official No application controls over input of purchase invoices Purchase ledger manually posted to general ledger Saving (deposit) bank accounts only reconciled every two months Payments to suppliers delayed Finance director only reviews the total of the payment list prior to payment authorising	
	Max	**17**
(b)	Up to 1 mark per well explained application control Document counts Control totals One for one checking Review of output to expected value Check digits Range checks Existence checks	
	Max	**3**
Total		**20**

Examiner's comments

Part (a) required a report to management which identifies and explains deficiencies, the implications and a recommendation for each of these deficiencies; in addition a covering letter was required.

This part of the question was answered very well and candidates were able to confidently identify four deficiencies from the scenario. However, candidates did not always adequately explain the implication of the deficiency to the business. For example, for the deficiency of purchase orders not being sequentially numbered, many candidates focused on the difficulties of agreeing invoices to orders, as opposed to the key issue of unfulfilled orders and hence stock outs. In addition many implications were vague such as 'there will be errors if application controls are not applied by the purchase ledger clerk' this answer does not give any examples of what type of errors and where they may occur. Candidates need to think in a practical manner and apply their knowledge when answering these types of questions.

The requirement to provide controls was, on the whole, well answered. Most candidates were able to provide good recommendations to address the deficiencies. However some of these recommendations were too brief, for example simply stating 'apply application controls' to address the deficiency of the purchase ledger clerk. The main recommendation where candidates failed to maximise their marks was for sequentially numbered purchase orders. Simply recommending 'that purchase orders should be sequentially numbered' only scored 1/2 marks, as the control is to undertake sequence checks, for which the orders need to be sequential. This demonstrated a lack of understanding of this type of control.

A covering letter to the report was required and there were 2 marks available. Despite this specific requirement a significant number of candidates provided their answers as a memo rather than as a letter. Adopting a memo format resulted in a failure to maximise marks. The two marks were allocated as 1/2 for a letterhead, 1/2 for an introductory paragraph, 1/2 for disclaimers and 1/2 for a courteous sign off of the letter, which requires more than just a signature.

Many candidates set their answer out in three columns being deficiency, implication and recommendation. However, those who explained all of the deficiencies, the implications and then separately provided all of the recommendations tended to repeat themselves and possibly wasted some time.

In many answers deficiencies were combined such as; 'purchase orders are not sequentially numbered and only orders over $5,000 require authorisation', the implications and recommendations would then also be combined. Combining answers leads to unstructured answers that are difficult to mark. Spending too much time on this part of the exam also puts candidates under time pressure for the rest of the paper.

Part (b) required application controls to ensure the completeness and accuracy of the input of purchase invoices. Performance on this question was quite unsatisfactory. Many candidates failed to pick up marks for this question; also this question was left unanswered by some candidates.

The requirement was for application controls, these could be computerised or manual, but they needed to address the specific area of INPUT of invoices. Many candidates gave general computer controls such as passwords or provided auditor's substantive tests. In addition candidates listed recommendations from part (b) such as 'sequentially numbered orders or regular bank reconciliations'; these have nothing to do with input of invoices. Some answers focused on auditing the purchase cycle, agreeing orders to goods received notes and to invoices. Candidates clearly either have a knowledge gap in this area or failed to read the question requirement carefully.

158 LILY WINDOW GLASS *Walk in the footsteps of a top tutor*

(a) Inventory count arrangements

> ***Top Tutor Tips***
>
> *Controls deficiencies and recommendations questions are usually quite straightforward, however, you must explain the deficiencies and controls in sufficient detail to score marks. If you are too brief you will only score ½ marks.*

Deficiencies	*Recommendations*
The warehouse manager is planning to supervise the inventory count. Whilst he is familiar with the inventory, he has overall responsibility for the inventory and so is not independent. He may want to hide inefficiencies and any issues that arise so that his department is not criticised.	An alternative supervisor who is not normally involved with the inventory, such as an internal audit manager, should supervise the inventory count. The warehouse manager and his team should not be involved in the count at all.
There are ten teams of counters, each team having two members of staff. However, there is no clear division of responsibilities within the team. Therefore, both members of staff could count together rather than checking each other's count; and errors in their count may not be identified.	Each team should be informed that both members are required to count their assigned inventory separately. Therefore, one counts and the second member checks that the inventory has been counted correctly.
The internal audit teams are undertaking inventory counts rather than reviewing the controls and performing sample test counts. Their role should be focused on confirming the accuracy of the inventory counting procedures.	The internal audit counters should sample check the counting undertaken by the ten teams to provide an extra control over the completeness and accuracy of the count.
Once areas are counted, the teams are not flagging the aisles as completed. Therefore there is the risk that some areas of the warehouse could be double counted or missed out.	All aisles should be flagged as completed, once the inventory has been counted. In addition, internal audit or the count supervisor should check at the end of the count that all 20 aisles have been flagged as completed.
Inventory not listed on the sheets is to be entered onto separate sheets, which are not sequentially numbered. Therefore the supervisor will be unable to ensure the completeness of all inventory sheets.	Each team should be given a blank sheet for entering any inventory count which is not on their sheets. This blank sheet should be sequentially numbered, any unused sheets should be returned at the end of the count, and the supervisor should check the sequence of all sheets at the end of the count.

Deficiencies	*Recommendations*
The sheets are completed in ink and are sequentially numbered, however, there is no indication that they are signed by the counting team. Therefore if any issues arise with the counting in an aisle, it will be difficult to follow up as the identity of the counting team will not be known.	All inventory sheets should be signed by the relevant team upon completion of an aisle. When the sheets are returned, the supervisor should check that they have been signed.
Damaged goods are not being stored in a central area, and instead the counter is just noting on the inventory sheets the level of damage. However, it will be difficult for the finance team to decide on an appropriate level of write down if they are not able to see the damaged goods. In addition, if these goods are left in the aisles, they could be inadvertently sold to customers or moved to another aisle.	Damaged goods should be clearly flagged by the counting teams and at the end of the count appropriate machinery should be used to move all damaged windows to a central location. This will avoid the risk of selling these goods. A senior member of the finance team should then inspect these goods to assess the level of any write down or allowance.
Lily Window Glass Co (Lily) undertakes continuous production and so there will be movements of goods during the count. Inventory records could be under/overstated if goods are missed or double counted due to movements in the warehouse.	It is not practical to stop all inventory movements as the production needs to continue. However, any raw materials required for 31 December should be estimated and put to one side. These will not be included as raw materials and instead will be work-in-progress. The goods which are manufactured on 31 December should be stored to one side, and at the end of the count should be counted once and included within finished goods. Any goods received from suppliers should be stored in one location and counted once at the end and included as part of raw materials. Goods to be despatched to customers should be kept to a minimum for the day of the count.
The warehouse manager is to assess the level of work-in-progress and raw materials. In the past, a specialist has undertaken this role. It is unlikely that the warehouse manager has the experience to assess the level of work-in-progress as this is something that the factory manager would be more familiar with.	A specialist should be utilised to assess both work-in-progress and the quantities of raw materials.

Deficiencies	*Recommendations*
In addition, whilst the warehouse manager is familiar with the raw materials, if he makes a mistake in assessing the quantities then inventory could be materially misstated.	With regards to the warehouse manager, he could estimate the raw materials and the specialist could check it. This would give an indication as to whether he is able to accurately assess the quantities for subsequent inventory counts.

(b) **Procedures during the inventory count**

Top Tutor Tips

During the inventory count the auditor will perform both tests of controls and substantive procedures therefore this gives plenty of scope for answers.

- Observe the counting teams of Lily to confirm whether the inventory count instructions are being followed correctly.
- Select a sample and perform test counts from inventory sheets to warehouse aisle and from warehouse aisle to inventory sheets.
- Confirm the procedures for identifying and segregating damaged goods are operating correctly.
- Select a sample of damaged items as noted on the inventory sheets and inspect these windows to confirm whether the level of damage is correctly noted.
- Observe the procedures for movements of inventory during the count, to confirm that no raw materials or finished goods have been omitted or counted twice.
- Obtain a photocopy of the completed sequentially numbered inventory sheets for follow up testing on the final audit.
- Identify and make a note of the last goods received notes (GRNs) and goods despatched notes (GDNs) for 31 December in order to perform cut-off procedures.
- Observe the procedures carried out by the warehouse manager in assessing the level of work-in-progress and consider the reasonableness of any assumptions used.
- Discuss with the warehouse manager how he has estimated the raw materials quantities. To the extent that it is possible, re-perform the procedures adopted by the warehouse manager.
- Identify and record any inventory held for third parties (if any) and confirm that it is excluded from the count.

ACCA marking scheme

		Marks
(a)	Up to 1 mark per well explained deficiency and up to 1 mark per recommendation. If not well explained then just give ½ mark for each. Warehouse manager supervising the count No division of responsibilities within each counting team Internal audit teams should be checking controls and performing sample counts No flagging of aisles once counting complete Additional inventory listed on sheets which are not sequentially numbered Inventory sheets not signed by counters Damaged goods not moved to central location Movements of inventory during the count Warehouse manager not qualified to assess the level of work-in-progress Warehouse manager not experienced enough to assess the quantities of raw materials	
	Max	**14**
(b)	Up to 1 mark per well described procedure Observe the counters to confirm if inventory count instructions are being followed Perform test counts inventory to sheets and sheets to inventory Confirm procedures for damaged goods are operating correctly Inspect damaged goods to confirm whether the level of damage is correctly noted Observe procedures for movements of inventory during the count Obtain a photocopy of the completed inventory sheets Identify and make a note of the last goods received notes and goods despatched notes Observe the procedures carried out by warehouse manager in assessing the level of work-in-progress Discuss with the warehouse manager how he has estimated the raw materials quantities Identify inventory held for third parties and ensure excluded from count	
	Max	**6**
Total		**20**

Examiner's comments

Part (a) required candidates to identify and explain, for the inventory count arrangements of Lily, deficiencies and suggest a recommendation for each deficiency.

Most candidates performed very well on this part of the question. They were able to confidently identify deficiencies from the scenario. However, some candidates did not address the question requirement fully as they did not 'identify and explain'. Candidates identified, but did not go on to explain why this was a deficiency. For example 'additional inventory sheets are not numbered' would receive 1/2 mark, however to obtain the other 1/2 mark they needed to explain how this could cause problems during the inventory count; such as 'the additional sheets could be lost resulting in understated inventory quantities'.

The requirement to provide controls was also well answered. Most candidates were able to provide practical recommendations to address the deficiencies. The main exception to this was with regards to the issue of continued movements of goods during the count. The scenario stated that Lily undertakes continuous production; therefore to suggest 'that production is halted for the inventory count' demonstrated a failure to read and understand the scenario. The scenario is designed to help candidates and so they should not ignore elements of it.

Some candidates incorrectly identified deficiencies from the scenario, demonstrating a fundamental lack of understanding of the purpose of an inventory count. For example, a significant minority believed that inventory sheets should contain inventory quantities when in fact this is incorrect, as this would encourage markers to just agree the stated quantities rather than counting properly. In addition candidates felt that counters should not use ink on the count sheets as pencil would be easier for adjustments, again this is incorrect, as if the counts are in pencil then the quantities could be erroneously amended after the count. Also candidates felt that there should be more warehouse staff involved in the count, despite the self- review risk.

Many candidates set their answer out in two columns being deficiency and recommendation. However, those who explained all of the deficiencies and then separately provided all of the recommendations tended to repeat themselves and possibly wasted some time. In addition, it was not uncommon to see candidates provide many more answers than required.

Part (b) required procedures the auditor should undertake during the inventory count of Lily. Performance was unsatisfactory on this part of the question.

The requirement stated in capitals that procedures DURING the count were required; however a significant proportion of candidates ignored this word completely and provided procedures both before and after the count. Many answers actually stated 'before the count...', candidates must read the question requirements properly.

Those candidates who had read the question properly often struggled to provide an adequate number of well described points. The common answers given were 'to observe the inventory counters' although candidates did not make it clear what they were observing for; or 'undertake test counts' but with no explanation of the direction of the test and whether it was for completeness or existence. Some candidates provided all possible inventory tests, in particular focusing on NRV testing. This demonstrated that candidates had learnt a standard list of inventory tests and rather than applying these to the question set just proceeded to list them all. This approach wastes time and does not tend to score well as of the six answers provided very few tended to be relevant.

159 PEAR INTERNATIONAL *Walk in the footsteps of a top tutor*

(a) **Pear International's internal control**

Top Tutor Tips

Controls deficiencies and recommendations questions are usually quite straightforward, however, you must explain the deficiencies and controls in sufficient detail to score marks. If you are too brief you will only score ½ marks.

When suggesting tests of controls remember that you are looking for evidence that the client has implemented the control effectively. Do not suggest the auditor should perform the control as this doesn't prove the client has performed the control. Also be careful not to give substantive procedures as these have a different purpose to a test of control and will not score marks.

Deficiency	*Control*	*Test of control*
Currently the website is not integrated into inventory system. This can result in Pear accepting customer orders when they do not have the goods in inventory. This can cause them to lose sales and customer goodwill.	The website should be updated to include an interface into the inventory system; this should check inventory levels and only process orders if adequate inventory is held. If inventory is out of stock, this should appear on the website with an approximate waiting time.	Test data could be used to attempt to process orders via the website for items which are not currently held in inventory. The orders should be flagged as being out of stock and indicate an approximate waiting time.
For goods despatched by local couriers, customer signatures are not always obtained. This can lead to customers falsely claiming that they have not received their goods. Pear would not be able to prove that they had in fact despatched the goods and may result in goods being despatched twice.	Pear should remind all local couriers that customer signatures must be obtained as proof of despatch and payment will not be made for any despatches with missing signatures.	Select a sample of despatches by couriers and ask Pear for proof of despatch by viewing customer signatures.
There have been a number of situations where the sales orders have not been fulfilled in a timely manner. This can lead to a loss of customer goodwill and if it persists will damage the reputation of Pear as a reliable supplier.	Once goods are despatched they should be matched to sales orders and flagged as fulfilled.	Review the report of outstanding sales orders. If significant, discuss with a responsible official to understand why there is still a significant time period between sales order and despatch date.
	The system should automatically flag any outstanding sales orders past a predetermined period, such as five days. This report should be reviewed by a responsible official.	Select a sample of sales orders and compare the date of order to the goods despatch date to ascertain whether this is within the acceptable predetermined period.

Deficiency	*Control*	*Test of control*
Customer credit limits are set by sales ledger clerks. Sales ledger clerks are not sufficiently senior and so may set limits too high, leading to irrecoverable debts, or too low, leading to a loss of sales.	Credit limits should be set by a senior member of the sales ledger department and not by sales ledger clerks. These limits should be regularly reviewed by a responsible official.	For a sample of new customers accepted in the year, review the authorisation of the credit limit, and ensure that this was performed by a responsible official. Enquire of sales ledger clerks as to who can set credit limits.
Sales discounts are set by Pear's sales team. In order to boost their sales, members of the sales team may set the discounts too high, leading to a loss of revenue.	All members of the sales team should be given authority to grant sales discounts up to a set limit. Any sales discounts above these limits should be authorised by sales area managers or the sales director.	Discuss with members of the sales team the process for setting sales discounts.
	Regular review of sales discount levels should be undertaken by the sales director, and this review should be evidenced.	Review the sales discount report for evidence of review by the sales director.
Supplier statement reconciliations are no longer performed. This may result in errors in the recording of purchases and payables not being identified in a timely manner.	Supplier statement reconciliations should be performed on a monthly basis for all suppliers and these should be reviewed by a responsible official.	Review the file of reconciliations to ensure that they are being performed on a regular basis and that they have been reviewed by a responsible official.
Changes to supplier details in the purchase ledger master file can be undertaken by purchase ledger clerks. This could lead to key supplier data being accidently amended or fictitious suppliers being set up, which can increase the risk of fraud.	Only purchase ledger supervisors should have the authority to make changes to master file data. This should be controlled via passwords. Regular review of any changes to master file data by a responsible official and this review should be evidenced.	Request a purchase ledger clerk to attempt to access the master file and to make an amendment, the system should not allow this. Review a report of master data changes and review the authority of those making amendments.

Deficiency	*Control*	*Test of control*
Pear has considerable levels of surplus plant and equipment. Surplus unused plant is at risk of theft. In addition, if the surplus plant is not disposed of then the company could lose sundry income.	Regular review of the plant and equipment on the factory floor by senior factory personnel to identify any old or surplus equipment. As part of the capital expenditure process there should be a requirement to confirm the treatment of the equipment being replaced.	Observe the review process by senior factory personnel, identifying the treatment of any old equipment. Review processed capital expenditure forms to ascertain if the treatment of replaced equipment is stated.
Purchase requisitions are authorised by production supervisors. Production supervisors are not sufficiently independent or senior to authorise capital expenditure.	Capital expenditure authorisation levels to be established. Production supervisors should only be able to authorise low value items, any high value items should be authorised by the board.	Review a sample of authorised capital expenditure forms and identify if the correct signatory has authorised them.

(b) **Impact on interim and final audit**

> ***Top Tutor Tips***
>
> *For this requirement you need to suggest how the internal audit function could help with the external audit at both the interim and final audit stages. Make sure you split your answer into the two stages of the audit and think about the types of activity the external auditor performs at each of those stages and whether the internal auditor may have already performed work of a similar nature that the external auditor could rely on.*

Interim audit

Apple & Co could look to rely on any internal control documentation produced by internal audit (IA) as they would need to assess whether the control environment has changed during the year.

If the IA department has performed testing during the year on internal control systems, such as the payroll, sales and purchase systems, then Apple & Co could review and possibly place reliance on this work. This may result in the workload reducing and possibly a decrease in the external audit fee.

During the interim audit, Apple & Co would need to perform a risk assessment to assist in the planning process. It is possible that the IA department may have conducted a risk assessment and so Apple could use this as part of their initial planning process.

Apple & Co would need to consider the risk of fraud and error and non-compliance with law and regulations resulting in misstatements in the financial statements. This is also an area for IA to consider, hence there is scope for Apple & Co to review the work and testing performed by IA to assist in this risk assessment.

Final audit

It is possible that the IA department may assist with year-end inventory counting and controls and so Apple & Co can place some reliance on the work performed by them, however, they would still need to attend the count and perform their own reduced testing.

ACCA marking scheme		
		Marks
(a)	Up to 1 mark per deficiency, up to 1 mark per well explained control and up to 1 mark for each well explained test of control, max of 5 for deficiencies, max of 5 for controls and max of 5 for tests of control. Website not integrated into inventory system Customer signatures Unfulfilled sales orders Customer credit limits Sales discounts Supplier statement reconciliations Purchase ledger master file Surplus plant and equipment Authorisation of capital expenditure	
	Max	**15**
(b)	Up to 1 mark per well explained point **Interim audit** Systems documentation Testing of systems such as payroll, sales, purchases Risk assessment Non-compliance with law and regulations Fraud and error **Final audit** Inventory count procedures	
	Max	**5**
Total		**20**

Examiner's comments

Part (a) required candidates to identify and explain deficiencies, suggest a control for each deficiency and recommend tests of controls to assess if the internal controls of Pear were operating effectively. Most candidates performed well on this part of the question. They were able to confidently identify deficiencies from the scenario. However, many candidates did not address the question requirement fully as they did not 'identify and explain'. Candidates identified, but did not go on to explain why this was a deficiency. For example 'couriers do not always record customer signatures as proof of delivery' would receive 1/2 mark, however to obtain the other 1/2 mark they needed to explain how this could cause problems for the company; such as customers could dispute receipt of goods and Pear would need to resend them. The requirement to provide controls was generally well answered. Some candidates gave objectives rather than controls for example 'Pear should ensure that all sales are forwarded to the despatch department' without explaining what the control should be to ensure that this happened. In addition some candidates provided controls which were just too vague to attain the 1 mark available per control.

The requirement to provide tests of control was not answered well. Many candidates simply repeated their controls and added 'to check that' or 'to make sure'. These are not tests of control. Also many candidates suggested that the control be tested through observation. For example 'observe the process for authorisation of sales discounts'. This is a weak test as it is likely that if the auditor is present that the control will operate effectively; instead a better test would be 'to review sales invoices for evidence of authorisation of discounts by sales manager.'

Many candidates set their answer out in three columns being deficiency, control and test of control. However those who set it out as identification of deficiency, explanation of deficiency and control and then separately addressed the requirement of test of controls tended to miss out some relevant tests of controls.

It was not uncommon to see candidates provide many more points than required. Often in one paragraph they would combine two or three points such as authorisation of credit limits and of sales discounts. When points were combined, some candidates did not fully provide controls and tests of controls for each of the given points, therefore failing to maximise their marks.

Part (b) required candidates to explain the impact on the external auditor's work at the interim and final audits if Pear was to establish an internal audit department. Performance on this question was unsatisfactory.

Where the question was attempted, many candidates failed to score more than 1 mark. What was required was an explanation of tasks that internal audit might perform that the external auditor might then look to rely on in either the interim or final audit. For example, they could utilise systems documentation produced by internal audit during the interim audit. Or they could rely on year-end inventory counts undertaken by internal audit as part of their inventory testing at the final audit.

Where candidates achieved 1 mark this was usually for a general comment about relying on the work of internal audit and so reducing substantive procedures.

Mistakes made by candidates were:

- Focusing on the role of internal audit in general.
- Giving lengthy answers on factors to consider when placing reliance on internal audit.
- Providing details of what an external auditor does at the interim and final audit stages.

160 GREYSTONE *Walk in the footsteps of a top tutor*

Top Tutor Tips

Part (a) is a tricky knowledge question. This question demonstrates the need for both breadth and depth of knowledge across the F8 syllabus, including knowing the objectives and key provisions of all of the examinable ISAs. If you don't know this, don't spend time thinking about it, move on to the next part of the question. It is only worth 3 marks so not worth wasting time over.

Part (b) is a very common style of question and should be practised before sitting the actual exam. Note that the question requires you to link part (ii) to the deficiencies you identified in part (i). For this reason a table format is appropriate for your answer. Your answer to part (b) requires application of knowledge to the specific information given in the question. You cannot 'knowledge dump' in your answer.

Part (c) asks for substantive procedures you could perform on the year-end trade payables balance of Greystone Co. However, as Greystone is a retail entity, the procedures over trade payables will not differ significantly from the standard procedures described in your learning materials.

The highlighted words are key phases that markers are looking for.

(a) Examples of matters the external auditor should consider in determining whether a deficiency in internal controls is significant include:

- The likelihood of the deficiencies leading to material misstatements in the financial statements in the future.
- The susceptibility to loss or fraud of the related asset or liability.
- The subjectivity and complexity of determining estimated amounts.
- The financial statement amounts exposed to the deficiencies.
- The volume of activity that has occurred or could occur in the account balance or class of transactions exposed to the deficiency or deficiencies.
- The importance of the controls to the financial reporting process.
- The cause and frequency of the exceptions detected as a result of the deficiencies in the controls.
- The interaction of the deficiency with other deficiencies in internal control.

Top tutor tips

Note that the requirement asks for matters which would mean an internal control deficiency is significant, NOT examples *of significant internal control deficiencies. Giving examples of deficiencies will not score any marks.*

Tutorial note

ISA 265 ***Communicating Deficiencies in Internal Control to those charged with Governance and Management*** *states that a significant deficiency in internal control is a deficiency or combination of deficiencies in internal control that, in the auditor's professional judgement, is of sufficient importance to merit the attention of those charged with governance.*

(b)

(i) **Deficiency**	**Explanation**	(ii) **Recommendation**
The purchasing manager decides on the inventory levels for each store without discussion with store or sales managers. The purchasing manager may not have the appropriate knowledge of the local market for a store.	This could result in stores ordering goods that are not likely to sell and hence require heavy discounting. In addition as a fashion chain, if customers perceive that the goods are not meeting the key fashion trends then they may cease to shop at Greystone at all.	The purchasing manager should initially hold a meeting with area managers of stores; if meeting all store managers is not practical, he should understand the local markets before agreeing jointly goods to be purchased.
The purchase orders are only reviewed and authorised by a purchasing director in a wholly aggregated manner (by specified regions of countries).	It will be difficult for the purchasing director to assess whether overall the correct buying decisions are being made as the detail of the orders is not being presented and he is the only level of authorisation. This could result in significant levels of goods being purchased that are not right for particular market sectors.	A purchasing senior manager should review the information prepared for each country and discuss with local purchasing managers the specifics of their orders. These should then be authorised and passed to the purchasing director for final review and sign off.
The store managers are responsible for re-ordering goods through the purchasing manager.	If the store managers forget or order too late, then as the ordering process can take up to four weeks, the store could experience significant stock outs leading to loss of income.	Automatic re-order levels should be set up in the inventory management systems. As the goods sold reach the re-order levels the purchasing manager should receive an automatic re-order request.

(i) **Deficiency**	**Explanation**	(ii) **Recommendation**
It is not possible for a store to order goods from other local stores for customers who request them. Instead they are told to contact the stores themselves, or use the company website.	Customers are less likely to contact individual stores themselves and this could result in the company losing out on valuable sales. In addition some goods which are slow moving in one store may be out of stock at another, if goods could be transferred between stores then overall sales may be maximised.	An inter-branch transfer system should be established between stores. This should help stores whose goods are below the re-order level but are awaiting their deliveries from the suppliers.
Deliveries from suppliers are accepted without being checked first.	The stores are receiving goods without checking that these are correct. Hence if a delivery is subsequently disputed there may be little recourse for the company.	Deliveries from suppliers should only be accepted between designated hours such as the first two hours of the morning when it is quieter. The goods should then be checked on arrival for quantity and quality prior to acceptance from the supplier. A responsible official at each store should produce the GRN from the supplier's delivery information.
In addition they are then checked by sales assistants to the supplier's delivery note to agree quantities but not quality.	If the sales assistants are only checking quantities then goods which are not of a saleable condition may be accepted.	
Sales assistants are producing the goods received note (GRN) on receipt of a supplier's delivery note.	The assistants may not be adequately experienced to produce the GRN, and this is an important document used in the invoice authorisation process. Errors could lead to under or overpayments.	
Goods are being received without any checks being made against purchase orders.	This could result in Greystone receiving and subsequently paying for goods it did not require. In addition if no check is made against order then the company may have significant purchase orders which are outstanding, leading to lost sales.	A copy of the authorised order form should be sent to the store. This should then be checked to the GRN. Once checked the order should be sent to head office and logged as completed. On a regular basis the purchasing clerk should review the order file for any outstanding items.

(i) Deficiency	Explanation	(ii) Recommendation
Purchase invoices are manually matched to a high volume of GRNs from the individual stores.	A manual checking process increases the risk of error, resulting in invoices being accepted or rejected erroneously.	The checked GRNs should be logged onto the purchasing system, matched against the relevant order number, then as the invoice is received this should be automatically matched. The purchasing clerk should then review for any unmatched items.
The purchase invoice is only logged onto the system as it is being authorised by the purchasing director.	If the invoice is misplaced then payables may not be settled on a timely basis. In addition at the year-end the purchase ledger may be understated as invoices relating to the current year have been received but are not in the purchase ledger.	Upon receipt of an invoice this should be logged into a file of unmatched invoices. As it is matched and authorised it should then be moved into the purchase ledger. At the year-end items in the unmatched invoices file should be accrued for, to ensure liabilities are not understated.

Tutorial note

The explanation in the table above has been separated from the identification to make it clear that this aspect of the requirement has been addressed. Answers which do not adequately explain the deficiency will only score ½ mark.

(c) **Substantive procedures over year-end trade payables**

- Obtain a listing of trade payables from the purchase ledger and agree to the general ledger and the financial statements.
- Reconcile the total of purchase ledger accounts with the purchase ledger control account, and cast the list of balances and the purchase ledger control account.
- Review the list of trade payables against prior years to identify any significant omissions.
- Calculate the trade payable days for Greystone and compare to prior years, investigate any significant differences.
- Review after date payments, if they relate to the current year then follow through to the purchase ledger or accrual listing to ensure completeness.
- Review after date invoices and credit notes to ensure no further items need to be accrued.
- Obtain supplier statements and reconcile these to the purchase ledger balances, and investigate any reconciling items.

- Select a sample of payable balances and perform a trade payables' circularisation, follow up any non-replies and any reconciling items between balance confirmed and trade payables' balance.
- Enquire of management their process for identifying goods received but not invoiced or logged in the purchase ledger and ensure that it is reasonable to ensure completeness of payables.
- Select a sample of goods received notes before the year-end and follow through to inclusion in the year-end payables balance, to ensure correct cut-off.
- Review the purchase ledger for any debit balances, for any significant amounts discuss with management and consider reclassification as current assets.
- Review the financial statements to ensure payables are included as current liabilities.

ACCA marking scheme

			Marks
(a)	Up to 1 mark per valid point		
	Likelihood of deficiencies leading to errors		
	Risk of fraud		
	Subjectivity and complexity		
	Financial statement amounts		
	Volume of activity		
	Importance of the controls		
	Cause and frequency of exceptions		
	Interaction with other deficiencies		
		Max	**3**
(b)	Up to 1 mark per well explained, deficiency and up to 1 mark per recommendation. If not well explained then just give ½ mark for each.		
	Purchasing manager orders goods without consulting stores		
	Purchase order reviewed in aggregate by purchasing director		
	Store managers re-order goods		
	No inter-branch transfer system		
	Deliveries accepted without proper checks		
	Sales assistants produce the goods received note		
	Goods received but not checked to purchase orders		
	Manual matching of goods received notes to invoice		
	Purchase invoice logged late		
		Max	**12**
(c)	Up to 1 mark per well explained substantive procedure		
	Agree purchase ledger to general and financial statements		
	Review payable to prior year		
	Calculate trade payables		
	After date payments review		
	After date invoices/credit notes review		
	Supplier statement reviews		
	Payables' circularisation		
	Goods received not invoiced		
	Cut-off testing		
	Debit balances review		
	Disclosure within current liabilities		
		Max	**5**
Total			**20**

161 SMOOTHBRUSH PAINTS *Walk in the footsteps of a top tutor*

Top Tutor Tips

*This question requires you to explain controls over the perpetual inventory system. Make sure that the controls you recommend specifically address the **completeness** and **accuracy** of inventory records.*

The highlighted words are key phases that markers are looking for.

Controls over the perpetual/continuous inventory system

Control	**Explanation**
The inventory count team should be independent of the warehouse team.	Currently the team includes a warehouse staff member and an internal auditor. There should be segregation of roles between those who have day-to-day responsibility for inventory and those who are checking it. If the same team are responsible for maintaining and checking inventory, then errors and fraud could be hidden.
Timetable of counts should be regularly reviewed to ensure that all areas are counted.	The warehouse has been divided into 12 areas that are each due to be counted once over the year. All inventory is required to be counted once a year, hence if the timetable is not monitored then some areas could be missed out.
Movements of inventory should be stopped from the designated areas during continuous/perpetual inventory counts.	Goods will continue to move in and out of the warehouse during the counts. Inventory records could be under/over stated if product lines are missed or double counted due to movements in the warehouse.
Inventory counting sheets should be pre-printed with a description or item code of the goods, but the quantities per the records should not be pre-recorded.	The inventory sheets produced for the count have the quantities pre-printed, therefore a risk arises that the counting team could just agree with the record quantities, making under counting more likely, rather than counting the inventory lines correctly.
A second independent team should check the counts performed by the inventory count team.	By counting the lines twice this should help to ensure completeness and accuracy of the counts, and hence that any inventory adjustments are appropriate.

Control	**Explanation**
Inventory checks should be performed from inventory physically present in the warehouse to the records.	Currently the team is comparing the records to the inventory in the warehouse. If the count is performed from the records to the warehouse then this will only ensure existence or overstatement of the records. To ensure completeness is addressed the inventory in the warehouse must be compared to the records as this will identify any goods physically present but not included in the records.
Any damaged or obsolete goods should be moved to a designated area, where a responsible official then inspects it, it should not be removed from the sheets.	Damaged or obsolete goods should be written down or provided against to ensure that they are stated at the lower of cost and NRV. This may not involve fully writing off the inventory item as is currently occurring. This is an assessment that should only be performed by a suitably trained member of the finance team, as opposed to the inventory count team.
After the count, the inventory count sheets should be compared to the inventory records, any adjustments should be investigated and if appropriate the records updated in a prompt manner by an authorised person.	At the year end the inventory of Smoothbrush will be based on the records maintained. Hence the records must be complete, accurate and valid. It is important that only individuals authorised to do so can amend records. Senior members of the finance team should regularly review the types and levels of adjustments, as recurring inventory adjustments could indicate possible fraud.

ACCA marking scheme	
	Marks
½ mark for each identification of a control and up to 1 mark per well explained description of the control	
– Team independent of warehouse	
– Timetable of counts	
– Inventory movements stopped	
– No pre-printed quantities on count sheets	
– Second independent team	
– Direction of counting floor to records	
– Damaged/obsolete goods to specific area	
– Records updated by authorised person	
Total	**10**

162 SHINY HAPPY WINDOWS *Walk in the footsteps of a top tutor*

Top Tutor Tips

Part (a) requires little more than pre-learnt knowledge.

Part (b) is a typical systems review question. You are asked to prepare a management letter of deficiencies to those charged with governance. This is a very common style of question and should be rehearsed before sitting the actual exam. Note that the question requires you to link parts (ii) and (iii) to the deficiencies you identified in part (i). For this reason a table format is appropriate for your answer. Your answer to part (b) requires application of knowledge to the specific information given in the question. You cannot 'knowledge dump' in your answer.

Part (c) asks for tests you could perform on any company's bank balance. You can therefore suggest general tests learnt from your study texts. You do not have to apply your answer to the scenario.

The highlighted words are key phases that markers are looking for.

(a) A control objective is the reason behind needing a control. The objective identifies a risk the company faces. For example there is a risk that purchase orders are placed by employees that are not for a valid business use.

A control procedure is the process or activity designed to mitigate a risk. For example authorisation of purchase orders to ensure they are for a valid business use.

A control procedure is therefore implemented to achieve the control objective.

(b)

Deficiency	**Control**	**Test of Control**
A junior clerk opens the post unsupervised. This could result in cash being misappropriated.	A second member of the accounts team or staff independent of the accounts team should assist with the mail, one should open the post and the second should record cash received in the cash log.	Observe the mail opening process, to assess if the control is operating effectively.
Cash and cheques are secured in a small locked box and only banked every few days. A small locked box is not adequate for security of considerable cash receipts, as it can easily be stolen.	Cash and cheques should be ideally banked daily, if not then it should be stored in a fire proof safe, and access to this safe should be restricted to supervised individuals.	Enquire of management where the cash receipts not banked are stored. Inspect the location to ensure cash is suitably secure.

Deficiency	**Control**	**Test of Control**
Cash and cheques are only banked every few days and any member of the finance team performs this.	Cash and cheques should be banked every day.	Inspect the paying-in-books to see if cash and cheques have been banked daily or less frequently. Review bank statements against the cash received log to confirm all amounts were banked promptly.
Cash should ideally not be held over-night as it is not secure. Also if any member of the team banks cash, then this could result in very junior clerks having access to significant amounts of money.	The cashier should prepare the paying-in-book from the cash received log. Then a separate responsible individual should have responsibility for banking this cash.	Enquire of staff as to who performs the banking process and confirm this person is suitably responsible.
The cashier updates both the cash book and the sales ledger. This is weak segregation of duties, as the cashier could incorrectly enter a receipt and this would impact both the cash book and the sales ledger. In addition weak segregation of duties could increase the risk of a 'teeming and lading' fraud.	The cashier should update the cash book from the cash received log. A member of the sales ledger team should update the sales ledger.	Observe the process for recording cash received into the relevant ledgers and note if the segregation of duties is occurring.
Bank reconciliations are not performed every month and they do not appear to be reviewed by a senior member of the finance department. Errors in the cash cycle may not be promptly identified if reconciliations are performed infrequently.	Bank reconciliations should be performed monthly. A responsible individual should then review them.	Review the file of reconciliations for evidence of regular performance and review by senior finance team members.

(c) **Substantive procedures over bank balance:**

- Obtain the company's bank reconciliation and cast to ensure arithmetical accuracy.
- Obtain a bank confirmation letter from the company's bankers.
- Verify the balance per the bank statement to an original year end bank statement and also to the bank confirmation letter.

- Verify the reconciliation's balance per the cash book to the year end cash book.
- Trace all of the outstanding lodgements to the pre year end cash book, post year end bank statement and also to paying-in-book pre year end.
- Examine any old unpresented cheques to assess if they need to be written back into the purchase ledger as they are no longer valid to be presented.
- Trace all unpresented cheques through to a pre year end cash book and post year end statement. For any unusual amounts or significant delays obtain explanations from management.
- Agree all balances listed on the bank confirmation letter to the company's bank reconciliations or the trial balance to ensure completeness of bank balances.
- Review the cash book and bank statements for any unusual items or large transfers around the year end, as this could be evidence of window dressing.
- Examine the bank confirmation letter for details of any security provided by the company or any legal right of set-off as this may require disclosure.

ACCA marking scheme		
		Marks
(a)	Up to 1 mark each for each point – Explanation of control objective – Explanation of control procedure – Control procedure achieves control objective	
	Max	**3**
(b)	Up to 1 mark for each deficiency identified and explained, up to 1 mark for each suitable control and up to 1 mark per test of control. – Junior clerk opens post – Small locked box – Cash not banked daily – Cashier updates cash book and sales ledger – Bank reconciliation not performed monthly	
	Maximum for deficiencies	**4**
	Maximum for controls	**4**
	Maximum for test of controls	**4**
(c)	Up to 1 mark per substantive procedure – Cast bank reconciliation – Obtain bank confirmation letter – Bank balance to statement/bank confirmation – Cash book balance to cash book – Outstanding lodgements – Unpresented cheques review – Old cheques write back – Agree all balances on bank confirmation – Unusual items/window dressing – Security/legal right set-off	
	Max	**5**
Total		**20**

163 MATALAS CO *Walk in the footsteps of a top tutor*

Top Tutor Tips

Read through the scenario line by line to identify the deficiencies in the petty cash system of Matalas. You must explain why they are deficiencies in order to earn the full mark. When suggesting recommendations, remember they must be commercially sensible and practical.

Internal control deficiencies – petty cash

Deficiency	**Suggested control**
The petty cash balance is approximately three months expenditure. This is excessive and will increase the possibility of petty cash being stolen or errors not being identified.	The petty cash balance should be $2,000, being about one month's expenditure.
The petty cash box itself is not secure; it is placed on a bookcase where any member of staff could steal it.	When not in use, the petty cash box should be kept in the branch safe, or at least a locked drawer in the accountant's desk.
Petty cash appears to be used for some larger items of expenditure (up to $500). Vouchers are only authorised after expenditure is incurred indicating that some significant expenditure can take place without authorisation.	A maximum expenditure limit (e.g. $50) should be set before which prior authorisation is required.
Petty cash vouchers are only signed by the person incurring the expenditure, indicating a lack of authorisation control for that expenditure.	All vouchers should be signed by an independent official showing that the expenditure has been authorised.
Petty cash only appears to be counted by the accounts clerk, who is also responsible for the petty cash balance. There is no independent check that the petty cash balance is accurate.	The counting of petty cash should be checked by the accountant to ensure that the clerk is not stealing the cash.
When the imprest cheque is signed, only the journal entry for petty cash is reviewed, not the petty cash vouchers. The accountant has no evidence that the journal entry actually relates to the petty cash expenditure incurred.	The petty cash vouchers should be available for review to provide evidence of petty cash expenditure.
Petty cash vouchers are not pre-numbered so it is impossible to check the completeness of vouchers; unauthorised expenditure could be blamed on 'missing' vouchers.	Petty cash vouchers should be pre-numbered and the numbering checked in the petty cash book to confirm completeness of recording of expenditure.

Examiner's comments

To obtain the full two marks per point, answers would normally take the format 'issue 1 is a petty cash deficiency in Matalas, because..... . This deficiency can be overcome by....' However, as the question requirement did not specify the number of points to make, then any number of valid points could be included in the answer. Most candidates included up to six fairly well explained points in their answer. Again, a minority of candidates provided limited or no explanation of the points made, limiting the marks awarded.

The most interesting point to mark in this question concerned the location of the petty cash box itself. Almost all candidates recognised that it was inappropriate to maintain the petty cash book in public view on a bookcase, with the reason that the box could be stolen easily. However, controls over this deficiency varied from simply keeping the box in a safe to using CCTV and employing security guards to ensure the box was not stolen. Given the (relatively) small amount of money in the box, some controls did appear excessive. However, they were normally marked as valid as certainly in some jurisdictions the control could well be appropriate.

Common errors and reasons why those errors did not obtain marks included:

-Not explaining the reason for deficiencies identified. For example, many candidates noted that petty cash was counted by the cashier – but not the deficiency that the cashier could report incorrect cash balances and steal some of the money.

-Suggesting deficiencies that were not mentioned in the scenario. The most common weakness in this respect was the comment that petty cash should be computerised. To gain full marks, the deficiency had to be clearly related to the information provided in scenario.

-Suggesting many, and sometimes completely impractical procedures for the control of petty cash. For example, suggesting that all petty cash vouchers had to be signed by the senior accountant or that a voucher should be signed by one person, recorded in the petty cash book by another and then a third person dispensed the actual cash. Awarding marks in these situations was limited because the controls were simply not practical or cost effective for any company.

-A significant number of candidates struggled to provide sufficient reasons.

The overall standard was satisfactory which was possibly more an indication that candidates were not always familiar with petty cash systems but that they could identify and comment on deficiencies.

ACCA marking scheme	
	Marks
2 marks for each control deficiency. 1 for explaining the deficiency and 1 for control over that deficiency.	
– Size of petty cash balance	
– Security of petty cash box	
– High value petty cash expenditure	
– individual items	
– Authorisation of petty cash expenditure	
– Counting of petty cash	
– No review of petty cash vouchers	
– signing of imprest cheque	
– Vouchers not pre-numbered	
Total	**10**

164 JACKDAW MOTORS *Walk in the footsteps of a top tutor*

Top Tutor Tips

This scenario describes very specific issues that have occurred during the year and your procedures need to focus on these issues rather than the balances in general. For example, in part (b), your procedures need to concentrate on the revaluation of land and buildings, purchased warehouse and work in progress valuation. Don't give general procedures over property, plant and equipment as this is not the requirement. You must answer the question set by the examiner.

Part (c) covers the impact on the audit report as a result of the directors refusing to amend the financial statements. State whether the report and opinion should be modified. State precisely how it should be modified to earn the marks.

(a) **Reliance on the work of an independent valuer**

ISA 500 *Audit Evidence* requires auditors to evaluate the competence, capabilities including expertise and objectivity of a management expert.

This would include consideration of the qualifications of the valuer and assessment of whether they were members of any professional body or industry association. The expert's independence should be ascertained, with potential threats such as undue reliance on Jackdaw or a self-interest threat such as share ownership considered.

In addition, Puffin & Co should meet with the expert and discuss with them their relevant expertise, in particular whether they have valued similar land and buildings to those of Jackdaw Motor Cars Co (Jackdaw) in the past. Puffin & Co should also consider whether the valuer understands the accounting requirements of IAS 16 *Property, Plant and Equipment* in relation to valuations.

The valuation should then be evaluated. The assumptions used should be carefully reviewed and compared to previous revaluations at Jackdaw. These assumptions should be discussed with both management and the valuer to understand the basis of any valuations.

(b) (i) Substantive procedures for land and buildings

- Obtain a schedule of land and buildings revalued this year and cast to confirm completeness and accuracy of the revaluation adjustment.
- On a sample basis agree the revalued amounts to the valuation statement provided by the valuer.
- Agree the revalued amounts for these assets are included correctly in the non-current assets register.
- Recalculate the total revaluation adjustment and agree correctly recorded in the revaluation surplus.
- Agree the initial cost for the warehouse addition to supporting documentation such as invoices to confirm cost.
- Confirm through a review of the title deeds that the warehouse is owned by Jackdaw.

- Recalculate the depreciation charge for the year to ensure that for assets revalued during the year, the depreciation was based on the correct valuation and for the warehouse addition that the charge was for nine months only.
- Review the financial statements disclosures of the revaluation to ensure they comply with IAS 16 *Property, Plant and Equipment*.

(ii) **Substantive procedures for work in progress (WIP)**

- Prior to attending the inventory count, discuss with management how the percentage completions are attributed to the WIP, for example, is this based on motor cars passing certain points in the production process.
- During the count, observe the procedures carried out by Jackdaw staff in assessing the level of WIP and consider the reasonableness of the assumptions used.
- Agree for a sample that the percentage completions assessed during the count are in accordance with Jackdaw's policies communicated prior to the count.
- Discuss with management the basis of the standard costs applied to the percentage completion of WIP, and how often these are reviewed and updated.
- Review the level of variances between standard and actual costs and discuss with management how these are treated.
- Obtain a breakdown of the standard costs and agree a sample of these costs to actual invoices or payroll records to assess their reasonableness.
- Cast the schedule of total WIP and agree to the trial balance and financial statements.
- Agree sample of WIP assessed during the count to the WIP schedule, agree percentage completion is correct and recalculate the inventory valuation.

(c) **Audit report**

Discuss with the management of Jackdaw why they are refusing to make the amendment to WIP.

Assess the materiality of the error; if immaterial, it should be added to the schedule of unadjusted differences. The auditor should then assess whether this error results in the total of unadjusted differences becoming material; if so, this should be discussed with management; if not, there would be no impact on the audit report.

If the error is material and management refuses to amend the financial statements, then the audit report will need to be modified. It is unlikely that any error would be pervasive as although WIP in total is material, it would not have a pervasive effect on the financial statements as a whole. As management has not complied with IAS 2 *Inventory* and if the error is material but not pervasive, then a qualified opinion would be necessary.

A basis for qualified opinion paragraph would need to be included before the opinion paragraph. This would explain the material misstatement in relation to the valuation of WIP and the effect on the financial statements. The opinion paragraph would be qualified 'except for'.

ACCA marking scheme

			Marks
(a)	Up to 1 mark per valid point. – ISA 500 requires consideration of competence and capabilities of expert – Consider if member of professional body or industry association – Assess independence – Assess whether relevant expertise of type of properties as Jackdaw Motor Cars Co – Evaluate assumptions		
		Maximum	5
(b)	Up to 1 mark per well explained procedure, overall max 6 marks for land and buildings and max of 4 marks for work in progress. (i) **Land and buildings** – Cast schedule of land and buildings revalued this year – Agree the revalued amounts to the valuation statement provided by the valuer – Agree the revalued amounts included correctly in the non-current assets register – Recalculate the total revaluation adjustment and agree recorded in the revaluation surplus – Agree the initial cost for the warehouse to invoices to confirm cost – Confirm through title deeds that the warehouse is owned by Jackdaw – Recalculate the depreciation charge for the year – Review the financial statements disclosures for compliance with IAS *16 Property, Plant and Equipment*		
		Maximum	6
	(ii) **Work in progress** – Discuss with management how the percentage completions are attributed to WIP – Observe the procedures carried out in the count in assessing the level of WIP; consider the reasonableness of the assumptions used – During the count, agree a sample of percentage completions are in accordance with Jackdaw's policies – Discuss with management the basis of the standard costs – Review the level of variances between standard and actual costs – Obtain a breakdown of the standard costs and agree a sample of these costs to actual invoices – Cast the schedule of total WIP and agree to the trial balance and financial statements – Agree sample of WIP assessed during the count to the WIP schedule, agree percentage completion is correct and recalculate the inventory valuation		
		Maximum	4
(c)	Up to 1 mark per well explained valid point. – Discuss with management why they are refusing to make the amendment – Assess the materiality of the error – If immaterial, add to the schedule of unadjusted differences and assess if total errors material – If material but not pervasive, modified audit report, material misstatement, qualified opinion – Basis for qualified opinion paragraph required – Opinion paragraph – except for		
		Maximum	5
Total			**20**

165 ROSE LEISURE CLUB *Walk in the footsteps of a top tutor*

Top Tutor Tips

This scenario describes very specific issues that have occurred during the year and your procedures need to focus on these issues rather than the balances in general. For example, in part (a), you are not testing the payables and accruals balance in general but specifically focussing on whether the client has captured all liabilities between 25 October and 31 October. For part (b) you need to suggest alternative procedures to the circularisation as there have been a number who have not responded, therefore alternative evidence must be obtained.

(i) **Substantive procedures – Trade payables and accruals**

- Calculate the trade payable days for Rose Leisure Clubs Co (Rose) and compare to prior years, investigate any significant difference, in particular any decrease for this year.
- Compare the total trade payables and list of accruals against prior year and investigate any significant differences.
- Discuss with management the process they have undertaken to quantify the understatement of trade payables due to the cut-off error and consider the materiality of the error.
- Discuss with management whether any correcting journal entry has been included for the understatement.
- Select a sample of purchase invoices received between the period of 25 October and the year end and follow them through to inclusion within accruals or as part of the trade payables journal adjustment.
- Review after date payments; if they relate to the current year, then follow through to the purchase ledger or accrual listing to ensure they are recorded in the correct period.
- Obtain supplier statements and reconcile these to the purchase ledger balances, and investigate any reconciling items.
- Select a sample of payable balances and perform a trade payables' circularisation, follow up any non-replies and any reconciling items between the balance confirmed and the trade payables' balance.
- Select a sample of goods received notes before the year end and after the year end and follow through to inclusion in the correct period's payables balance, to ensure correct cut-off.

(ii) **Substantive procedures – Receivables**

- For non-responses, with the client's permission, the team should arrange to send a follow up circularisation.
- If the receivable does not respond to the follow up, then with the client's permission, the senior should telephone the customer and ask whether they are able to respond in writing to the circularisation request.
- If there are still non-responses, then the senior should undertake alternative procedures to confirm receivables.
- For responses with differences, the senior should identify any disputed amounts, and identify whether these relate to timing differences or whether there are possible errors in the records of Rose.
- Any differences due to timing, such as cash in transit, should be agreed to post year-end cash receipts in the cash book.
- The receivables ledger should be reviewed to identify any possible mispostings as this could be a reason for a response with a difference.
- If any balances have been flagged as disputed by the receivable, then these should be discussed with management to identify whether a write down is necessary.

ACCA marking scheme

		Marks
(i)	Up to 1 mark per well described procedure	
	Trade payables and accruals	
	– Calculate trade payable days	
	– Compare total trade payables and list of accruals against prior year	
	– Discuss with management process to quantify understatement of payables	
	– Discuss with management whether any correcting journal adjustment posted	
	– Sample invoices received between 25 October and year end and follow to inclusion in year-end accruals or trade payables correcting journal	
	– Review after date payments	
	– Review supplier statements reconciliations	
	– Perform a trade payables' circularisation	
	– Cut-off testing pre and post year-end GRN	
	Max	**5**
(ii)	**Receivables**	
	– For non-responses arrange to send a follow up circularisation	
	– With the client's permission, telephone the customer and ask for a response	
	– For remaining non-responses, undertake alternative procedures to confirm receivables	
	– For responses with differences, identify any disputed amounts, identify whether these relate to timing differences or whether there are possible errors in the records	
	– Cash in transit should be vouched to post year-end cash receipts in the cash book	
	– Review receivables ledger to identify any possible mispostings	
	– Disputed balances, discuss with management whether a write down is necessary	
	Max	**5**
Total		**10**

Examiner's comments

Part (i) required substantive procedures for an issue on trade payables and accruals with regards to an early cut off of the purchase ledger resulting in completeness risk. Performance on this question was unsatisfactory.

Candidates were unable to tailor their knowledge of general substantive procedures to the specific issue in the scenario. Most saw that the scenario title was trade payables and accruals and proceeded to list all possible payables tests. This is not what was required and hence did not score well. The scenario was provided so that candidates could apply their knowledge; however it seems that many did not take any notice of the scenario at all. What was required was tests to specifically address the risk of cut off and completeness due to the purchase ledger being closed one week early.

Common mistakes made by candidates were:

- Providing procedures to address assertions such as rights and obligation for example 'review year end purchase invoices to ensure in the company name'.
- Giving objectives rather than procedures 'ensure that cut off is correct', this is not a substantive procedure and so would not score any marks.
- Lack of detail in tests such as 'perform analytical procedures over payables', this would score no marks as the actual analytical review procedure has not been given.
- Thinking that 'obtaining a management representation' is a valid answer for all substantive procedure questions.
- Not providing enough tests, candidates should assume 1 mark per valid procedure.

Part (ii) for 5 marks required substantive procedures for an issue on trade receivables circularisations with regards to non-responses and responses with differences. Performance on this question was also unsatisfactory. As above, candidates failed to identify the specific issue from the scenario and instead provided a general list of receivables tests. Some candidates failed to recognise that analytical review procedures were unlikely to be of any benefit as Rose's receivables had changed significantly on the prior year due to a change in the business model. Also Rose was a leisure club and so provided services rather than goods; however candidates still recommended 'reviewing goods despatch notes for cut off'. This again demonstrates that candidates are learning generic lists of procedures and just writing them into their answers with little thought or application to the scenario. This approach will score very few if any marks at all.

166 PINEAPPLE BEACH HOTEL *Walk in the footsteps of a top tutor*

Top Tutor Tips

This scenario describes very specific issues that have occurred during the year and your procedures need to focus on these issues rather than the balances in general. Audit procedures should be specific. They should be clear instructions to an audit team member.

Substantive procedures

Depreciation

- Review the reasonableness of the depreciation rates applied to the new leisure facilities and compare to industry averages.
- Review the capital expenditure budgets for the next few years to assess whether there are any plans to replace any of the new leisure equipment, as this would indicate that the useful life is less than 10 years.
- Review profits and losses on disposal of assets disposed of in the year, to assess the reasonableness of the depreciation policies.
- Select a sample of leisure equipment and recalculate the depreciation charge to ensure that the non-current asset register is correct.
- Perform a proof in total calculation for the depreciation charged on the equipment, discuss with management if significant fluctuations arise.
- Review the disclosure of the depreciation charges and policies in the draft financial statements.

Food poisoning

- Review the correspondence from the customers claiming food poisoning to assess whether Pineapple has a present obligation as a result of a past event.
- Send an enquiry letter to the lawyers of Pineapple to obtain their view as to the probability of the claim being successful.
- Review board minutes to understand whether the directors believe that the claim will be successful or not.
- Review the post year-end period to assess whether any payments have been made to any of the claimants.
- Discuss with management as to whether they propose to include a contingent liability disclosure or not, consider the reasonableness of this.
- Obtain a written management representation confirming management's view that the lawsuit is unlikely to be successful and hence no provision is required.
- Review the adequacy of any disclosures made in the financial statements.

ACCA marking scheme	
	Marks
Up to 1 mark per relevant substantive procedure, max of 5 marks for each issue.	
Depreciation	
Review the reasonableness of the depreciation rates and compare to industry averages	
Review the capital expenditure budgets	
Review profits and losses on disposal for assets disposed of in year	
Recalculate the depreciation charge for a sample of assets	
Perform a proof in total calculation for the depreciation charged on the equipment	
Review the disclosure of depreciation in the draft financial statements	
Max	**5**
Food poisoning	
Review the correspondence from the customers	
Send an enquiry to the lawyers as to the probability of the claim being successful	
Review board minutes	
Review the post year-end period to assess whether any payments have been made	
Discuss with management as to whether they propose to include a contingent liability disclosure	
Obtain a written management representation	
Review any disclosures made in the financial statements	
Max	**5**
Total	**10**

Examiner's comments

This question required substantive procedures for depreciation and a contingent liability for a food poisoning case. Performance on this question was unsatisfactory. A significant minority did not even attempt this part of the question.

Candidates' answers for depreciation tended to be weaker than for the food poisoning. On the depreciation many candidates did not focus their answer on the issue identified, which related to the depreciation method adopted for the capital expenditure incurred in the year. In the scenario the issue was headed up as depreciation and so this should have given candidates a clue that they needed to focus just on depreciation. However, a significant proportion of answers were on general PPE tests often without any reference at all to depreciation. In addition many felt that generic tests such as 'get an expert's advice' or 'obtain management representation' were appropriate tests; they are not.

The food poisoning issue tended to be answered slightly better; however again tests tended to be too brief, 'read board minutes', 'discuss with management' or 'discuss with the lawyer' did not score any marks as they do not explain what is to be discussed or what we are looking for in the board minutes. In addition a minority of candidates focused on auditing the kitchen and food hygiene procedures with tests such as 'observing the kitchen process' or 'writing to customers to see if they have had food poisoning.' This is not the focus of the auditor and does not provide evidence with regards to the potential contingent liability.

Substantive procedures are a core topic area and future candidates must focus on being able to generate specific and detailed tests.

167 TIRROL *Walk in the footsteps of a top tutor*

Online question assistance

Top Tutor Tips

Part (a) requires both repetition and application of basic knowledge regarding the use of CAAT's. However, the latter carries the majority of the marks and for this reason candidates must refer to the specific information to obtain good quality marks. Simple repetition of learned facts regarding the drawbacks of CAATs will not obtain good marks for this reason.

For each point of explanation relevant to Tirrol you will be awarded 1 mark. Therefore for part (i) you need to make four points of explanation. For part (ii) you need 5 explained problems and five methods of overcoming those problems.

Part (b) again requires a mix of basic knowledge (i.e. what procedures must be performed before reliance is placed on the documentation produced by the internal audit department) and application to the facts presented in the scenario.

The highlighted words are key phases that markers are looking for.

(a) (i) **Benefits of using audit software**

Standard systems at client

The same computerised systems and programs as used in all 25 branches of Tirrol Co. This means that the same audit software can be used in each location providing significant time savings compared to the situation where client systems are different in each location.

Use actual computer files not copies or printouts

Use of audit software means that the Tirrol Co's actual inventory files can be tested rather than having to rely on printouts or screen images. The latter could be incorrect, by accident or by deliberate mistake. The audit firm will have more confidence that the 'real' files have been tested.

Test more items

Use of software will mean that more inventory records can be tested – it is possible that all product lines could be tested for obsolescence rather than a sample using manual techniques. The auditor will therefore gain more evidence and have greater confidence that inventory is valued correctly.

Cost

The relative cost of using audit software decreases the more years that software is used. Any cost overruns this year could be offset against the audit fees in future years when the actual expense will be less.

(ii) **Problems on the audit of Tirrol**

Timescale – six week reporting deadline – audit planning

The audit report is due to be signed six weeks after the year end. This means that there will be considerable pressure on the auditor to complete audit work without compromising standards by rushing procedures.

This problem can be overcome by careful planning of the audit, use of experienced staff and ensuring other staff such as second partner reviews are booked well in advance.

Timescale – six week reporting deadline – software issues

The audit report is due to be signed about six weeks after the year end. This means that there is little time to write and test audit software, let alone use the software and evaluate the results of testing.

This problem can be alleviated by careful planning. Access to Tirrol Co's software and data files must be obtained as soon as possible and work commenced on tailoring Cal & Co's software following this. Specialist computer audit staff should be booked as soon as possible to perform this work.

First year audit costs

The relative costs of an audit in the first year at a client tend to be greater due to the additional work of ascertaining client systems. This means that Cal & Co may have a limited budget to document systems including computer systems.

This problem can be alleviated to some extent again by good audit planning. The manager must also monitor the audit process carefully, ensuring that any additional work caused by the client not providing access to systems information including computer systems is identified and added to the total billing cost of the audit.

Staff holidays

Most of the audit work will be carried out in July, which is also the month when many of Cal & Co staff take their annual holiday. This means that there will be a shortage of audit staff, particularly as audit work for Tirrol Co is being booked with little notice.

The problem can be alleviated by booking staff as soon as possible and then identifying any shortages. Where necessary, staff may be borrowed from other offices or even different countries on a secondment basis where shortages are acute.

Non-standard systems

Tirrol Co's computer software is non-standard, having been written specifically for the organisation. This means that more time will be necessary to understand the system than if standard systems were used.

This problem can be alleviated either by obtaining documentation from the client or by approaching the software house (with Tirrol Co's permission) to see if they can assist with provision of information on data structures for the inventory systems. Provision of this information will decrease the time taken to tailor audit software for use in Tirrol Co.

Issues of live testing

Cal & Co has been informed that inventory systems must be tested on a live basis. This increases the risk of accidental amendment or deletion of client data systems compared to testing copy files.

To limit the possibility of damage to client systems, Cal & Co can consider performing inventory testing on days when Tirrol Co is not operating e.g. weekends. At the worst, backups of data files taken from the previous day can be re-installed when Cal & Co's testing is complete.

Computer systems

The client has 25 locations, with each location maintaining its own computer system. It is possible that computer systems are not common across the client due to amendments made at the branch level.

This problem can be overcome to some extent by asking staff at each branch whether systems have been amended and focusing audit work on material branches.

Usefulness of audit software

The use of audit software at Tirrol Co does appear to have significant problems this year. This means that even if the audit software is ready, there may still be some risk of incorrect conclusions being derived due to lack of testing, etc.

This problem can be alleviated by seriously considering the possibility of using a manual audit this year. The manager may need to investigate whether a manual audit is feasible and if so whether it could be completed within the necessary timescale with minimal audit risk.

(b) **Reliance on internal audit documentation**

There are two issues to consider; the ability of internal audit to produce the documentation and the actual accuracy of the documentation itself.

The ability of the internal audit department to produce the documentation can be determined by:

- Ensuring that the department has staff who have appropriate qualifications. Provision of a relevant qualification e.g. membership of a computer related institute would be appropriate.
- Ensuring that this and similar documentation is produced using a recognised plan and that the documentation is tested prior to use. The use of different staff in the internal audit department to produce and test documentation will increase confidence in its accuracy.
- Ensuring that the documentation is actually used during internal audit work and that problems with documentation are noted and investigated as part of that work. Being given access to internal audit reports on the inventory software will provide appropriate evidence.

Regarding the actual documentation:

- Reviewing the documentation to ensure that it appears logical and that terms and symbols are used consistently throughout. This will provide evidence that the flowcharts, etc. should be accurate.
- Comparing the documentation against the 'live' inventory system to ensure it correctly reflects the inventory system. This comparison will include tracing individual transactions through the inventory systems.
- Using part of the documentation to amend Cal & Co's audit software, and then ensuring that the software processes inventory system data accurately. However, this stage may be limited due to the need to use live files at Tirrol Co.

ACCA marking scheme			
			Marks
(a)	(i) **Benefits of audit software** 1 mark per benefit – 0.5 for identifying the benefit and 0.5 for explaining the benefit. • Standard systems • Use actual computer files • Test more items • Cost		
		Max	**4**
	(ii) **Problems in the audit of Tirrol** 2 marks for each problem. 1 for explaining the problem and 1 for explaining how to alleviate the problem. • Six week reporting deadline • Timescale – software issues • First year audit costs • Staff holidays • Non-standard systems • Live testing • Usefulness of audit software		
		Max	**10**
(b)	Reliance on internal audit documentation 1 mark per point • Appropriate qualifications • Produced according to plan • Problems with use noted • Documentation logical • Compare to live system • Use documentation to amend audit software		
		Max	**6**
Total			**20**

Examiner's comments

Part (a)

In part (i), most candidates demonstrated basic knowledge of the use of audit software. A few candidates made some good links to the scenario, for example, explaining how data could be amalgamated to avoid having to visit the 25 branches in the company.

In part (ii), again most candidates provided a range of valid points and obtained decent marks. However, common deficiencies in this section included:

Not explaining how to overcome the deficiency either by omitting this comment or by making unrealistic comments. E.g. in terms of potential damage to client systems from the use of test data, suggesting the deficiency would be overcome by 'being careful' or in a handful of answers by simply not accepting the audit engagement.

Suggesting deficiencies that were not mentioned in the scenario. For example, suggesting that inventory valuation would be difficult as experts on car parts were difficult to find, or that the auditor had to attend all 25 locations simultaneously to prevent the client double counting inventory in more than one location.

Recommending amendments to the client systems for other perceived deficiencies. For example, stating that a distributed processing system was not appropriate for the client and recommending a centralised system instead. Even if this was a recommendation to the client, it would not affect audit planning now and so was not relevant as a current audit problem.

Part (b)

Most candidates obtained a marginal result explaining either how the internal audit department itself could be relied on or the documentation; only a minority of answers mentioned both. Marks were generally obtained from:

Considering the work of internal audit in areas such as experience in computer systems, and quality of documentation provided, and

Testing the documentation itself for example, in comparison to the actual system using walk-through or similar testing methods, or obtaining advice from external specialists.

There were relatively few less relevant points in this section. The main area of weakness related to candidates spending too much time explaining the appointment and general work of internal audit rather than placing reliance on this function.

168 CONTROLS

(a) **Internal control components**

ISA 315 *Identifying and Assessing the Risks of Material Misstatement through Understanding the Entity and Its Environment* considers the components of an entity's internal control. It identifies the following components:

(i) **Control environment**

The control environment has many elements such as communication and enforcement of integrity and ethical values, commitment to competence, participation of those charged with governance, management's philosophy and operating style, organisational structure, assignment of authority and responsibility and human resource policies and practices.

(ii) **Entity's risk assessment process**

For financial reporting purposes, the entity's risk assessment process includes how management identifies business risks relevant to the preparation of financial statements in accordance with the entity's applicable financial reporting framework. It estimates their significance, assesses the likelihood of their occurrence, and decides upon actions to respond to and manage them and the results thereof.

(iii) **Information system, including the related business processes, relevant to financial reporting, and communication**

The information system relevant to financial reporting objectives, which includes the accounting system, consists of the procedures and records designed and established to initiate, record, process, and report entity transactions (as well as events and conditions) and to maintain accountability for the related assets, liabilities, and equity.

(iv) **Control activities relevant to the audit**

Control activities are the policies and procedures that help ensure that management directives are carried out. Control activities, whether within information technology or manual systems, have various objectives and are applied at various organisational and functional levels.

(v) **Monitoring of controls**

Monitoring of controls is a process to assess the effectiveness of internal control performance over time. It involves assessing the effectiveness of controls on a timely basis and taking necessary remedial actions. Management accomplishes the monitoring of controls through ongoing activities, separate evaluations, or a combination of the two. Ongoing monitoring activities are often built into the normal recurring activities of an entity and include regular management and supervisory activities.

(b) **Advantages and Disadvantages of methods of recording the system**

Narrative Notes

Advantages

The main advantage of narrative notes is that they are simple to record, after discussion with the company these discussions are easily written up as notes.

Additionally, as the notes are simple to record, this can facilitate understanding by all members of the team, especially more junior members who might find alternative methods too complex.

Disadvantages

Narrative notes may prove to be too cumbersome, especially if the system is complex.

This method can make it more difficult to identify missing internal controls as the notes record the detail but do not identify control exceptions clearly.

Questionnaires

Internal control questionnaires are used to assess whether controls exist which meet specific objectives or prevent or detect errors and omissions.

Advantages

Questionnaires are quick to prepare, which means they are a cost effective method for recording the system.

They ensure that all controls present within the system are considered and recorded; hence missing controls or deficiencies are clearly highlighted.

Questionnaires are simple to complete and therefore any members of the team can complete them and they are easy to use and understand.

Disadvantages

It can be easy for the company to overstate the level of the controls present as they are asked a series of questions relating to potential controls.

Without careful tailoring of the questionnaire to make it company specific, there is a risk that controls may be misunderstood and unusual controls missed.

ACCA marking scheme		
		Marks
(a)	Up to 1 mark per well explained component, being 0.5 for stating the component and 0.5 for an explanation Control environment – governance and management function, attitudes awareness and actions of management Control environment – made up of a number of elements (need to list at least 2 of these to score 1 mark) Entity's risk assessment – process for identifying risk Information system relevant to financial reporting – procedures and records to record an entity's transactions, assets and liabilities and to maintain accountability Control activities – policies and procedures to help ensure management directives are carried out Monitoring controls – assess effectiveness of internal controls	
	Max	**5**
(b)	Up to 1 mark per valid point **Notes:** Simple to understand Facilitate understanding by all team Cumbersome especially if complex system Difficult to identify missing controls **Questionnaires:** Quick to prepare and hence cost effective All internal controls considered and missing controls identified Easy to complete and use Easy to overstate controls Easy to misunderstand controls and miss unusual controls	
	Max	**5**
Total		**10**

Examiner's comments

Part (a) for 5 marks required candidates to state and briefly explain the components of an entity's internal control as per ISA 315 *Identifying and Assessing the Risks of Material Misstatements through Understanding the Entity and Its Environment*. Candidates' performance was unsatisfactory on this question, with a number of candidates not even attempting it.

A significant minority of candidates did not understand the question requirement, or did not have sufficient technical knowledge of this area and so instead of providing components, such as, control environment and control activities relevant to audit, they focused on providing a list of internal controls such as authorisation or segregation of duties controls. Candidates are reminded to read the question requirements carefully and to answer the question asked and not the one they wish had been asked.

ISA 315 is an important element of the F8 syllabus and candidates need to ensure that they have a better knowledge of this area.

Part (b) required candidates to describe the advantages and disadvantages of narrative notes and internal control questionnaires (ICQs) as methods for documenting the system. Candidates' performance was unsatisfactory on this question, with a number of candidates not even attempting it. A significant minority of candidates did not understand the question requirement fully, and so instead of providing advantages and disadvantages for notes and then for ICQs, they provided answers which were of a general nature and just covered advantages and disadvantages of documenting the internal control system. It is possible that these candidates did not carefully read the scenario paragraph preceding the requirement. This paragraph laid out that there were various methods available for documenting internal controls and it identified notes and ICQs, the requirement then followed on with the advantages and disadvantages of these two methods. Candidates must take the time to read and understand any scenario paragraphs; these are intended to help candidates understand the question requirements.

Those candidates who understood the requirement often made the following mistakes:

- Lack of detail, the requirement was to 'describe' and often candidates provided bullet point notes, this is not a sufficient level of detail to be awarded the 1 mark available per point.
- Some candidates were confused as to who prepared the systems documentation, thinking that ICQs were produced by management, and so identified irrelevant advantages and disadvantages.
- Providing definitions and explanations of what notes and ICQs are, rather than answering the question requirement. Definitions will not score marks unless they are a specific part of the question requirement.
- Listing points in relation to internal control evaluation questionnaires (ICEQ)s rather than ICQs. This is another method for documenting systems but was not part of the question requirement and hence scored no marks.

169 AUDIT PROCEDURES AND EVIDENCE

(a) **Test of control and substantive procedures**

(i) Tests of control evaluate the operating effectiveness of controls in preventing, or detecting and correcting, material misstatements at the assertion level. **Example tests of control over wages and salaries**

- Inspect numerical sequence of clock cards/timesheets; if any breaks in the sequence are noted, enquire of management as to missing payroll records.
- Review a sample of timesheets/clock cards for evidence of authorisation of overtime by a responsible official.
- Observe whether there is adequate segregation of duties between human resources and payroll departments.

(ii) Substantive procedures are aimed at detecting material misstatements at the assertion level. They include tests of details of transactions, balances, disclosures and substantive analytical procedures.

Example substantive procedures over wages and salaries

- Perform a proof in total of total payroll taking into account joiners and leavers and any annual pay rise, compare any trends to prior years and discuss significant fluctuations with management.
- For a sample of employees, recalculate the gross and net pay and agree to the payroll records to verify accuracy.
- Re-perform calculation of statutory deductions to confirm whether correct deductions for this year have been included within the payroll expense.

Tutorial note

Marks will be awarded for any other relevant wages and salaries tests/procedures.

(b) **Reliability of audit evidence**

The following factors or generalisations can be made when assessing the reliability of audit evidence:

- The reliability of audit evidence is increased when it is obtained from independent sources outside the entity.
- The reliability of audit evidence which is generated internally is increased when the related controls, including those over its preparation and maintenance, imposed by the entity are effective.
- Audit evidence obtained directly by the auditor is more reliable than audit evidence obtained indirectly or by inference.
- Audit evidence in documentary form, whether paper, electronic or other medium, is more reliable than evidence obtained orally.

- Audit evidence provided by original documents is more reliable than audit evidence provided by photocopies or facsimiles, the reliability of which may depend on the controls over their preparation and maintenance.

(c) **Substantive procedures to confirm revenue:**

- Compare the overall level of revenue against prior years and budget and investigate any significant fluctuations.
- Obtain a schedule of sales for the year broken down into the major revenue streams and compare this to the prior year breakdown and for any unusual movements discuss with management.
- Calculate the gross margin and compare this to the prior year and investigate any significant fluctuations.
- Select a sample of sales invoices for larger customers and recalculate the discounts allowed to ensure that these are accurate.
- Recalculate for a sample of invoices that the sales tax has been correctly applied to the sales invoice.
- Select a sample of customer orders and agree these to the despatch notes and sales invoices through to inclusion in the sales ledger to ensure completeness of revenue.
- Select a sample of despatch notes both pre and post the year end, follow these through to sales invoices in the correct accounting period to ensure that cut-off has been correctly applied.
- Select a sample of credit notes issued after the year end and follow through to sales invoice to ensure the returns were recorded in the proper period.

ACCA marking scheme		
		Marks
(a)	Up to 1 mark each for definitions of test of control (TOC) and substantive procedure and up to 1 mark each for example test of controls and substantive procedures. – Definition of TOC – Example TOC – Definition of substantive test – Example substantive test	
	Max	4
(b)	Up to 1 mark per well explained point, maximum of 3 points. – Reliability increased when it is obtained from independent sources – Internally generated evidence more reliable when the controls are effective – Evidence obtained directly by the auditor is more reliable than evidence obtained indirectly or by inference – Evidence in documentary form is more reliable than evidence obtained orally – Evidence provided by original documents is more reliable than evidence provided by copies	
	Max	**3**

(c)	Up to 1 mark per well explained procedure Analytical review over revenue compared to budget and prior year Analytical review of major revenue streams compared to prior year Gross margin review Recalculate discounts allowed for larger customers Recalculate sales tax Follow order to goods despatched note to sales invoice to sales ledger Sales cut-off Review post year-end credit notes	
	Max	**3**
Total		**10**

Examiner's comments

Part (a) for 4 marks required candidates to define 'tests of control' and 'substantive procedures' as well as provide an example for each relevant to the audit of wages and salaries. Candidates' performance was mixed on this question. Many candidates were able to adequately define tests of controls but did not define substantive procedures as well, the definitions were often incomplete. This is a core area of the syllabus and it is disappointing that candidates are unable to provide clear definitions of procedures that are frequently examined. The requirement to provide examples of each type of procedure was answered unsatisfactorily by a significant proportion of candidates. Rather than giving tests of control many candidates provided example controls, these would not have scored any marks. The substantive procedures examples given were often vague and some candidates were confused in that they gave tests of controls here rather than substantive tests.

As has been noted in previous examiner's reports, candidates are often confused with the differences between tests of controls and substantive tests. Both are methods for obtaining evidence and are key elements of the F8 syllabus. Future candidates must ensure that they understand when tests of controls are required and when substantive procedures are needed. They need to learn the difference between them and should practice questions requiring the generation of both types of procedures.

Part (b) for 3 marks required candidates to identify and explain three factors which influence the reliability of audit evidence. This question was answered well by most candidates, with many scoring full marks.

Where candidates did not score full marks this tended to be because they misunderstood the question and discussed sufficiency of evidence with points on materiality of the area and the level of judgements required.

Part (c) required substantive procedures the auditor should perform on revenue. This requirement was not answered well. Some candidates confused this requirement with receivables tests. In addition a significant number of candidates provided procedures to confirm bank and cash rather than revenue. Perhaps they confused cash receipts with revenue and so thought that if they confirmed cash receipts this would confirm revenue.

Those candidates who performed well were able to provide a good mixture of analytical procedures such as, 'compare revenue to prior year or to budget' and 'review monthly sales against prior year' and also detailed tests such as confirming cut -off of sales.

170 EXPERTS/SAMPLING/ASSERTIONS *Walk in the footsteps of a top tutor*

Top Tutor Tips

This is a straightforward knowledge based question. Note that three responses are required for parts (a) and (c) for three marks and that four responses are required for (b) for four marks,

The highlighted words are key phases that markers are looking for.

(a) **Competence and objectivity of experts**

- The expert's professional qualification. The expert should be a member of a relevant professional body or have the necessary licence to perform the work.
- The experience and reputation of the expert in the area in which the auditor is seeking audit evidence.
- The objectivity of the expert from the client company. The expert should not normally be employed by the client.

(b) **Sampling methods**

Methods of sampling in accordance with ISA 530 *Audit Sampling and Other Means of Testing:*

Random selection. Ensures each item in a population has an equal chance of selection, for example by using random number tables.

Systematic selection. In which a number of sampling units in the population is divided by the sample size to give a sampling interval.

Haphazard selection. The auditor selects the sample without following a structured technique – the auditor would avoid any conscious bias or predictability.

Sequence or block. Involves selecting a block(s) of continguous items from within a population.

Monetary Unit Sampling. This selection method ensures that each individual $1 in the population has an equal chance of being selected.

(c) **Tangible non-current assets – assertions**

- Completeness – Physically verify assets from the premises back to the register to ensure that all non-current assets are recorded in the non-current asset register.
- Existence – Trace a sample of assets from the register and physically see the asset to ensure non-current assets exist.
- Valuation and allocation – Recalculate depreciation charge to ensure assets are correctly valued.
- Rights and obligations – Inspect a sample of purchase invoices for the name of the client to verify rights.

Tutorial note

Marks will be awarded for any other relevant tests/procedures.

Note: Only three assertions were required.

ACCA marking scheme			
			Marks
(a)	1 mark per 0.5 for identifying. 0.5 for explanation. Qualifications Experience/reputation Objectivity		
		Max	**3**
(b)	1 mark for each method. 0.5 for stating the method and 0.5 for brief explanation. Random Systematic Haphazard Sequence MUS		
		Max	**4**
(c)	0.5 for each assertion and 0.5 for each procedure. Completeness Existence Valuation Rights and obligations		
		Max	**3**
Total			**10**

Examiner's comments

Part b was worth 4 marks and required candidates to explain four methods of obtaining a sample of items to test from a population.

Most candidates provided up to four methods, and a significant minority obtained full marks. There were two overall weaknesses in many answers:

Firstly, not explaining the method of sampling, or explaining the method incorrectly. For example, stating that statistical sampling meant that the auditor used judgement to determine which items to sample.

Secondly, listing general methods of collecting audit evidence (enquiry, computation, etc.) as methods of obtaining audit samples.

In summary, the question was well-answered.

171 SAMPLING

Key answer tips

This question is a straightforward knowledge based question.

Part (a) and (b) require definitions rote learned from the study materials.

Part (c) requires a little more thought about how the auditor can reduce detection risk but separated into the elements of sampling and non-sampling risk which is slightly trickier.

(a) **Sampling**

The application of audit procedures to less than 100% of the items within a population of relevance such that each item has a chance of selection in order to provide the auditor with a reasonable basis on which to draw conclusions about the entire population.

(b) **Sampling risk**

Sampling risk is the possibility that the auditor's conclusion, based on a sample, may be different from the conclusion reached if the entire population were subjected to the audit procedure. The auditor may conclude from the results of testing that either material misstatements exist, when they do not, or that material misstatements do not exist when in fact they do.

Non-sampling risk

Non-sampling risk arises from any factor that causes an auditor to reach an incorrect conclusion that is not related to the size of the sample.

Examples of non-sampling risk include the use of inappropriate procedures, misinterpretation of evidence or the auditor simply 'missing' an error.

(c) Sampling risk is controlled by the audit firm

– Using a valid method of selecting items from a population.

– Increasing the sample size.

Non-sampling risk is controlled by

– Providing appropriate training for staff so they know which audit techniques to use and will recognise an error when one occurs.

– Allocating sufficiently experienced staff to audit areas of particular risk.

– Allowing sufficient time for the audit to ensure the work is performed properly.

– Allocating sufficient resources to the audit.

ACCA marking scheme			
			Marks
(a)	2 marks for full definition. 0.5 for each element below. Less than 100% tested From a relevant population Each has chance of selection Reasonable basis to form a conclusion		
		Max	**2**
(b)	1 mark per point. Sampling risk definition Sampling risk explanation Non-sampling risk definition Non-sampling risk explanation		
		Max	**4**
(c)	1 mark for each method. Must be under the correct headings. **Sampling risk** Appropriate sampling method Increase sample size **Non-sampling risk** Training for staff Experience staff Sufficient time Sufficient resource		
		Max	**4**
Total			**10**

172 RELIABILITY/ASSERTIONS/INTERIM AND FINAL AUDITS

Walk in the footsteps of a top tutor

Top Tutor Tips

This question requires little more than pre-learnt knowledge. Take care to offer the appropriate number of responses requested in the question.

The highlighted words are key phases that markers are looking for.

(a) The following five factors that influence the reliability of audit evidence are taken from ISA 500 *Audit Evidence*:

(i) Audit evidence is more reliable when it is obtained from independent sources outside the entity.

(ii) Audit evidence that is generated internally is more reliable when the related controls imposed by the entity are effective.

(iii) Audit evidence obtained directly by the auditor (for example, observation of the application of a control) is more reliable than audit evidence obtained indirectly or by inference (for example, inquiry about the application of a control).

(iv) Audit evidence is more reliable when it exists in documentary form, whether paper, electronic, or other medium. (For example, a contemporaneously written record of a meeting is more reliable than a subsequent oral representation of the matters discussed.)

(v) Audit evidence provided by original documents is more reliable than audit evidence provided by photocopies or facsimiles.

Other examples are:

(vi) Evidence created in the normal course of business is better than evidence specially created to satisfy the auditor.

(vii) The best-informed source of audit evidence will normally be management of the company (although management's lack of independence may reduce its value as a source of such evidence).

(viii) Evidence about the future is particularly difficult to obtain and is less reliable than evidence about past events.

(b) **Assertions – classes of transactions**

Occurrence. The transactions and events that have been recorded have actually occurred and pertain to the entity.

Completeness. All transactions and events that should have been recorded have been recorded.

Accuracy. The amounts and other data relating to recorded transactions and events have been recorded appropriately.

Cut-off. Transactions and events have been recorded in the correct accounting period.

Classification. Transactions and events have been recorded in the proper accounts.

Tutorial note

It is important to learn which assertions are relevant to transactions and events and which are relevant to account balances.

(c) **Interim audit**

- Usually performed before the year end.
- Risk assessment.
- Recording of internal control system.
- Performing tests of controls to evaluate effectiveness of the controls.
- May perform testing on material transactions to date.

Final audit

- Usually performed after the year end.
- Focuses on testing of account balances and remaining transactions.
- Obtaining external confirmation of year end balances.
- Follow up of items noted at the inventory count.
- Includes testing of overall disclosure and presentation.
- Completion activities e.g. going concern and subsequent events reviews.

Tutorial note

Management representations, third party confirmations, the review of working papers, and reporting to those charged with governance and management could also be mentioned.

ACCA marking scheme

			Marks
(a)	1 marks for each factor. Independently generated Effective controls Evidence obtained directly by the auditor Written evidence Original documents Normal course of business Informed management		
		Max	**3**
(b)	0.5 mark per assertion. 0.5 per explanation. Occurrence Completeness Accuracy Cut-off Classification		
		Max	**4**
(c)	1 mark per point. **Interim audit** Before year end Risk assessment Tests of controls Other material transaction testing **Final audit** After year end Account balances Disclosure		
		Max	**3**
Total			**10**

173 EXTERNAL CONFIRMATIONS *Walk in the footsteps of a top tutor*

(a) External confirmations are obtained to provide externally generated evidence which is more reliable than client generated evidence.

(b) **Steps to obtain a bank confirmation letter**

- Ask the client to provide authority to the bank to disclose information to the audit firm if not already in place.
- Obtain details from the client of all bank accounts that require confirmation including main bank account number, name and address.
- The auditor will produce a confirmation letter in accordance with local audit regulations and practices.
- The auditor will send the letter to the bank. Ideally the letter should be sent before the end of the accounting period to enable the bank to complete it on a timely basis e.g. at the year-end.
- The bank will complete the letter and send it back directly to the auditor.

Top Tutor Tip

The easiest approach to this requirement is to think logically about what the auditor must do in order to obtain the confirmation. Break the process down into individual steps. This will help generate sufficient points.

(c) Other types of external confirmation

Accounts receivable letter

This letter provides evidence of the existence of the receivable when a reply is returned from that receivable direct to the auditor.

Solicitor letter

A solicitor letter provides evidence as to the existence of claims at the period end as the solicitor will confirm specific claims.

Inventory held by third parties

A letter from the third party holding the inventory will provide evidence of the existence of that inventory because the third party has confirmed this in writing.

Supplier confirmations

Where supplier statements are not available, the auditor may obtain direct confirmation from the supplier regarding the payables balance outstanding at the year end to verify completeness.

ACCA marking scheme		
		Marks
(a)	1 marks for reason Externally generated evidence – more reliable	
	Max	1
(b)	1 mark per step. Ensure authority is in place Obtain bank details Produce letter Send letter Receive reply from bank	
	Max	**5**
(c)	1 mark per external confirmation Accounts receivable Solicitor Inventory Supplier/payables	
	Max	**4**
Total		**10**

174 AUDIT PROCEDURES – PROVISIONS

(a) **Reorganisation**

- Review the board minutes where the decision to reorganise the business was taken, ascertain if this decision was made pre year end.
- Review the announcement to shareholders in late October, to confirm that this was announced before the year end.
- Obtain a breakdown of the reorganisation provision and confirm that only direct expenditure from restructuring is included.
- Review the expenditure to confirm that there are no retraining costs included.
- Cast the breakdown of the reorganisation provision to ensure correctly calculated.
- For the costs included within the provision, agree to supporting documentation to confirm validity of items included.
- Obtain a written representation confirming management discussions in relation to the announcement of the reorganisation.
- Review the adequacy of the disclosures of the reorganisation in the financial statements to ensure they are in accordance with IAS 37 Provisions, Contingent Liabilities and Contingent Assets.

(b) **Substantive procedures to verify redundancy provision**

- Discuss with the directors of Chuck Industries as to whether they have formally announced their intention to make the sales ledger department redundant, to confirm that a present obligation exists at the year end.
- If announced before the year end, review a copy of the announcement to verify that the decision has been formally announced.
- Review the board minutes to ascertain whether it is probable that the redundancy payments will be paid.
- Obtain a breakdown of the redundancy calculations by employee and cast it to ensure completeness.
- Recalculate the redundancy provision to confirm completeness and agree components of the calculation to HR records detailing redundancy terms, length of service and salary.
- Review the post year-end period to identify whether any redundancy payments have been made, compare actual payments to the amounts provided to assess whether the provision is reasonable.
- Obtain a written representation from management to confirm the completeness of the provision.
- Review the disclosure of the redundancy provision to ensure compliance with IAS 37 *Provisions, Contingent Liabilities and Contingent Assets*.

ACCA marking scheme		
		Marks
(a)	**Reorganisation**	
	Up to 1 mark per well described procedure	
	– Review the board minutes where decision taken	
	– Review the announcement to shareholders in late October	
	– Obtain a breakdown and confirm that only direct expenditure from restructuring is included	
	– Review expenditure to ensure retraining costs excluded	
	– Cast the breakdown of the reorganisation provision	
	– Agree costs included to supporting documentation	
	– Obtain a written representation	
	– Review the adequacy of the disclosures	
	Max	**5**
(b)	**Redundancy**	
	Up to 1 mark per substantive procedure	
	– Discuss with directors whether formal announcement made of redundancies	
	– Review supporting documentation to confirm present obligation	
	– Review board minutes to confirm payment probable	
	– Cast breakdown of redundancy provision	
	– Recalculate provision and agree components of calculation to supporting documentation	
	– Review post year-end period to compare actual payments to amounts provided	
	– Written representation to confirm completeness	
	– Review disclosures for compliance with IAS 37 Provisions, Contingent Liabilities and Contingent Assets	
	Max	**5**
Total		**10**

Examiner's comments

Part (a) required substantive procedures for an issue on a reorganisation announced just before the year end. Performance on this question was also unsatisfactory; a significant minority did not even attempt this part of the question. Those candidates who scored well focused on gaining evidence of the provision, therefore they provided valid procedures like 'recalculating the provision', 'discussing the basis of the provision with management', 'obtaining a written representation confirming the assumptions and basis of the provision' and 'reviewing the board minutes to confirm management have committed to the reorganisation'. Some candidates failed to read the question properly and assumed that the reorganisation had already occurred as opposed to being announced just before the year end. Therefore many provided answers aimed at confirming that assets had been disposed of and staff had been retrained. In addition some candidates focused on whether the company was making the correct business decisions by reorganising. Many procedures also lacked sufficient detail to score the available 1 mark per test. This commonly occurred with tests such as; 'reviewing board minutes' and 'obtain written representation'. These procedures need to be phrased with sufficient detail to obtain credit, therefore if we consider the following candidates answers:

- 'Obtain a written representation from management' – this would not have scored any marks as it does not specify what the representation is for.
- 'Obtain a written representation from management in relation to the provision' – this would have scored 1/2 marks as it did not specify what element of the provision we wanted confirmation over.
- 'Obtain a written representation from management confirming the assumptions and basis of the provision'– this would have scored 1 mark as it clearly states what is required from management, and in relation to which balance and for which element. As stated in previous examiner reports, substantive procedures are a core topic area and future candidates must focus on being able to generate specific and detailed tests which are applied to any scenario provided.

Part (b) required substantive procedures the auditor should perform on Chuck Industries' redundancy provision. This requirement was answered unsatisfactorily by many candidates.

Candidates who did not score well tended to focus on whether the redundancy was legal or not; therefore wanted the auditor to focus on reviewing redundancy law and contacting the company lawyer. Others wanted to focus on the outsourcing of the sales ledger, which was irrelevant in confirming the provision. Some candidates wanted to undertake a proof in total of the redundancy provision; however with only 14 employees this procedure would not have been practical. In addition some candidates wanted to compare this provision to an industry average, which was impractical and demonstrated that candidates seem to learn generic lists of procedures. Candidates must tailor their knowledge to the scenario in order to pick up application marks.

Those candidates who performed well were able to produce detailed procedures which related to the scenario. In addition sufficient breadth was given including recalculation of the provision, discussion with management with regards to the basis of the provision, reviewing disclosures, reviewing post year-end period for payment of the provision and obtaining written representations.

In relation to the popular answer of obtaining written representations this procedure needs to be phrased with sufficient detail to obtain credit. Therefore if we consider the following candidates answers:

- 'Obtain a written representation from management' – this would not have scored any marks as it does not specify what the representation is for.
- 'Obtain a written representation from management in relation to the provision' – this would have scored 1/2 marks as it did not specify which assertion we wanted confirmation over.
- 'Obtain a written representation from management confirming the completeness of the provision'– this would have scored 1 mark as it clearly states what is required from management, and in relation to which balance and for which assertion.

175 CAATS

(i) **Audit procedures using CAATS**

- Calculate inventory days for the year-to-date to compare against the prior year to identify whether inventory is turning over slower, as this may be an indication that it is overvalued.
- Audit software can be utilised to produce an aged inventory analysis to identify any slow moving goods, which may require write down or an allowance.
- Cast the inventory listing to confirm the completeness and accuracy of inventory.
- Audit software can be used to select a representative sample of items for testing to confirm net realisable value and/or cost.
- Audit software can be utilised to recalculate cost and net realisable value for a sample of inventory.
- CAATs can be used to verify cut-off by testing whether the dates of the last GRNs and GDNs recorded relate to pre year end.
- CAATs can be used to confirm whether any inventory adjustments noted during the count have been correctly updated into final inventory records.

(ii) **Advantages of using CAATS**

- CAATs enable the audit team to test a large volume of inventory data accurately and quickly.
- As long as the client does not change their inventory systems, they can be cost effective after setup.
- CAATs can test program controls within the inventory system as well as general IT controls, such as passwords.
- Allows the team to test the actual inventory system and records rather than printouts from the system which could be incorrect.
- CAATs reduce the level of human error in testing and hence provide a better quality of audit evidence.

- CAATs results can be compared with traditional audit testing; if these two sources agree, then overall audit confidence will increase.
- The use of CAATs frees up audit team members to focus on judgemental and high risk areas, rather than number crunching.

(iii) **Disadvantages of using CAATS**

- The cost of using CAATs in this first year will be high as there will be significant set up costs, it will also be a time-consuming process which increases costs.
- When it is the first time that CAATs will be used on the audit, then the team may require training on the specific CAATs to be utilised.
- If the inventory system is likely to change in the foreseeable future, then costly revisions may be required to the designed CAATs.
- The inventory system may not be compatible with the audit firm's CAATs, in which case bespoke CAATs may be required, which will increase the audit costs.
- If testing is performed over the live inventory system, then there is a risk that the data could be corrupted or lost.
- If testing is performed using copy files rather than live data, then there is the risk that these files are not genuine copies of the actual files.
- In order to perform CAATs, there must be adequate systems documentation available. If this is not the case, then it will be more difficult to devise appropriate CAATs due to a lack of understanding of the inventory system.

ACCA marking scheme		
		Marks
(i)	Up to 1 mark per well described procedure, max of 4 procedures Calculate inventory days Produce an aged inventory analysis to identify any slow moving goods Cast the inventory listing Select a sample of items for testing to confirm net realisable value (NRV) and/or cost Recalculate cost and NRV for sample of inventory Computer-assisted audit techniques (CAATs) can be used to confirm cut-off CAATs can be used to confirm whether inventory adjustments noted during the count have been updated to inventory records.	
	Max	**4**
(ii)	Up to 1 mark per well explained advantage Test a large volume of inventory data accurately and quickly Cost effective after setup CAATs can test program controls as well as general IT controls Test the actual inventory system and records rather than printouts from the system CAATs reduce the level of human error in testing CAATs results can be compared with traditional audit testing Free up audit team members to focus on judgemental and high risk areas	
	Max	**3**

(iii)	Up to 1 mark per well explained disadvantage Costs of using CAATs in this first year will be high Team may require training on the specific CAATs to be utilised Changes in the inventory system may require costly revisions to the CAATs The inventory system may not be compatible with the audit firm's CAATs If testing the live system, there is a risk the data could be corrupted or lost If using copy files rather than live data, there is the risk that these files are not genuine copies Adequate systems documentation must be available	
	Max	**3**
Total		**10**

Examiner's comments

Part (i) required a description of four audit procedures that could be carried out for inventory using CAATs. Performance on this question was unsatisfactory.

Candidates needed to apply their knowledge of CAATs to inventory procedures, many failed to do this. Again lots of candidates did not read the question properly and so despite the requirement to apply their answer to inventory, they proceeded to refer to tests on receivables and payables. Also many candidates appear not to actually understand what CAATs are, who uses them and how they work. Therefore many answers focused on the company using CAATs rather than the auditor, many procedures given were not related to CAATs for example 'discuss inventory valuation with the directors' or 'agree goods received notes to purchase invoices'.

Those candidates who scored well tended to mainly focus on analytical review procedures for inventory that could be undertaken as part of audit software tests.

Part (ii) required an explanation of the advantages of using CAATs. This question was on the whole answered well.

Candidates were able to identify an adequate number of advantages to score well on this part of the question. The main advantages given related to saving time; reducing costs; improving the accuracy of testing and the ability to test larger samples. A minority of candidates failed to explain their advantages; answers such as 'saves time' were commonly provided, this is not an explanation and so would not have scored well.

Part (iii) required an explanation of the disadvantages of using CAATs. Again, this part of the question was answered well. Candidates were able to identify an adequate number of points to score well. The main disadvantages given related to increased costs; training requirements and the corruption of client data. It was apparent that candidates had learnt a standard list of points for CAATs.

176 AUDIT PROCEDURES – PURCHASES *Walk in the footsteps of a top tutor*

Top Tutor Tips

This is a straightforward knowledge requirement asking for audit procedures apart from external confirmation. Note the verb of the requirement – state and explain. You need to explain what the procedures entail but without using those terms in your explanation. Don't expect to receive marks for saying inspection means to inspect something. Marks will be awarded for any other relevant purchases and expenses tests not shown in the answer.

Inspection

Inspection involves examining records or documents, whether internal or external, in paper form, electronic form, or other media, or a physical examination of an asset.

- Inspect a sample of purchase invoices and agree the amount is included correctly within the purchase ledger.
- Inspect purchase orders for evidence of authorisation by a responsible official.

Observation

Observation consists of looking at a process or procedure being performed by others.

- Observe the process for logging purchase invoices into the system to ensure that all invoices are entered completely and accurately.
- Observe the goods received department to assess whether goods received are checked against purchase orders and reviewed for adequate quality.

Analytical procedures

Analytical procedures consist of evaluations of financial information through analysis of plausible relationships among both financial and non-financial data. Analytical procedures also encompass such investigation as is necessary of identified fluctuations or relationships that are inconsistent with other relevant information or that differ from expected values by a significant amount.

- Calculate the operating profit margin/overhead ratio and compare it to last year and budget and investigate any significant differences.
- Review monthly other expenses to identify any significant fluctuations and discuss with management.

Inquiry

Inquiry consists of seeking information of knowledgeable persons, both financial and non-financial, within the entity or outside the entity.

- Discuss with management whether there have been any changes in the key suppliers used and compare this to the purchase ledger to assess completeness and accuracy of purchases.
- Inquire of department heads the process they follow in authorising orders to ensure that it follows the specified company authorisation process.

Recalculation

Recalculation consists of checking the mathematical accuracy of documents or records. Recalculation may be performed manually or electronically.

- Recalculate the accuracy of a sample of purchase invoices.
- Recalculate the prepayments and accruals charged at the year end to ensure the accuracy of the other expenses.

Reperformance

Reperformance involves the auditor's independent execution of procedures or controls that were originally performed as part of the entity's internal control.

- Reperform the purchase ledger control account reconciliation to ensure accuracy.
- Select a sample of purchase orders and match them to the goods received notes and purchase invoices to ensure completeness of the purchase cycle.

ACCA marking scheme	
	Marks
Up to 1 mark per well explained procedure and up to 1 mark for a valid audit test, overall maximum of 2 marks per type of procedure and test.	
Inspection	
Observation	
Analytical procedures	
Inquiry	
Recalculation	
Reperformance	
Total	**10**

Examiner's comments

Part (i) required five procedures, other than external confirmation, for obtaining evidence and then part (aii) for 5 marks required an example of each procedure relevant to the audit of purchases and expenses. This question was knowledge based, and candidates performed satisfactorily.

Where candidates did not score full marks this was because they failed to read the question properly. The scenario clearly excluded the procedure of external confirmation, however, a significant minority of candidates gave confirmations as a procedure. This scored no marks. Some saw the word 'confirmation' and then proceeded to provide a lengthy answer only relating to this procedure. Candidates must read the question carefully.

In addition some candidates confused procedures for obtaining evidence with financial statement assertions and so gave answers which focused on completeness, valuation and existence. A number of candidates provided example procedures which were not related to purchases and expenses, but instead focused on inventory, payables or non-current assets. Again this was due to a failure to read the question requirement.

ETHICS

177 CINNAMON *Walk in the footsteps of a top tutor*

Ethical risks and steps to reduce the risks

> ***Top Tutor Tips***
>
> *This was an unusual ethics question as it didn't focus on threats to objectivity specifically. There were other fundamental principles affected with this question. Don't expect every exam question to look similar to the ones that have been on previous exams. So long as you know the knowledge and can apply it to different situations you can score well.*

Ethical risk	*Steps to reduce the risks*
Salt & Pepper has guaranteed that their audit will not last longer than two weeks and will minimise disruption to companies.	Salt & Pepper should cease this advertising campaign immediately as it is not in compliance with ACCA's *Code of Ethics and Conduct*.
Every audit engagement is different and hence will require a differing amount of time. Complex audits cannot possibly be completed within two weeks as the team would not be able to gather sufficient and appropriate audit evidence in this time, leading to an incorrect opinion.	For any potential clients who have approached Salt & Pepper as a result of this advert, the firm should inform them that the audit duration will be based on the level of audit risk present, and this could be considerably longer than two weeks.
Salt & Pepper has offered all new audit clients a free accounts preparation service for the first year of the engagement. Whilst Salt & Pepper is able to prepare accounts for unlisted clients, this does increase the risk of self-review as the audit team could be auditing their own work.	For engagements where Salt & Pepper is to prepare the accounts, they must ensure that this work is undertaken by a team separate to the audit team.
Additionally, if this service is offered for free, then in order to make a profit on the total engagement, Salt & Pepper could be inclined to substantially reduce the procedures undertaken on the audit engagement.	In addition, the firm should ensure that all audit engagements are conducted in accordance with International Standards on Auditing.
The firm is not updating engagement letters for existing clients on the basis that they do not change much on a yearly basis. This is not in accordance with ISA 210 *Agreeing the Terms of Audit Engagements* as even if engagement letters are not changed, they should still be reviewed to ensure that they are still relevant and up to date.	Salt & Pepper should comply fully with ISA 210 and annually review the need for revising the engagement letters.

Ethical risk	*Steps to reduce the risks*
An existing client of Salt & Pepper has proposed an audit fee based on a percentage of the client's final pre-tax profit. This is a contingent fee arrangement and is prohibited as it creates a self-interest threat which cannot be reduced to an adequate level.	Salt & Pepper should politely decline the proposed contingent fee arrangement as it would be a breach of ACCA's *Code of Ethics and Conduct*. Instead they should inform the client that the fees will be based on the level of work required to obtain sufficient and appropriate audit evidence.
Salt & Pepper intends to use junior staff for the audit of their new client Cinnamon as the timing of the audit is when the firm is very busy. As a new engagement, Salt & Pepper has little knowledge of the risks associated with this audit. If they use too junior staff, they will not be competent enough to assess whether they have performed adequate work, and the risk of giving an incorrect audit opinion is increased.	Salt & Pepper should review the staffing of Cinnamon and make changes to increase the amount of experienced team members. If this is not possible, they should discuss with the directors of Cinnamon to see whether the timing of the audit could be moved to a point where the firm has adequate staff resources.
Salt & Pepper has not contacted Cinnamon's previous auditors. Contacting the previous auditors is important as the firm needs to understand why Cinnamon has changed their auditors. They may have been acting unethically and their previous auditors therefore refused to continue. In addition, it is professional courtesy to contact the previous auditors.	Salt & Pepper should contact the previous auditors to identify if there are any ethical issues which would prevent them from acting as auditors of Cinnamon.

ACCA marking scheme	
Ethical risks	*Marks*
Up to 1 mark per well explained ethical risk and up to 1 mark per well explained step to reduce risk, max of 5 marks for risks and max 5 marks for steps to reduce.	
Duration of audit no more than two weeks	
Free accounts preparation service	
Engagement letters not updated	
Contingent fees	
Timing of audit	
Contact previous auditor of Cinnamon Brothers Co	
Total	**10**

Examiner's comments

This question was based on the audit firm Salt & Pepper & Co and tested candidates' knowledge of ethical threats.

The question required an identification and explanation of five ethical risks which arise from the audit firm's actions and how these risks may be reduced. This question was answered well by most candidates.

Candidates were able to identify from the scenario the ethical risks arising from the firm's actions. Some candidates did not explain the risks correctly or in sufficient detail, sometimes just identifying the risk and not explaining correctly how this was an ethical issue. For example, many identified the risk of the audit fee being based on a percentage of the client's pre-tax profit; however this was incorrectly explained as being an issue of fee dependence rather than it being a contingent fee. As the risk was incorrectly explained this resulted in an irrelevant action for reducing the ethical risk. Therefore only the identification 1/2 marks would have been awarded.

In addition some candidates incorrectly thought that there was an ethical risk because Cinnamon wanted their audit complete by February. The ethical risk was that in order to meet the client's deadline the firm would be using more junior staff and hence increased the risk of giving an incorrect opinion.

The second part of this question required steps for reducing the ethical risks. Candidates' performance was generally satisfactory although some answers tended to be quite brief. For example for the risk of the engagement letters not being updated, the response given by some candidates was 'Update the engagement letters,' this is not a sufficiently detailed explanation.

Some candidates thought that a risk had to be identified for each of the ethical threats of self-review, self-interest etc. This resulted in them trying to identify a situation from the scenario to fit each of the types of threats. This is not the correct approach to take as it is unlikely that the scenario will be based around one of each of the five ethical threats.

178 GOOFY *Walk in the footsteps of a top tutor*

Top Tutor Tips

This is a straightforward knowledge based requirement on conflicts of interest and should not pose too many problems.

(a) **Safeguards to be adopted to address the conflict of interest of auditing both Goofy Co and Mickey Co:**

- Both Goofy Co and Mickey Co should be notified that NAB & Co would be acting as auditors for each company and, if necessary, consent obtained.
- Advising one or both clients to seek additional independent advice.
- The use of separate engagement teams, with different engagement partners and team members; once an employee has worked on one audit such as Goofy Co then they would be prevented from being on the audit of Mickey Co for a period of time. This separation of teams is known as building a 'Chinese wall'.

- Procedures to prevent access to information, for example, strict physical separation of both teams, confidential and secure data filing.
- Clear guidelines for members of each engagement team on issues of security and confidentiality. These guidelines could be included within the audit engagement letters.
- Potentially the use of confidentiality agreements signed by employees and partners of the firm.
- Regular monitoring of the application of the above safeguards by a senior individual in NAB & Co not involved in either audit.

(b) **Ethical threats and managing these risks**

Top Tutor Tips

This is a typical ethical threats question focusing on threats to objectivity. Remember to explain the threat properly, don't just state the name of the threat but explain how it could affect the auditor's behaviour when performing the audit.

A familiarity threat arises where an engagement partner is associated with a client for a long period of time. NAB & Co's partner has been involved in the audit of Goofy Co for six years and hence may not maintain her professional scepticism and objectivity.	NAB & Co should monitor the relationship between engagement and client staff, and should consider rotating engagement partners when a long association has occurred. In addition, *ACCA's Code of Ethics and Conduct* recommends that engagement partners rotate off an audit after seven years for listed and public interest entities. Therefore consideration should be given to appointing an alternative audit partner.
The engagement partner's son has accepted a job as a sales manager at Goofy Co. This could represent a self-interest/familiarity threat if the son was involved in the financial statement process.	It is unlikely that as a sales manager the son would be in a position to influence the financial statements and hence additional safeguards would not be necessary.
A self-interest threat can arise when an audit firm has a financial interest in the company. In this case the partner's son will receive shares as part of his remuneration. As the son is an immediate family member of the partner then if he holds the shares it will be as if the partner holds these shares, and this is prohibited.	In this case as holding shares is prohibited by *ACCA's Code of Ethics and Conduct* the engagement partner should be removed from the audit.

Fees based on the outcome or results of work performed are known as contingent fees and are prohibited by *ACCA's Code of Ethics and Conduct.* Hence Goofy Co's request that 20% of the external audit fee is based on profit after tax would represent a contingent fee.	NAB & Co will not be able to accept contingent fees and should communicate to Goofy Co that the external audit fee needs to be based on the time and level of work performed.

ACCA marking scheme

		Marks
(a)	Up to 1 mark per well explained safeguard Notify Goofy Co and Mickey Co Advise seek independent advice Separate engagement teams Procedures prevent access to information Clear guidelines on security and confidentiality Confidentiality agreements Monitoring of safeguards	
	Max	**4**
(b)	Up to 1 mark per well explained threat and up to 1 mark for method of managing risk, overall maximum 6 marks Familiarity threat – long association of partner Self-interest threat – son gained employment at client company Self-interest threat – financial interest (shares) in client company Contingent fees	
	Max	**6**
Total		**10**

Examiner's comments

Part (a) for 4 marks required an explanation of the safeguards NAB should implement to manage the potential conflict of interest between their two competing clients. Candidates performed satisfactorily on this part of the question. Most candidates were able to identify safeguards such as separate audit teams and informing both parties and therefore scored half of the available marks. However, many candidates then provided procedures which were a repeat of separate teams, such as separate engagement partners. In addition some candidates' listed general ethical safeguards rather than focusing on the specific requirement of conflicts of interest.

Part (b) for 6 marks required an explanation of the ethical threats with respect to the audit of Goofy Co and how these threats may be reduced. This question was answered well by most candidates, and many scored full marks. Candidates were able to clearly identify from the scenario the ethical issues impacting the audit of Goofy Co. Some candidates did not explain the threats in sufficient detail, sometimes just identifying the issue and not explaining how this was an ethical threat. For example, many identified the issue of the engagement partner having been in place for six years, however if they did not then go on to explain that this was a familiarity threat, or they gave an incorrect threat such as self-interest, they would have only gained 1/2 rather than 1 mark.

The second part of this question required methods for reducing the threats. Candidates' performance was generally satisfactory although some answers tended to be quite brief. In addition some candidates confused the issue of contingent fees with undue fee dependence and so focused on ways to reduce the proportion of fees from Goofy Co.

In addition many candidates provided more points than were necessary. The requirement was for six marks and had two elements to it: the marking guide awarded 1 mark per threat and 1 per method for reducing risk, hence 3 threats and methods were required for full marks. Yet some candidates listed up to five threats and methods, this then put them under time pressure and led to later questions being impacted.

179 ORANGE FINANCIALS *Walk in the footsteps of a top tutor*

Ethical threats and managing these risks

Top Tutor Tips

This is a typical ethical threats question focusing on threats to objectivity. Remember to explain the threat properly, don't just state the name of the threat but explain how it could affect the auditor's behaviour when performing the audit.

Ethical Threat	*Managing Risk*
Orange Financials Co (Orange) has asked the engagement partner of Currant & Co to attend meetings with potential investors. This represents an advocacy threat as the audit firm may be perceived as promoting investment in Orange and this threatens objectivity.	The engagement partner should politely decline this request from Orange, as it represents too great a threat to independence.
Due to the stock exchange listing, Orange has requested that Currant & Co produce the financial statements. This represents a self-review threat. As Orange is currently not a listed company then Currant & Co are permitted to produce the financial statements and also audit them. However, Orange is seeking a listing and therefore these financial statements will be critical to the potential investors and this increases audit risk.	Ideally, Currant & Co should not undertake the preparation of the financial statements. Due to the imminent listing, this would probably represent too high a risk. If Currant & Co choose to produce the financial statements then separate teams should undertake each assignment and the audit team should not be part of the accounts preparation process.
The assistant finance director of Orange has joined Currant & Co as a partner and has been proposed as the review partner. This represents a self-review threat, as he was in a position to influence the financial statements whilst working at Orange; if he is the review partner there could be a risk of him reviewing his own work.	This partner must not be involved in the audit of Orange for a period of at least two years. An alternative review partner should be appointed

Ethical Threat	*Managing Risk*
Orange has several potential assurance assignments available and Currant & Co wish to be appointed to these. There is a potential self-interest threat as these assurance fees along with the external audit fee could represent a significant proportion of Currant & Co's fee income.	The firm should assess whether these assignments along with the audit fee would represent more than 15% of gross practice income for two consecutive years. These assurance assignments will only arise if the company obtains its listing and hence will be a public interest company. If the recurring fees are likely to exceed 15% of annual practice income then additional consideration should be given as to whether these assignments should be sought by the firm.
Orange has implied to Currant & Co that they must complete the audit quickly and with minimal questions/issues if they wish to obtain the assurance assignments. This creates an intimidation threat on the team as they may feel pressure to cut corners and not raise issues, and this could compromise the objectivity of the audit team.	The engagement partner should politely inform the finance director that the team will undertake the audit in accordance with all relevant ISAs and their own quality control procedures. This means that the audit will take as long as is necessary to obtain sufficient, appropriate evidence to form an opinion. If any residual concerns remain or the intimidation threat continues then Currant & Co may need to consider resigning from the engagement.
The finance director has offered the team a free weekend away at a luxury hotel. This represents a self-interest threat as the acceptance of goods and services, unless insignificant in value, is not permitted.	As it is unlikely that a weekend at a luxury hotel for the whole team has an insignificant value, then this offer should be politely declined.
The finance director has offered a senior team member a loan at discounted interest rates. Orange does provide loans and hence the provision of a loan is within the normal course of business. However, if the loan is on preferential rates, as this is, then it would represent a self-interest threat.	This loan must not be accepted by the audit senior due to the preferential terms. However, if the terms of the loan are amended so that the interest rate charged is in line with Orange's normal levels, then the provision of the loan is acceptable.

ACCA marking scheme	
	Marks
Up to 1 mark per ethical threat and up to 1 mark per managing method, max of 5 for threats and max 5 for methods	
Engagement partner attending listing meeting	
Preparation of financial statements	
Assistant finance director as review partner on audit	
Total fee income	
Pressure to complete audit quickly and with minimal issues	
Weekend away at luxury hotel	
Provision of loan at preferential rates	
Total	**10**

Examiner's comments

This question required an explanation of ethical threats from the scenario and a method for reducing each of these threats. This was very well answered with many candidates scoring full marks. Ethics questions are often answered well by candidates and the scenario provided contained many possible threats.

Where candidates did not score well this was usually because they only identified rather than explained the ethical threat. In addition some candidates identified the threat but when explaining them they came up with incorrect examples of the type of threat; such as attending the weekend away at a luxury hotel gave rise to a familiarity threat rather than a self-interest threat.

The threat which candidates struggled with the most was the intimidation threat caused by management requesting the audit team ask minimal questions. The response given by many candidates was to decline the assurance engagement; this does not address the intimidation threat. Instead candidates needed to stress that this issue needed to be discussed with the finance director and that appropriate audit procedures would be undertaken to ensure the quality of the audit was not compromised.

In addition when explaining issues some candidates listed many examples of ethical threats; such as 'the assistant finance director being the review partner gives rise to a familiarity, self-review and self-interest threat.' This scatter gun approach to questions is not recommended as it wastes time.

180 LV FONES CO *Walk in the footsteps of a top tutor*

Online question assistance

Top Tutor Tips

This question requires you to apply your knowledge of ethics to the specific circumstances in the scenario. For that reason you cannot simply 'knowledge dump' pre-learnt facts and phrases. Given that the two elements of the question are linked, a table format is appropriate for your answer.

The highlighted words are key phases that markers are looking for.

Ethical threat	Managing risk
The audit team has in previous years been offered a staff discount of 10% on purchasing luxury mobile phones. This is a self-interest threat. It would need to be confirmed if this discount is to be offered to this year's team as well, as only goods of an insignificant value are allowed to be accepted. A discount of 10% may not appear to be significant, but as these are luxury mobile phones then this may still be a	The audit firm should ascertain whether the discount is to be offered to staff this year. If it is then the discount should be reviewed for significance. If it is deemed to be of significant value then the offer of discount should be declined.

Ethical threat	**Managing risk**
significant value.	
An audit senior of Jones & Co has been on secondment as the financial controller of LV Fones and is currently part of the audit team. There is a self-review threat if the senior has prepared records or schedules that support the year end financial statements and he then audits these same documents.	The firm should clarify exactly what areas the senior assisted the client on. If he worked on areas not related to the financial statements then he may be able to remain in the audit team. However, it is likely that he has worked on some related schedules and therefore he should be removed from the audit team to ensure that independence is not threatened.
The total fee income from LV Fones is 16% of the total fees for the audit firm. If the fees for audit and recurring work exceed 15% then there is a self-interest threat. The fees for LV Fones include tax and audit that are assumed to be recurring, however the secondment fees would not recur each year.	The firm should assess if the recurring fees will exceed 15%. If this is the case then it might need to consider whether the appearance of independence will still be met if the tax and audit work is retained. No further work should be accepted in the current year from the client, and it might be advisable to perform external quality control reviews. It may also become necessary to consider resigning from either the tax or the audit engagement.
The partner and the finance director know each other socially and have holidayed together. Personal relationships between the client and members of the audit team can create a familiarity or self-interest threat. ACCA's *Code of Ethics and Conduct* does not specifically prohibit friendships between the audit client and the team. However, due to the senior positions held by both parties then there is a risk that independence may be perceived to have been threatened.	The personal relationship should be reviewed in line with Jones's ethical policies. Consideration should be given to rotating the partner off this engagement and replacing with an alternative partner.
Last year's audit fee is still outstanding. This amounts to 20% of the total fee and is likely to be a significant value. A self-interest threat can arise if the fees remain outstanding, as Jones & Co may feel pressure to agree to certain accounting adjustments in order to have the previous year and the current year fee paid. In addition outstanding fees could be perceived as a loan to a client, this is strictly prohibited.	Jones & Co should chase the outstanding fees. If they remain outstanding, the firm should discuss with those charged with governance the reasons for the continued non-payment, and ideally agree a payment schedule which will result in the fees being settled before much more work is performed for the current year audit.

ACCA marking scheme	
	Marks
Up to 1 mark per ethical threat and up to 1 mark per managing method	
Staff discount	
Secondment	
Total fee income	
Finance director and partner good friends	
Outstanding fees	
Maximum for threats	**5**
Maximum for methods	**5**
Total	**10**

181 ETHICS

(a) **Fundamental principles**

Integrity – to be straightforward and honest in all professional and business relationships.

Objectivity – to not allow bias, conflict of interest or undue influence of others to override professional or business judgements.

Professional Competence and Due Care – to maintain professional knowledge and skill at the level required to ensure that a client receives competent professional services, and to act diligently and in accordance with applicable technical and professional standards.

Confidentiality – to respect the confidentiality of information acquired as a result of professional and business relationships and, therefore, not to disclose any such information to third parties without proper authority, nor use the information for personal advantage.

Professional Behaviour – to comply with relevant laws and regulations and avoid any action that discredits the profession.

(b) **Safeguards**

Familiarity

- Partner rotation – to reduce threat from long association.
- Review composition of the audit team when a previous audit firm employee joins the audit client in a key finance role.
- Remove individuals from the audit team that have a close personal relationship with a key member of client staff.

Self-review

- Separate engagement teams when non audit services are provided to audit clients.

Self interest

- Monitoring of fee levels for public interest entities – to safeguard against fee dependency.
- Ensure significant outstanding fees are paid before commencement of audit.
- Don't make loans to or receive loans from a client.
- Don't accept gifts/hospitality unless clearly trivial.

Conflicts of interest

- Information barriers – to help manage a conflict of interest.
- Independent review partner to ensure ethical threats have been properly managed.

ACCA marking scheme		
		Marks
(a)	Up to 1 mark per well explained point, being ½ mark for the principle and ½ mark for the explanation. Integrity Objectivity Professional competence and due care Confidentiality Professional behaviour	
	Max	**5**
(b)	Up to 1 mark per explained safeguard. ½ if only identified. Partner rotation Review composition of audit team Remove individual from audit team Separate engagement teams Monitor fee levels Significant outstanding fees paid before commencing audit No loans to/from client Don't accept gifts/hospitality unless trivial Information barriers Independent review partner	
	Max	**5**
Total		**10**

182 ETHICAL THREATS

(i) Compliance with ACCA's Code of Ethics and Conduct fundamental principles can be threatened by a number of areas. The five categories of threats, which may impact on ethical risk, are:

- Self-interest – auditor has financial or other interest in the client which might cause the auditor to be reluctant to take actions that would be adverse to the interests of the audit firm.
- Self-review – arises when the results of non-audit services are reflected in the financial statements and in the course of the audit, the auditor may need to re-evaluate the work performed.
- Advocacy – arises when the audit firm undertakes work that involves supporting a position taken by management in an adversarial context.
- Familiarity – arises when the auditor is predisposed to accept or is insufficiently questioning of the client.
- Intimidation – arises when the auditor's conduct is influenced by fear of threats.

(ii) Examples for each category (Only one example required per threat):

Self-interest

- Undue dependence on fee income from one client – monitor fee levels.
- Close personal or business relationships – remove audit team members from the audit where a relationship exists with key client personnel.
- Financial interest in a client – dispose of any shareholdings in the client.
- Incentive fee arrangements – contingent fees or incentives should not be accepted.
- Gifts and hospitality – only accept if clearly insignificant.

Self-review

- Member of assurance team being or recently having been employed by the client in a position to influence the subject matter being reviewed – don't assign to the audit for a period of two years.
- Involvement in implementation of financial system and subsequently reporting on the operation of said system – use separate teams for audit and non-audit work.
- Same person reviewing decisions or data that prepared them – use separate teams for audit and non-audit work.
- Performing a service for a client that directly affects the subject matter of an assurance engagement – use separate teams for audit and non-audit work.

Advocacy

- Acting as an advocate on behalf of a client in litigation or disputes
- Promoting shares in a listed audit client
- Commenting publicly on future events in particular circumstances
- Where information is incomplete or advocating an argument which is unlawful.
- Safeguard – cannot promote or represent audit clients.

Familiarity

- Long association with a client – partner rotation after 7 years for listed clients.
- Acceptance of gifts or preferential treatment (significant value) – only accept if clearly insignificant, otherwise reject.
- Former partner of firm being employed by client – cannot audit the client for a period of 2 years.
- A person in a position to influence financial or non-financial reporting or business decisions having an immediate or close family member who is in a position to benefit from that influence – remove that person from the audit team.

Intimidation

- Threat of litigation.
- Threat of removal as assurance firm.
- Dominant personality of client director attempting to influence decisions.
- Pressure to reduce inappropriately the extent of work performed in order to reduce fees.
- Safeguard: acceptance and continuance procedures to assess integrity of management and reject or resign from clients that lack integrity and are more likely to try and intimidate the auditor. Communicate with the audit committee any intimidating behaviour by management.

ACCA marking scheme			
			Marks
(i)	½ mark for each threat and ½ per explanation of a threat Self-interest Self-review Advocacy Familiarity Intimidation		
		Max	**5**
(ii)	Up to ½ mark per example and up to ½ mark per managing method		
		Max	**5**
Total			**10**

183 CONFIDENTIALITY *Walk in the footsteps of a top tutor*

Top Tutor Tips

Part (a) is theoretical and requires that you have learned the key ethical aspects of the syllabus. The mark allocation is quite high, but this often implies that the marking guide will be generous so do not be intimidated. Make sure you adhere to the principles of good presentation with each mark-scoring point being clearly separated.

Part (b) is slightly more unusual and requires some thought as to why the profession has the fundamental principle of confidentiality.

(a) **Confidential information**

General rules

Information obtained during an audit is normally held to be confidential; that is it will not be disclosed to a third party. However, client information may be disclosed where:

- consent has been obtained from the client
- there is a public duty to disclose
- there is a legal or professional right or duty to disclose.

However, these rules are general principles only; more detailed guidance is also available to accountants, as explained below.

ACCA's Code of ethics – obligatory disclosure

As noted above, ACCA's Code of ethics confirms that when a member agrees to work for a client in a professional capacity, it is an implied term of that agreement that the member will not disclose a client's affairs to any other person.

The recognised exceptions to this rule are where a member knows or suspects that his client has committed treason, or is involved in drug trafficking terrorist offences, or money laundering offences. In this situation, information must be disclosed to the relevant authority. The actual disclosure will depend on the laws of the jurisdiction where the auditor is located.

The auditor may also be obliged to provide information where a court demands disclosure. Refusal to provide information is likely to be considered contempt of court with the auditor being liable for this offence.

If ACCA or another professional body requires disclosure, the auditor must also comply. Refusal in this instance may lead to disciplinary procedures.

ACCA Code of ethics – voluntary disclosure

A member may also disclose client confidential information voluntarily, that is without client permission, in a limited number of situations. Examples include:

- To protect a member's interest, e.g. to allow a member to sue a client for unpaid fees or defend an action for negligence.
- Where there is a public duty to disclose, e.g. the client has committed an action against the public interest such as unauthorised release of toxic chemicals.
- Where there is a breach of a specific legal or regulatory provision – in these cases the information must be disclosed to the relevant legal or regulatory authority.

(b) **Confidential information**

Confidential information is information not in the public domain. This information is available to auditors through their right to access all information of a client for the purpose of the audit.

Confidentiality is important for auditors as clients need to be able to trust the auditor with their information.

Such information may be commercially sensitive and disclosure could jeopardise the client's commercial success.

Confidentiality is one of the fundamental ethical principles and therefore auditors must comply with the principle in order to comply with the Code of Ethics.

ACCA marking scheme

			Marks
(a)	Up to 1 mark per situation		
	Consent of client		
	Money laundering		
	Other legal requirement – court order		
	Professional body requires disclosure		
	Protect member's interest		
	Public duty		
	Breach of regulations requiring disclosure		
		Max	**6**
(b)	Up to 1 mark per point		
	Information not in the public domain		
	Trust		
	Commercially sensitive		
	Fundamental ethical principle		
		Max	4
Total			**10**

CORPORATE GOVERNANCE AND INTERNAL AUDIT

184 BLUEBIRD ENTERPRISES *Walk in the footsteps of a top tutor*

Top Tutor Tips

This question focuses on the audit framework and regulation syllabus area. Benefits of establishing an audit committee should be straightforward in part (a).

Part (b) requires knowledge of the Corporate Governance Code to identify the advantages and disadvantages of each of the potential non-executive directors. Work through on a line by line basis and consider whether each of the candidates has relevant experience, skills or independence. Explain why you think they would be appropriate candidates.

(a) **Benefits of audit committee for Bluebird Enterprises Co**

Appointing an audit committee will benefit Bluebird in the following ways:

- Bluebird does not currently have any non-executive directors, hence once appointed, they will bring considerable external experience to the board as well as challenging the decisions of executive directors and contributing to independent judgements.
- The finance director will benefit in that he will be able to raise concerns and discuss accounting issues with the audit committee.
- It will help to improve the quality of the financial reporting of Bluebird; whilst the company already has a finance director, the audit committee will assist by reviewing the financial statements.
- The establishment of an audit committee can help to improve the internal control environment of the company. The audit committee is able to devote more time and attention to areas such as internal controls.
- If Bluebird has an internal audit (IA) department, then establishing an audit committee will also improve the independence of IA.
- The audit committee can also provide advice on risk management to the executive directors. They can create a climate of discipline and control and reduce the opportunity for fraud, and increase public confidence in the credibility and objectivity of the financial statements.
- The audit committee will assume responsibility for appointing and liaising with the external audit firm, thus ensuring the independence of the external auditor especially in cases of dispute with management.

(b) **Advantages and disadvantages of potential non-executive directors (NEDs)**

Advantages

(i) Antony Goldfinch already has experience of being a NED for another company and he has sat on an audit committee, hence he will be familiar with what the role entails and will be able to bring experience of being a NED to Bluebird.

In addition, Antony Goldfinch has indicated he is agreeable to being paid a fixed fee which is not profit related; this is important as an independent NED's remuneration should be unrelated to the performance of the company.

(ii) Jacob Mallard is currently a finance director and so he possesses recent and relevant financial experience which is required for at least one member of the audit committee.

In addition, he operates in the retail industry and so would be aware of key issues facing companies like Bluebird and so would have an appropriate mix of experience and knowledge.

Disadvantages

(i) Appointing Antony Goldfinch as a NED has disadvantages as he works for a banking company and so would not have relevant experience of companies such as Bluebird; hence he could lack the critical skills and relevant experience needed to provide meaningful advice to the executive directors.

In addition, Antony Goldfinch is already an executive director for a large multinational company and a NED for another company; it might be difficult for him to devote sufficient time to his role at Bluebird.

(ii) Jacob Mallard is the brother of the chief executive and therefore he is not an independent NED. He might be inclined to agree with the chief executive as he is his brother rather than providing the level of objective judgement required from a NED.

Also he wants a contract as a NED for a period of seven years; all directors including NEDs must be subject to re-election at regular intervals not exceeding three years.

ACCA marking scheme	
	Marks
(a) Up to 1 mark per well explained point. – Non-executives will bring outside experience to the board – The finance director will be able to raise concerns with the audit committee – Improve the quality of the financial reporting – Improve the internal control environment of the company – Establishing an audit committee will improve the independence of internal audit – Provide advice on risk management to the executive directors – Responsibility for appointing and liaising with external auditors; reducing the work load of the finance directors	
Maximum	4

(b) Up to 1 mark per well explained point, max of 3 marks for advantages and max of 3 marks for disadvantages. Max of 3 marks for each director, overall max of 6 marks in total.

Advantages

– Antony Goldfinch has experience as a NED and of audit committee role
– Antony Goldfinch has agreed to a non-profit related fee
– Jacob Mallard has relevant and recent financial experience as he is a finance director
– Jacob Mallard operates in the retail industry

Disadvantages

– Antony Goldfinch could lack critical skills and relevant experience of the retail industry
– Antony Goldfinch may not have sufficient time as he has a number of roles already
– Jacob Mallard is the brother of the chief executive and so is not independent
– Jacob Mallard wants a seven-year fixed contract which is contrary to corporate governance principles

Maximum	6
Total	**10**

185 SAXOPHONE ENTERPRISES *Walk in the footsteps of a top tutor*

Top Tutor Tips

This question focuses on the audit framework and regulation syllabus area. Advantages and disadvantages of outsourcing internal audit should be straightforward in part (a).

Part (b) requires corporate governance weaknesses within the scenario to be explained and a recommendation provided for each. Knowledge of the Corporate Governance Code is required here. Work through on a line by line basis and consider whether the information suggests that the company is being properly managed and controlled in the best interests of the shareholders.

(a) **Advantages/disadvantages of outsourcing internal audit department**

Saxophone

Advantages

Staffing: Saxophone Enterprises Co (Saxophone) wishes to expand its internal audit department in terms of size and specialist skills. If they outsource, then there will be no need to spend money in recruiting further staff as Cello & Co (Cello) will provide the staff members.

Immediate solution: As the current internal audit department is small, then outsourcing can provide the number of staff needed straight away.

Skills and experience: Cello is likely to have a large pool of staff available to provide the internal audit service to Saxophone. In addition, the audit firm is likely to have staff with specialist skills already available.

Cost savings: Outsourcing can be an efficient means to control the costs of internal audit as any associated costs such as training will be eliminated as Cello will train its own employees. In addition, the costs for the internal audit service will be agreed in advance. This will ensure that Saxophone can budget accordingly.

Flexibility: If the internal audit department is outsourced, Saxophone will have total flexibility in its internal audit service. Staff can be requested from Cello to suit the company's workloads and requirements. This will ensure that, when required, extra staff is readily available for as long or short a period as needed.

Disadvantages

Existing internal audit department: Saxophone has an existing internal audit department; if they cannot be redeployed elsewhere in the company, then they may need to be made redundant and this could be costly for Saxophone. Staff may oppose the outsourcing if it results in redundancies.

Increased costs: As well as the cost of potential redundancies, the internal audit fee charged by Cello may over a period of time increase, proving to be very expensive.

Knowledge of company: Cello will allocate available staff members to work on the internal audit assignment; this may mean that each visit the staff members are different and hence they may not fully understand the systems of Saxophone. This will decrease the quality of the services provided and increase the time spent by Saxophone's employees in explaining the system to the auditors.

Loss of in-house skills: If the current internal audit team is not deployed elsewhere in the company, valuable internal audit knowledge and experience may be lost. If Saxophone then decided at a future date to bring the service back in-house, this might prove to be too difficult.

Confidentiality: Knowledge of company systems and confidential data will be available to Cello. Although the engagement letter would provide confidentiality clauses, this may not stop breaches of confidentiality.

Control: Saxophone currently has more control over the activities of its internal audit department; however, once outsourced it will need to discuss areas of work and timings well in advance with Cello.

Cello

Advantages

Additional fees for Cello: The audit firm will benefit from the internal audit service being outsourced as this will generate additional fee income. However, the firm will need to monitor the fees to ensure that they do not represent too high a percentage of their total fee income. As a public interest company, fee income should not represent more than 15% of gross practice income for two consecutive years.

Disadvantages

Independence: If Cello provides both external audit and internal audit services, there may be a self-review threat especially where the internal audit work is relied upon by the external auditor team. The firm would need to take steps to ensure that separate teams are put in place as well as additional safeguards.

(b) **Corporate governance weaknesses and recommendations**

(i) **Weakness**	(ii) **Recommendation**
Bill Bassoon is now the chairman; however, until last year he was the chief executive. The chairman is supposed to be an independent non-executive director and hence cannot have previously been the chief executive. The roles of chairman and chief executive are both very important and carry significant responsibilities; hence this prevents too much power residing in the hands of one individual.	Bill Bassoon should return to his role as chief executive as this will fill the current vacancy and an independent non-executive director should be recruited to fill the role of chairman.
The board is comprised of five executives and only three non-executive directors. There should be an appropriate balance of executives and non-executives, to ensure that the board makes the correct objective decisions, which are in the best interest of the stakeholders of the company, and no individual or group of individuals dominates the board's decision-making.	At least half of the board should be comprised of non-executive directors. Hence the board of Saxophone should consider recruiting and appointing an additional one to two non-executive directors.
Bill Bassoon is considering appointing his close friend as a non-executive director; the friend has experience of running a manufacturing company. Non-executives bring valuable experience to a company, but they must also exercise their independent judgment over the whole board. If this director is a close friend of Bill Bassoon, then it is possible that he will not be independent. In addition, other than being a former chief executive, he does not have any relevant experience of the insurance industry and so it is questionable what value he will add to Saxophone.	Only independent non-executives with relevant experience and skills should be appointed to the board of Saxophone. The close friend of Bill Bassoon is unlikely to meet these criteria, as he has no experience in the insurance industry, and so should not be appointed.
The remuneration for directors is set by Jessie Oboe, the finance director. However, no director should be involved in setting their own remuneration as this may result in excessive levels of pay being set.	There should be a fair and transparent policy in place for setting remuneration levels. The non-executive directors should decide on the remuneration of the executives. The finance director or chairman should decide on the pay of the non-executives.

(i) **Weakness**	(ii) **Recommendation**
All directors' remuneration is in the form of an annual bonus. However, the pay should motivate the directors to focus on the long-term growth of the business. Annual targets can encourage short-term strategies rather than maximising shareholder wealth.	The remuneration of executives should be restructured to include a significant proportion aimed at long-term company performance. Perhaps they could be granted share options, as this would help to move the focus to the longer term.
In addition, non-executive directors' pay should not be based on meeting company targets as their pay should be independent of how the company performs.	Non-executives should be paid an annual fee for their services, which is unrelated to how Saxophone performs.
Saxophone does not currently have an audit committee. Audit committees undertake an important role in that they help the directors to satisfy their responsibility of accountability with regards to maintaining an appropriate relationship with the company's auditor.	Saxophone should appoint an audit committee as soon as possible. The committee should be comprised of at least three independent non-executives, one of whom should have relevant financial experience. The three current non-executives should be appointed to the audit committee, assuming they meet the requirements of independence.
A new sales director was appointed nine months ago, however, he has not undergone any board training. All directors should receive induction training when they first join the board so that they are fully aware of their responsibilities.	The new sales director should immediately receive relevant training from Bill Bassoon to ensure that he has a full understanding of his role and responsibilities.
Saxophone is not planning to hold an annual general meeting (AGM) as the number of shareholders are such that it would be too costly and impractical. However, the AGM is an important meeting in that it gives the shareholders an opportunity to raise any concerns, receive an answer and vote on important resolutions. The proposal to send the financial statements and resolutions by email is not appropriate as it does not allow shareholders an opportunity to raise relevant questions.	The company should continue to hold the AGM. Sending information by email in advance of the meeting may be practical and save some costs; however, this should not be seen as a replacement for the AGM.

ACCA marking scheme		
		Marks
(a)	Up to 1 mark per well explained advantage/disadvantage. Overall maximum of 8 marks for Saxophone and 2 marks for Cello. **Saxophone** Staffing gaps addressed Immediate solution Skills and experience increased Costs savings Flexibility of service Existing internal audit department staff, cost of potential redundancies Increased costs as fees by Cello & Co may increase over time Knowledge of company and systems reduced Loss of in-house skills Confidentiality issues Control of department reduced **Cello** Additional fees for Cello & Co Independence issues for audit firm	
	Maximum	**10**
(b)	Up to 1 mark per well explained weakness and up to 1 mark per recommendation. Overall maximum of 5 marks for weaknesses and 5 marks for recommendations. Chief executive is now chairman Currently only three of eight directors are non-executive, should be at least half Chairman considering appointing his friend as a non-executive Finance director decides on the remuneration for the directors Remuneration for all directors in form of annual bonus No audit committee at present No induction training for new sales director No AGM planned as felt impractical and too costly	
	Maximum	**10**
Total		**20**

Examiner's comments

This 20-mark question was based on a listed company which sold insurance services, Saxophone Enterprises Co (Saxophone). This question tested candidates' knowledge of outsourcing internal audit and corporate governance.

Part (a) for 10 marks required advantages and disadvantages for Saxophone and its audit firm, Cello, of outsourcing the internal audit department. Candidates performed well on this question. Many candidates were able to identify a good range of points for both Saxophone and Cello, and the mark allocation of 8 and 2 marks respectively was adhered to. Many answers were well structured with a section for each company with sub headings for advantages and disadvantages; this facilitated the marking of this question. Those candidates who did not score well tended to provide very little detail in their answers, such as for advantages simply stated 'lower costs' or 'more flexibility' these are far too brief to score the 1 mark available per point. The requirement asked candidates to 'explain' their points and this does not provide adequate explanation. Candidates must pay attention to the requirement verb and provide the required level of detail. In addition some candidates included incorrect points such as for advantages the fact that the internal audit work would be quicker as the external auditors knew the company, or that the audit fee would reduce implying that the same team would be used for both tasks or that the work would automatically be relied on which was not appropriate.

Part (b) for 10 marks required an identification and explanation of five corporate governance weaknesses as well as a recommendation for each. Candidates performed well on this question.

Most candidates were able to confidently identify weaknesses from the scenario. However many could not explain the weakness, relying on explanations such as 'this is not good corporate governance'. This was not sufficient to score the extra ½ marks available for each point. Candidates needed to be able to explain how these weaknesses impacted the company. In addition a significant proportion of candidates misread the scenario and thought the chairman and chief executive was the same person. This was not correct; Bill Bassoon had been the chief executive and was now the chairman. Hence answers focused on these key roles being held by the same person rather than the chairman not being independent and failed to score marks as a result. Candidates must read the scenario carefully before they start to write. The recommendations provided were not adequate in many cases and often answers gave corporate governance objectives rather than recommendations, such as, 'the board should be balanced between executive and nonexecutives'. This is an objective; the recommendation should have been to 'appoint additional non-executive directors to ensure a balanced board'.

186 BUSH-BABY HOTELS

(a) **Preventing and detecting fraud and error**

The directors of Bush-Baby Hotels Co (Bush-Baby) are responsible for the prevention and detection of fraud and error. However, the new internal audit department can help the directors by assessing the main areas of fraud risk, assessing the adequacy and effectiveness of control systems and helping to develop controls to mitigate key risks.

Having developed the controls, they can undertake regular reviews of compliance by each hotel of these controls. Where non-compliance is identified, they can instigate further training if necessary or report suspected frauds to senior management.

Where fraud is suspected, the internal audit department can undertake a detailed fraud investigation to identify who is involved, likely sums stolen and gather evidence for any subsequent police investigation.

In addition, the presence of an internal audit department can itself act as a fraud deterrent, as the risk of being discovered means individuals are less likely to undertake fraudulent activities.

(b) **Limitations of establishing and maintaining an internal audit department**

The internal auditors of Bush-Baby will be employees of the company and so this can impair their independence, as they may not report issues to those charged with governance for fear of losing their job.

Although some internal auditors are professionally qualified, there is no requirement to be qualified, as there is for external auditors. Hence, there may be gaps in the experience and technical knowledge of the internal audit department.

The cost of establishing an internal audit department can be significant; hence prior to recruiting a team, the management of Bush-Baby should consider carefully the roles the team can perform and whether this will generate sufficient value for money.

As Bush-Baby has not previously had any form of internal audit, there may be some resistance from employees of the company. They may be uncomfortable with the idea of their work being reviewed, especially if the first role of the department is to undertake fraud investigations.

(c) **Additional functions for Bush-Baby's internal audit department**

Monitoring asset levels

The internal audit department could undertake inventory counts at the restaurants of the 18 hotels. There is likely to be a significant level of goods held at each hotel. Internal audit could count actual levels of goods held and compare them to the hotels' records. If consistent negative differences occur for a hotel, then this may be an early indicator of fraud. If positive differences are highlighted, then it could be because employees have not been adequately trained on how to record inventory.

Cash controls at hotels

Bush-Baby's internal auditors could undertake controls testing over cash receipts and cash counts. It is likely that cash at each hotel will be significant as there would be cash at the reception, restaurant and leisure club. Each hotel should have tight controls over the cash receipts process. These controls should be tested at each location as well as performance of a cash count to reduce the level of errors.

Customer satisfaction levels

In order to improve the overall guest experience in the hotel, members of the internal audit department could undertake 'mystery guest' reviews, where they enter the hotel as a guest, stay the night, eat and drink in the restaurant and visit the leisure club. They then rate the overall hotel experience. This is fed back to each hotel to improve customer service and can provide the basis for further training, if necessary.

Overall review of financial/operational controls

The department could undertake reviews of controls at head office, as well as individual hotels and make recommendations to management over such areas as the purchasing process as well as the payroll cycle.

IT system reviews

Bush-Baby is likely to have a relatively complex computer system linking all of the tills in the hotels to head office. The internal audit department could be asked to perform a review over the computer environment and controls.

Value for money review

The internal audit department could be asked to assess whether Bush-Baby is obtaining value for money in areas such as capital expenditure.

Regulatory compliance

Bush-Baby's operations include leisure clubs, restaurants and hotel rooms. There will be various laws and regulations such as health and safety, food hygiene and fire prevention that impact Bush-Baby. The internal audit department could help to monitor compliance with these regulations.

ACCA marking scheme		
		Marks
(a)	Up to 1 mark per well explained point Internal audit (IA) can assess fraud risk and develop controls to mitigate fraud Regular reviews of compliance with these controls Where fraud suspected, IA can undertake detailed fraud investigation Existence of IA department acts as a fraud deterrent	
	Max	**3**
(b)	Up to 1 mark per well described limitation Lack of independence as employees of the company No requirement to be professionally qualified Cost of establishing department Possible resistance from existing employees to idea of being audited	
	Max	**2**
(c)	Up to 1 mark per well described point Monitoring asset levels Cash controls testing Customer satisfaction levels Financial/operational controls IT system review Value for money review Regulatory compliance	
	Max	**5**
Total		**10**

Examiner's comments

Part (a) for 3 marks required an explanation of how the new internal audit (IA) department of Bush-Baby could assist the directors in preventing and detecting fraud and error. Performance was mixed on this question.

Most candidates were able to gain a mark by suggesting controls that IA could help to develop and monitor to prevent fraud and error. However answers needed to be broader and rather than focusing in excessive detail on internal controls, candidates needed to give more of a general outline in how IA could help, such as fraud investigations.

Part (b) for 2 marks required a description of the limitations of an IA department. Performance was satisfactory on this question.

Many candidates were able to identify the cost outweighing the benefit as being the main limitation or independence issues as they were employees of Bush-Baby. Unfortunately a significant minority of candidates could only provide one of these points. Some candidates referred to the size of the hotel chain as being a limitation, where it was not.

Part (c) for 5 marks required a description of additional functions, other than fraud investigations, the IA department could be asked by the directors to undertake. Performance was mixed on this question.

Candidates were able to easily describe different functions such as internal controls reviews, value for money (VFM) audits, review of compliance with laws and regulations and risk assessment/management.

Some candidates just identified these types of functions with no description of what these functions were; answers such as 'the IA department could undertake a VFM audit' were common. Candidates must consider the question requirement verb, a describe requirement requires some detailed descriptions.

There was also some confusion as to the types of functions IA would perform, for example they should not prepare financial statements. In addition some candidates focused exclusively on the IA department liaising with the external auditor.

187 CONOY *Walk in the footsteps of a top tutor*

Top Tutor Tips

It is vital to apply knowledge to the specific information given. Simple repetition of rote learned facts from study texts will probably not provide sufficient marks to achieve a good pass. Use your knowledge on the benefits of audit committee's and relate it to the scenario. For this part you should try and make six points. 1 mark will be awarded for identifying the basic benefit and 1 for applying it to Conoy.

The highlighted words are key phases that markers are looking for.

Benefits of audit committee in Conoy Co

Assistance with financial reporting (no finance expertise)

The executive directors of Conoy Co do not appear to have any specific financial skills – as the financial director has recently left the company and has not yet been replaced. This may mean that financial reporting in Conoy Co is limited or that the other non-financial directors spend a significant amount of time keeping up to date on financial reporting issues.

An audit committee will assist Conoy Co by providing specialist knowledge of financial reporting on a temporary basis – at least one of the new appointees should have relevant and recent financial reporting experience under codes of corporate governance. This will allow the executive directors to focus on running Conoy Co.

Enhance internal control systems

The board of Conoy Co do not necessarily understand the work of the internal auditor, or the need for control systems. This means that internal control within Conoy Co may be inadequate or that employees may not recognise the importance of internal control systems within an organisation.

The audit committee can raise awareness of the need for good internal control systems simply by being present in Conoy Co and by educating the board on the need for sound controls. Improving the internal control 'climate' will ensure the need for internal controls is understood and reduce control errors.

Reliance on external auditors

Conoy Co's internal auditors currently report to the board of Conoy Co. As previously noted, the lack of financial and control expertise on the board will mean that external auditor reports and advice will not necessarily be understood – and the board may rely too much on external auditors.

If Conoy Co report to an audit committee this will decrease the dependence of the board on the external auditors. The audit committee can take time to understand the external auditor's comments, and then via the non-executive director, ensure that the board take action on those comments.

Appointment of external auditors

At present, the board of Conoy Co appoint the external auditors. This raises issues of independence as the board may become too familiar with the external auditors and so appoint on this friendship rather than merit.

If an audit committee is established, then this committee can recommend the appointment of the external auditors. The committee will have the time and expertise to review the quality of service provided by the external auditors, removing the independence issue.

Corporate governance requirements – best practice

Conoy Co do not need to follow corporate governance requirements (the company is not listed). However, not following those requirements may start to have adverse effects on Conoy. For example, Conoy Co's bank is already concerned about the lack of transparency in reporting.

Establishing an audit committee will show that the board of Conoy Co are committed to maintaining appropriate internal systems in the company and providing the standard of reporting expected by large companies. Obtaining the new bank loan should also be easier as the bank will be satisfied with financial reporting standards.

Given no non-executives – independent advice to board

Currently Conoy Co does not have any non-executive directors. This means that the decisions of the executive directors are not being challenged by other directors independent of the company and with little or no financial interest in the company.

The appointment of an audit committee with one non-executive director on the board of Conoy Co will start to provide some non-executive input to board meetings. While not sufficient in terms of corporate governance requirements (about equal numbers of executive and non-executive directors are expected) it does show the board of Conoy Co are attempting to establish appropriate governance systems.

Advice on risk management

Finally, there are other general areas where Conoy Co would benefit from an audit committee. For example, lack of corporate governance structures probably means Conoy Co does not have a risk management committee. The audit committee can also provide advice on risk management, helping to decrease the risk exposure of the company.

ACCA marking scheme	
	Marks
Benefits of audit committee	
Up to 2 marks for each point. 1 for the benefit and 1 for application to the scenario. 1 mark only where point stated in general terms	
Assistance with financial reporting	
Enhance internal control systems	
Reliance on external auditors	
Appointment of external auditors	
Best practice – corporate governance	
Independent advice to board	
Advice on risk management	
Other valid points e.g. may be cost benefits over time.	
Total	**10**

Examiner's comments

In some answers, the marking guide was recognised and some satisfactory answers showing how an audit committee could assist the company in the scenario were produced. Many answers, however, tended to list the benefits of an audit committee with little or no reference to the detail in the scenario. These answers still obtained 1 mark per point for identifying and explaining the benefit and obviously needed double the number of points to obtain full marks.

The main weakness in many answers was explaining the constitution of the audit committee or the work of other committees rather than the benefit of an audit committee. Overall, this question was answered well. The question obviously benefited those candidates who could apply knowledge to a scenario and those who had good knowledge.

188 MONTEHODGE CO

For establishing an internal audit department

Value for money (VFM) audits

MonteHodge has some relatively complex systems such as the stock market monitoring systems. Internal audit may be able to offer VFM services or review potential upgrades to these systems checking again whether value for money is provided.

Accounting system

While not complex, accounting systems must provide accurate information. Internal audit can audit these systems in detail ensuring that fee calculations, for example, are correct.

Computer systems

Maintenance of computer systems is critical to MonteHodge's business. Without computers, the company cannot operate. Internal audit could review the effectiveness of backup and disaster recovery arrangements.

Internal control systems

Internal control systems appear to be limited. Internal audit could check whether basic control systems are needed, recommending implementation of controls where appropriate.

Effect on audit fee

Provision of internal audit may decrease the audit fee where external auditors can place reliance on the work of internal audit. This is unlikely to happen during the first year of internal audit due to lack of experience.

Image to clients

Provision of internal audit will enable MonteHodge Co to provide a better 'image' to its clients. Good controls imply client monies are safe with MonteHodge.

Corporate governance

Although MonteHodge does not need to comply with corporate governance regulations, internal audit could still recommend policies for good corporate governance. For example, suggesting that the chairman and chief executive officer roles are split.

Compliance with regulations

MonteHodge is in the financial services industry. In most jurisdictions, this industry has a significant amount of regulation. An internal audit department could help ensure compliance with those regulations, especially as additional regulations are expected in the future.

Assistance to financial accountant

The financial accountant in MonteHodge is not qualified. Internal audit could therefore provide assistance in compliance with financial reporting standards, etc. as well as recommending control systems.

Against establishing of internal audit department

No statutory requirement

As there is no statutory requirement, the directors may see internal audit as a waste of time and money and therefore not consider establishing the department.

Accounting systems

Many accounting systems are not necessarily complex so the directors may not see the need for another department to review their operations, check integrity, etc.

Family business

MonteHodge is owned by a few shareholders in the same family. There is therefore not the need to provide assurance to other shareholders on the effectiveness of controls, accuracy of financial accounting systems, etc.

Potential cost

There would be a cost of establishing and maintaining the internal audit department. Given that the directors consider focus on profit and trusting employees to be important, then it is unlikely that they would consider the additional cost of establishing internal audit.

Review threat

Some directors may feel challenged by an internal audit department reviewing their work (especially the financial accountant). They are likely therefore not to want to establish an internal audit department.

Examiner's comments

The scenario contained many 'clues' as to why an internal audit department would be useful (or not) and candidates were expected to identify those points and make specific reference to them in their answers.

The requirement verb discuss indicated that some comment was needed to show why the points made were relevant. The marking scheme allowed one mark for mentioning the specific area and a second mark for applying this to the scenario. Many candidates recognised this requirement and provided sufficient well-explained comments to obtain full marks. Other candidates did not relate their comments to the scenario at all, which limited the number of marks obtainable per point to 1.

Common errors included:

- Not linking the points made to the scenario. As mentioned above, this limited the number of marks available per point to 1.
- Not fully explaining the points made. Brief comments such as 'internal audit would be expensive' only attracted ½ of a mark.

ACCA marking scheme	
	Marks
Up to 2 marks for each well-explained point	
For internal audit	
– VFM audits	
– Accounting system	
– Computer systems	
– Internal control systems	
– Effect on audit fee	
– Image to clients	
– Corporate governance	
– Lack of control	
– Law change	
– Assistance to financial accountant	
– Nature of industry (financial services)	
Against internal audit	
– No statutory requirement	
– Family business	
– Potential cost	
– Review threat	
Total	**10**

189 INTERNAL AUDIT

(a) **Need for Internal Audit**

Having an internal audit department is generally considered to be 'best practice,' rather than being required by law. This allows flexibility in the way internal audit is established to suit the needs of a business.

In small, or owner managed businesses there is unlikely to be a need for internal audit because the owners are able to exercise more direct control over operations, and are accountable to fewer stakeholders.

The need for internal audit will therefore depend on:

- Scale, diversity and complexity of activities.
- Number of employees.
- Cost/benefit considerations.
- The desire of senior management to have assurance and advice on risk and control.
- The desire to be seen to be adopting best practice voluntarily to increase confidence of shareholders and other stakeholders.

(b) Additional assignments for an internal audit department

Performing cash counts

Performance of a cash count to reduce the level of fraud and error.

Mystery shopper reviews

In order to improve the customer experience, an internal audit department could undertake 'mystery shopper' reviews, where they pose as a customer and rate the overall shopping experience. This is then fed back to improve customer service and can provide the basis for further training if necessary.

Overall review of financial/operational controls

The department could undertake reviews of controls and make recommendations to management on areas of improvement.

Fraud investigations

Internal audit could be asked to review the main areas of fraud risk and develop controls to mitigate these risks. If fraud is suspected then internal audit could be asked to investigate these cases further.

IT system reviews

Where a company uses relatively complex computer systems, the internal audit department could be asked to perform a review over the computer environment and controls.

Value for money

The internal audit department assess whether the company is obtaining value for money i.e. obtaining the best price for the required quality of inputs.

Regulatory compliance

The internal audit department could help ensure compliance with relevant laws and regulations to reduce the risk of the company incurring fines and penalties.

ACCA marking scheme			
			Marks
(a)	1 mark per point Scale, diversity, complexity of operations Number of employees Cost/benefit analysis Management need for assurance on risk and controls Increase confidence of shareholders and stakeholders		
		Max	**5**
(b)	Up to 1 mark per well explained point Cash controls testing Mystery shopper Financial/operational controls Fraud investigations IT system review Value for money review Regulatory compliance		
		Max	**5**
Total			**10**

COMPLETION AND REPORTING

190 BULLFINCH *Walk in the footsteps of a top tutor*

Top Tutor Tips

Part (a) requires four elements of an unmodified report with an explanation of why they are included. Stating what the elements are is not the same as explaining why they are included. Think about the purpose of each of the elements.

Part (b) deals with a subsequent event and requires you to state whether the financial statements require amendment and the audit procedures to form a conclusion on the matter. Notice that the requirement does not ask for audit reporting implications. Therefore there are no marks in the marking scheme for talking about audit reports. Keep to the requirement to avoid wasting time writing unnecessary answers.

(a) **Audit report elements and why included**

The following elements should be included within an auditor's report along with why:

Title – The auditor's report shall have a title which clearly indicates that it is the report of an independent auditor, this distinguishes this report from any other.

Addressee – The auditor's report shall be addressed as required by the circumstances of the engagement, this is determined by law or regulation but is usually to the shareholders. This clarifies who may rely on the opinion and who may not, such as third parties.

Introductory paragraph – The introductory paragraph in the auditor's report shall identify the entity whose financial statements have been audited, state that the financial statements have been audited, identify the title of each statement which comprises the financial statements, refer to the summary of significant accounting policies and other explanatory information and specify the date or period covered by each financial statement. This paragraph aims to clarify what time period the audit covers and which pages of the financial statement have been audited, as not every page is audited.

Management's responsibility for the financial statements – This section of the auditor's report describes the responsibilities of those in the organisation who are responsible for the preparation of the financial statements. This paragraph along with that of the auditor's responsibilities looks to make clear what the role of management is, as well as what the role of the auditor is. It seeks to reduce the expectation gap.

Auditor's responsibility – The auditor's report shall state that the responsibility of the auditor is to express an opinion on the financial statements based on the audit and that the audit was conducted in accordance with International Standards on Auditing and ethical requirements and that the auditor plans and performs the audit to obtain reasonable assurance about whether the financial statements are free from material misstatement. Along with the management's responsibility paragraph, it seeks to make clear the role of the auditor and also what management's role is. Also this paragraph seeks to explain what an audit involves and that only material misstatements are considered, as opposed to all errors.

Opinion paragraph – When expressing an unmodified opinion, the auditor's opinion shall either state that the financial statements 'present fairly' or 'give a true and fair view' in accordance with the applicable financial reporting framework. This paragraph details whether the financial statements are true and fair or not.

Other reporting responsibilities – If the auditor addresses other reporting responsibilities in the auditor's report, these shall be addressed in a separate section in the auditor's report titled 'Report on Other Legal and Regulatory Requirements'. This is important where there is local legislation which requires reporting on; this needs to be clearly identified in the report as this is in addition to the requirement of the ISAs.

Signature of the auditor – The auditor's report must be signed, this can be either the personal name of the auditor or, the signature is on behalf of the firm, depending on the jurisdiction in which the auditor is operating. This clarifies which firm or auditor has performed the audit engagement.

Date of the auditor's report – The auditor's report shall be dated no earlier than the date on which the auditor has obtained sufficient appropriate audit evidence on which to base the auditor's opinion on the financial statements. The date of the audit report is important in the case of subsequent events which impact the financial statements; the auditor's role is different depending on whether the audit report was signed or not when the subsequent event came to light.

Auditor's address – The auditor's report shall name the location where the auditor practises. This is useful in case shareholders need to contact the auditors.

(b) **Subsequent event**

A key customer of Bullfinch.com has just notified the company that they are experiencing cash flow difficulties and are unlikely to make any payments for the foreseeable future. This information was received after the year end but provides further evidence of the recoverability of the receivable balance at the year end. If the customer is experiencing cash flow difficulties just a few months after the year end, then it is highly unlikely that the year-end receivable was recoverable as at 31 October and hence is an adjusting event.

The receivables balance is overstated and consideration should be given to adjusting this balance, if material, through the use of an allowance for receivables or by being written off. The total amount outstanding at the year end was $283,000 and is material as it represents 7.4% (0.283/3.8m) of profit before tax and 2.5% (0.283/11.2m) of revenue. Hence, the directors should amend the 2014 financial statements by writing down or writing off the receivable balance.

The following audit procedures should be applied to form a conclusion as to the level of the adjustment:

- The correspondence with the customer should be reviewed to assess whether there is any likelihood of payment.
- Discuss with management as to why they feel an adjustment is not required in the 2014 financial statements.
- Review the post year-end period to see if any payments have been received from the customer.

ACCA marking scheme

		Marks
(a)	Up to 1 mark per well described element and explanation of why included. – Title – Addressee – Introductory paragraph – Management responsibility – Auditor's responsibility – Opinion paragraph – Other reporting responsibilities – Signature of the auditor – Date of the auditor's report – Auditor's address	
	Maximum	4
(b)	Up to 1 mark per valid point, max of 3 marks for whether financial statements require amendment and max of 3 marks for procedures. – Provides evidence of conditions at the year end – Adjusting event – Calculation of materiality – Receivable to be written down or an allowance for receivable used – Customer correspondence reviewed – Discuss with management why no adjustment in 2014 financial statements – Review the post year-end period for payments	
	Maximum	6
Total		**10**

191 CLARINET *Walk in the footsteps of a top tutor*

Top Tutor Tips

Going concern is the assumption that the company will continue to trade for the foreseeable future. Part (a) asks for indicators that the company is not a going concern i.e. will not be able to continue to trade. Look for indicators that the company will not have enough cash to settle its debts when they fall due as cash flow is the main contributor to going concern problems.

Part (b) asks for the impact on the audit report if the auditor believes the company is a going concern but a material uncertainty exists. State whether the report and opinion will be modified and if so, how. State the name of the opinion as well as the key words of that opinion to earn the marks available.

(a) **Going concern indicators**

A new competitor, Drums Design Co (Drums), has entered the market and gained considerable market share from Clarinet through competitive pricing. There is a risk that if Clarinet continues to lose market share this will impact on future cash flows. In addition, there may be pressure on Clarinet to drop their prices in order to compete, which will impact profits and cash flows.

A significant customer has stopped trading with Clarinet and moved its business to Drums. This could result in a significant loss of future revenues and profit, and unless this customer can be replaced, there will be a reduction of future cash flows.

A number of Clarinet's specialist developers have left the company and joined Drums and the company has found it difficult to replace these employees due to their experience and skills. The company is looking to develop new products and in order to do this, it needs sufficiently trained staff. If it cannot recruit enough staff, then it could hold up the product development and stop the company from increasing revenue.

Clarinet's main supplier who provides specialist equipment has just stopped trading. If the equipment is highly specialised, there is a risk that Clarinet may not be able to obtain these products from other suppliers which would impact on their ability to trade. More likely, there are other suppliers available but they may be more expensive which will increase the outflows of Clarinet and worsen the cash flow forecast.

Clarinet needs to raise finance to develop new products in order to gain market share; they approached their shareholders for further finance but they declined to invest further. If Clarinet is unable to obtain suitable finance, then it may be that the shareholders deem Clarinet to be too risky to invest in further. They may be concerned that Clarinet will not be able to offer them a suitable return on their investment, suggesting cash flow problems. In addition, if Clarinet cannot obtain alternative finance, then it will not be able to develop the products it needs to.

Clarinet's overdraft has grown significantly during the year. If the bank does not renew the overdraft and the company is unable to obtain alternative finance, then it may not be able to continue to trade.

Clarinet's cash flow forecast shows a significantly worsening position for the coming 12 months. If the company continues to have cash outflows, then it will increase its overdraft further and will start to run out of available cash.

One of Clarinet's customers is planning to sue the company for loss of revenue due to hardware being installed by Clarinet in the customer's online ordering system not operating correctly. If the customer is successful, then Clarinet may have to pay a significant settlement which will put further pressure on cash flows. In addition, it is unlikely that this customer will continue to trade with Clarinet and if the problems become known to other customers, this may lead to a further loss of revenue and cash flows as well as impact on Clarinet's reputation.

(b) **Audit report**

The directors of Clarinet have agreed to make going concern disclosures; however, the impact on the audit report will be dependent on the adequacy of these disclosures. If the disclosures are adequate, then the audit report will be modified as an emphasis of matter paragraph would be required.

The paragraph will state that the audit opinion is not modified, indicate that there is a material uncertainty and will cross reference to the disclosure note made by management. It would be included immediately after the opinion paragraph.

If the disclosures made by management are not adequate, the audit opinion will need to be modified as there is a material misstatement. Depending on the materiality of the issue, this will be either qualified or an adverse opinion.

A paragraph describing the matter giving rise to the modification will be included just before the opinion paragraph and this will clearly identify the lack of disclosure over the going concern uncertainty. The opinion paragraph will be amended to state 'except for' or the financial statements are not fairly presented.

ACCA marking scheme		
		Marks
(a)	Up to 1 mark per explanation of why this could indicate going concern problems, if just identify indicator then max of ½ mark, overall maximum of 6 indicators. New competitor taking market share from Clarinet Loss of large customer Loss of specialist staff Main supplier ceased to trade Shareholders refused to provide further finance for product development Overdraft facility due for renewal and increased significantly Cash flow shows worsening position Customer potentially suing for loss of revenue	
	Maximum	**6**
(b)	Up to 1 mark per well described point. Depends on adequacy of disclosures Adequately disclosed – modified report Emphasis of matter paragraph after opinion – opinion unmodified Not adequately disclosed – modified opinion as material misstatement Depending on materiality either qualified or adverse opinion. Add paragraph before opinion and impact on opinion paragraph	
	Maximum	**4**
Total		**10**

Examiner's comments

This question was based on a computer hardware specialist, Clarinet Co (Clarinet) and tested candidates' knowledge of going concern and audit reports.

Part (a) for 6 marks required an explanation of six indicators the company was not a going concern. Candidates performed well on this question. Most candidates were able to identify six indicators from the scenario; this resulted in them achieving 3 marks. However in order to gain the final 3 marks, candidates were required to explain why this indicator could impact the going concern of Clarinet. Many did not do this, or the explanations provided did not give sufficient depth often simply stating 'this could impact the going concern status'. This would not have scored marks as it does not make clear how the going concern status could be impacted. The requirement verb was to 'explain' therefore sufficient detail was required to score the 1 mark available per point. Once again candidates are reminded to look carefully at the verb at the beginning of the question requirement, as this should help them to understand the level of detail required for their answers. A small minority of candidates misread the requirement and provided indicators from the scenario that Clarinet was a going concern, rather than was not. This can only be due to a failure to read the question requirement properly.

Part (b) for 4 marks required a description of the impact on the audit report if the auditor believes the company is a going concern but is subject to a material uncertainty. Candidates performed disappointingly on this question. Unfortunately many candidates approached this requirement by suggesting every possible impact on the audit report. Very few candidates seemed to realise that the key issue was whether the disclosures given by the directors were adequate or not and so did not approach the answer in a methodical way. It appears that there is a lack of knowledge in relation to the differences between a modified report and a modified opinion and that if the inclusion of an emphasis of matter paragraph is considered appropriate the report but not the opinion is modified. Once again future candidates are reminded that audit reports are a key element of the syllabus and hence an understanding of how an audit report can be modified and in which circumstances, is considered very important for this exam.

192 PAPRIKA *Walk in the footsteps of a top tutor*

Top Tutor Tips

This was an unusual requirement asking for the amendments needed to the draft audit report. Use your knowledge of audit reports to identify the wording that needs to be amended. You must explain why the statements are wrong and hence why the amendment is needed to earn all of the marks.

Audit report elements

Extract 1

'Our responsibility is to express an opinion on all pages of the financial statements.' This is incomplete as the auditor is required to list the components of the financial statements which have been audited, being: statement of financial position, statement of profit or loss (income statement), statement of cash flows, summary of significant accounting policies and other explanatory information detailed in the notes to the financial statements.

'We conducted our audit in accordance with most of the International Standards on Auditing (ISAs).' An auditor is required to perform their audit in accordance with all ISAs and cannot just choose to apply some. They must state that they follow all ISAs.

Extract 2

'Obtain maximum assurance as to whether the financial statements are free from all misstatements.' The auditor is not able to obtain maximum assurance and they cannot confirm that the financial statements contain no errors. This is because they do not test every transaction or balance as it is not practical. They only test a sample of transactions and may only consider material balances. Hence auditors give reasonable assurance that financial statements are free from material misstatements.

Extract 3

'We have a responsibility to prevent fraud and error.' This is not correct as it is in fact management's and not the auditor's responsibility to prevent and detect fraud and error. The auditor only has a responsibility to detect material misstatements whether caused by fraud or error.

'We prepare the financial statements.' Again this is a responsibility of management, as they prepare the financial statements. The auditor provides an opinion on the truth and fairness of the financial statements.

Extract 4

'The procedures selected depend on the availability and experience of audit team members.' The auditor is required to obtain sufficient and appropriate evidence and therefore should carry out any necessary procedures. Availability and experience of team members should not dictate the level of testing performed.

'We express an opinion on the effectiveness of these internal controls.' The audit report is produced for the shareholders of Paprika Co and the auditor provides an opinion on the truth and fairness of the financial statements. Brown & Co will review the effectiveness of the internal controls and they will report on any key deficiencies identified during the course of the audit to management.

Extract 5

'We did not evaluate the overall presentation of the financial statements as this is management's responsibility.' Management is responsible for producing the financial statements and so will consider the overall presentation as part of this. However, the auditors also have a responsibility to review the overall presentation to ensure that it is in accordance with relevant accounting standards and in line with their audit findings.

'We considered the reasonableness of any new accounting estimates.' The auditor is required to consider all material accounting estimates made by management, whether these are brought forward from prior years or are new. Estimates from prior years, such as provisions, need to be considered annually as they may require amendment or may no longer be required.

'We did not review the appropriateness of accounting policies as these are the same as last year.' Accounting policies must be reviewed annually as there could be a change in Paprika's circumstances which means a change in accounting policy may be required. In addition, new accounting standards may have been issued which require accounting policies to change.

'We relied on the work undertaken by an independent expert.' Auditors are not expected to have knowledge of all elements of a company and hence it is acceptable to rely on the work of an independent expert. However, it is not acceptable for Brown & Co to refer to this in their audit report, as this implies that they are passing responsibility for this account balance to a third party. The auditor is ultimately responsible for the true and fair opinion and so cannot refer in their report to reliance on any third parties.

ACCA marking scheme	
	Marks
Up to 1 mark for each element identified and up to 1 mark per explanation.	
– Opinion on all pages	
– Audit in accordance with most International Standards on Auditing	
– Maximum assurance, free from all misstatements	
– Responsibility to prevent and detect fraud and error	
– We prepare financial statements	
– Procedures depend on availability and experience of team members	
– We express opinion on effectiveness of internal controls	
– Did not evaluate overall presentation of financial statements	
– Considered reasonableness of new accounting estimates	
– Did not review accounting policies	
– Relied on work of independent expert	
Total	**10**

Examiner's comments

This question required an identification and explanation of elements of the draft audit report provided which required amendment. Candidates' performance was mixed on this question.

Reviewing a draft audit report and identifying areas that require amendment was a different style of audit report question than in previous diets. However, many candidates answered this question satisfactorily. These recognised that there were two parts to the requirement, a need to identify the element from the scenario and then a need to explain why this sentence needed amending. Those candidates who scored well also tended to use a two column approach of identify and explain. This resulted in them maximising their marks as they easily identified the elements from the scenario and then for each explained why there was a problem.

Those candidates who did not score as well tended to ignore the 'identify' requirement and jumped straight into the explanation. This is not what the question wanted as there were clearly two requirements 'identify' and 'explain' and both needed to be addressed to score well. In addition many candidates focused on redrafting the audit report extracts even though this was specifically excluded from the question requirement.

In this question it was also common to see many more points being provided. All points made are reviewed but marks are only allocated to the best points up to the maximum specified. Candidates would do better if they focused on the quality of points made rather than the quantity.

193 PANDA *Walk in the footsteps of a top tutor*

(a) **Subsequent events**

Top Tutor Tips

Subsequent events are typically misunderstood by students as they confuse the accounting treatment with the auditors' responsibilities leading to very jumbled answers. Keep in mind that the client should prepare the financial statements in accordance with IAS 10. The auditor then performs audit procedures to obtain evidence to see if IAS 10 has been complied with.

Explosion

An explosion has occurred in one of the offsite storage locations and property, plant and equipment and inventory valued at $0.9 million have been damaged and now have no scrap value. The directors do not believe they are likely to be able to claim insurance for the damaged assets. This event occurred after the year end and the explosion would not have been in existence at 30 April, and hence this event indicates a non-adjusting event.

The damaged assets of $0.9 million are material as they represent 16.1% (0.9/5.6) of profit before tax and 1.6% (0.9/55) of revenue. As a material non-adjusting event, the assets should not be written down to zero; however, the directors should consider including a disclosure note detailing the explosion and the value of assets impacted.

The following audit procedures should be applied to form a conclusion on any amendment:

- Obtain a schedule showing the damaged property, plant and equipment and agree the net book value to the non-current assets register to confirm what the value of damaged assets was.
- Obtain the latest inventory records for this storage location to ascertain the likely level of inventory at the time of the explosion.
- Discuss with the directors whether they will disclose the effect of the explosion in the financial statements.
- Discuss with the directors why they do not believe that they are able to claim on their insurance; if a claim was to be made, then only uninsured losses would require disclosure, and this may be an immaterial amount.

(b) **Audit report**

Top Tutor Tips

Note that for part (b) the requirement asks for audit reporting implications 'should this issue remain unresolved'. There is no point wasting time writing an answer considering if the issue is resolved.

The explosion is a non-adjusting post year-end event and the level of damaged assets are material. Hence a disclosure note should be included in the 2013 financial statements and the write down of assets would be included in the 2014 financial statements.

If the directors refuse to make the subsequent event disclosures, then the financial statements are materially misstated and as the lack of disclosure is material but not pervasive, the audit report will be modified and a qualified opinion will be necessary.

A basis for qualified opinion paragraph would need to be included before the opinion paragraph. This would explain the misstatement in relation to the lack of subsequent events disclosure and the effect on the financial statements. The opinion paragraph would be qualified 'except for'.

ACCA marking scheme		
		Marks
(a)	Up to 1 mark per valid point, overall maximum of 6 marks	
	Explosion	
	Provides evidence of conditions that arose subsequent to the year end	
	Non-adjusting event, requires disclosure if material	
	Calculation of materiality	
	Obtain schedule of damaged property, plant and equipment and agree values to asset register	
	Obtain latest inventory records to confirm damaged inventory levels	
	Discuss with the directors if they will make disclosures	
	Discuss with directors why no insurance claim will be made	
	Max	**6**

(b)	Up to 1 mark per well explained valid point Disclosure required in 2013 financial statements and adjustment to the assets in 2014 financial statements Material but not pervasive misstatement, modified audit report, qualified opinion Basis for qualified opinion paragraph required Opinion paragraph – except for	
	Max	**4**
Total		**10**

Examiner's comments

Part (a) required an explanation of whether the financial statements should be amended and audit procedures that should be performed by the auditor to form a conclusion on any required amendment. Performance was mixed on this question.

Many candidates were able to correctly identify whether the event was adjusting or non-adjusting. However the justification for this was not always correct; for example stating that 'the explosion was non-adjusting as it occurred after the year end'. Many candidates were able to calculate the materiality of the potential error, using the numbers provided. The decision as to whether the financial statements required amendment was not answered well as many candidates did not seem to realise that adding a disclosure note is an amendment.

With regards to procedures to undertake to form a conclusion on any required amendment, candidates seemed to struggle with this. Many procedures lacked sufficient detail to score the available 1 mark per test. This commonly occurred with tests such as; 'reviewing board minutes' and 'obtain written representation'. These procedures need to be phrased with sufficient detail to obtain credit and must be tailored to the scenario. In addition a significant minority of candidates wanted to contact Panda's insurance company; this is not a realistic procedure.

In addition some candidates wasted time by discussing the impact on the audit report; this was not part of the question requirement for part (a) and so would not have generated any marks. Candidates once again are reminded to only answer the question set.

Part (b) required the impact on the audit report should the explosion issue remain unresolved. Performance on this question was unsatisfactory.

Candidates still continue to recommend an emphasis of matter paragraph for all audit report questions, this is not the case and it was not relevant for this issue. Candidates need to understand what an emphasis of matter paragraph is and why it is used. In addition some candidates are confused with regards to audit report terms and used phrases such as 'qualify the report' rather than modify the report and 'modified opinion' rather than qualified opinion.

A significant number of candidates were unable to identify the correct audit report modification, giving multiple options and some candidates seemed to believe that the opinion did not require qualification as it was only the disclosure, as opposed to any numbers that were incorrect. Also some answers contradicted themselves such as 'the issue is material therefore an unqualified opinion can be given'. Additionally many candidates ignored the question requirement to only consider the audit report impact if the issue was unresolved. Lots of answers started with 'if resolved the audit report .....' this was not required. Once again future candidates are reminded that audit reports are the only output of a statutory audit and hence an understanding of how an audit report can be modified and in which circumstances, is considered very important for this exam.

194 VIOLET & CO *Walk in the footsteps of a top tutor*

Top Tutor Tips

This is a straightforward audit reporting question and the requirement gives you an approach to use. Discuss the issue, consider if it is material, recommend further procedures and describe the impact on the audit report.

When discussing the impact on the audit report remember that the opinion is only one element of the report. Consider whether there is a need for any further modifications such as a 'basis for' paragraph if you are suggesting the opinion should be modified or an emphasis of matter paragraph if there are material uncertainties which have been adequately disclosed by the client.

Daisy Designs Co (Daisy)

(i) Daisy's sales ledger has been corrupted by a computer virus; hence no detailed testing has been performed on revenue and receivables. The audit team will need to see if they can confirm revenue and receivables in an alternative manner. If they are unable to do this, then two significant balances in the financial statements will not have been confirmed. Revenue and receivables are both higher than the total profit before tax (PBT) of $2m; receivables are 170% of PBT and revenue is nearly eight times the PBT; hence this is a very material issue.

(ii) Procedures to be adopted include:

- Discuss with management whether they have any alternative records which detail revenue and receivables for the year.
- Attempt to perform analytical procedures, such as proof in total or monthly comparison to last year, to gain comfort in total for revenue and for receivables.

(iii) The auditors will need to modify the audit report as they are unable to obtain sufficient appropriate evidence in relation to two material and pervasive areas, being receivables and revenue. Therefore a disclaimer of opinion will be required.

A basis for disclaimer of opinion paragraph will be required to explain the limitation in relation to the lack of evidence over revenue and receivables. The opinion paragraph will be a disclaimer of opinion and will state that we are unable to form an opinion on the financial statements.

Fuchsia Enterprises Co (Fuchsia)

(i) Fuchsia is facing going concern problems as it has experienced difficult trading conditions and it has a negative cash outflow. However, the financial statements have been prepared on a going concern basis, even though it is possible that the company is not a going concern. The prior year financial statements showed a profit of $1.2m and the current financial statements show a loss before tax of $4.4m, the net cash outflow of $3.2m represents 73% of this loss (3.2/4.4m) and hence is a material issue.

(ii) Management are confident that further funding can be obtained; however, the team is sceptical and so the following procedures should be adopted:

- Discuss with management whether any finance has now been secured.
- Review the correspondence with the finance provider to confirm the level of funding that is to be provided and this should be compared to the net cash outflow of $3.2m.
- Review the most recent board minutes to understand whether management's view on Fuchsia's going concern has altered.
- Review the cash flow forecasts for the year and assess the reasonableness of the assumptions adopted.

(iii) If management refuse to amend the going concern basis of the financial statements or at the very least make adequate going concern disclosures, then the audit report will need to be modified. As the going concern basis is probably incorrect and the error is material and pervasive, then an adverse opinion would be necessary.

A basis for adverse opinion paragraph will be required to explain the inappropriate use of the going concern assumption. The opinion paragraph will be an adverse opinion and will state that the financial statements do not give a true and fair view.

ACCA marking scheme	
	Marks
Up to 1 mark per valid point, overall maximum of 5 marks PER ISSUE	
Discussion of issue	
Calculation of materiality	
Procedures at completion stage – 1 mark only	
Type of audit report modification required	
Impact on audit report	
Total	**10**

Examiner's comments

This question required a discussion of two issues; an assessment of the materiality of each; procedures to resolve each issue and the impact on the audit report if each issue remained unresolved. Performance was mixed on this question. There were a significant minority of candidates who did not devote sufficient time and effort to this question bearing in mind the mark allocation.

The requirement to discuss the two issues of Daisy's corrupted sales ledger and Fuchsia's going concern problem was on whole, answered well by most candidates. In addition many candidates correctly identified that each issue was clearly material. A significant minority seemed to believe the corruption of the sales ledger was an adjusting event and so incorrectly proceeded to focus on subsequent events.

With regards to procedures to undertake at the completion stage, candidates seemed to struggle with Daisy. Given that the sales ledger had been corrupted procedures such as 'agree goods despatch notes to sales invoices to the sales ledger' or 'reconcile the sales ledger to the general ledger' were unlikely to be possible. Most candidates correctly identified relevant analytical review procedures and a receivables circularisation. Candidates performed better on auditing the going concern of Fuchsia, however some candidates wasted time by providing a long list of going concern tests when only one was needed.

Performance on the impact on the audit report if each issue remained unresolved was unsatisfactory. Candidates still continue to recommend an emphasis of matter paragraph for all audit report questions, this is not the case and it was not relevant for either issue. Candidates need to understand what an emphasis of matter paragraph is and why it is used.

A significant number of candidates were unable to identify the correct audit report modification, suggesting that Daisy's should be qualified or adverse, as opposed to disclaimer of opinion. Also some answers contradicted themselves with answers of 'the issue is not material therefore qualify the opinion'. Additionally many candidates ignored the question requirement to only consider the audit report impact if the issue was unresolved. Lots of answers started with 'if resolved the audit report .....' this was not required. In relation to the impact on the audit report, many candidates were unable to describe how the opinion paragraph would change and so failed to maximise their marks.

Once again future candidates are reminded that audit reports are the only output of a statutory audit and hence an understanding of how an audit report can be modified and in which circumstances, is considered very important for this exam.

195 STRAWBERRY KITCHEN DESIGNS *Walk in the footsteps of a top tutor*

(a) **Going concern procedures**

Top Tutor Tips

Generate procedures which are related to the scenario, rather than giving a list of generic going concern procedures. There is plenty of information to work with in the scenario. Your procedures should focus on trying to identify whether any of the issues mentioned could pose a problem to the going concern status.

- Perform a sensitivity analysis on the cash flows to understand the margin of safety the company has in terms of its net cash in/out flow.
- Discuss with the finance director whether the sales director has yet been replaced and whether any new customers have been obtained to replace the one lost.
- Review the company's post year-end sales and order book to assess if the levels of trade are likely to increase and if the revenue figures in the cash flow forecast are reasonable.
- Review the loan agreement and recalculate the covenant which has been breached. Confirm the timing and amount of the loan repayment.
- Review any agreements with the bank to determine whether any other covenants have been breached, especially in relation to the overdraft.
- Discuss with the directors whether they have contacted any alternative banks for finance to assess whether they have any other means of repaying the loan of $4.8m.
- Review any correspondence with shareholders to assess whether any of these are likely to increase their equity investment in the company.

- Review post year-end correspondence with suppliers to identify if any others have threatened legal action or refused to supply goods.
- Enquire of the lawyers of Strawberry as to the existence of any additional litigation and request their assessment of the likely amounts payable to the suppliers.
- Perform audit tests in relation to subsequent events to identify any items that might indicate or mitigate the risk of going concern not being appropriate.
- Review the post year-end board minutes to identify any other issues that might indicate further financial difficulties for the company.
- Review post year-end management accounts to assess if in line with cash flow forecast.
- Consider whether the going concern basis is appropriate for the preparation of the financial statements.
- Obtain a written representation confirming the director's view that Strawberry is a going concern.

(b) (i) **Reporting in relation to going concern to the directors of Strawberry Kitchen Designs Co**

Kiwi & Co has a responsibility to report to the directors in relation to any events or conditions which may cast doubt on Strawberry's ability to continue as a going concern. These include:

- Whether the events or conditions constitute a material uncertainty;
- Whether the use of the going concern assumption is appropriate in the preparation of the financial statements; and
- The adequacy of related disclosures in the financial statements.

(ii) **Audit report**

Top Tutor Tips

When discussing the impact on the audit report remember that the opinion is only one element of the report. Consider whether there is a need for any further modifications such as a 'basis for' paragraph if you are suggesting the opinion should be modified or an emphasis of matter paragraph if there are material uncertainties which have been adequately disclosed by the client.

The directors do not wish to make any amendments to the financial statements. However, if we believe that Strawberry is not a going concern then the audit report will need to be modified. An adverse opinion will be required regardless of whether or not the financial statements include disclosure of the inappropriateness of management's use of the going concern assumption as the financial statements are materially misstated, and the misstatements are material and pervasive to the financial statements.

The basis for adverse opinion paragraph will require an explanation that the use of the going concern basis is inappropriate. The opinion paragraph will state that the financial statements do not present fairly or are not true and fair.

ACCA marking scheme			
			Marks
(a)		Up to 1 mark per well explained point Review cash flow forecasts Sensitivity analysis Discuss if sales director replaced and new customers obtained Review post year-end sales and order book Review the loan agreement and recalculate the covenant breached to confirm timing and amount of the loan repayment Review bank agreements, breach of covenants Review bank correspondence Discuss if alternative finance obtained Review shareholders' correspondence Review suppliers' correspondence Enquire of lawyers any further litigation by suppliers Subsequent events Board minutes Management accounts Consider going concern basis appropriate Written representation	
		Max	**5**
(b)	(i)	Up to 1 mark per well explained point Events or conditions constitute a material uncertainty Use of the going concern assumption is appropriate Adequacy of disclosures in the financial statements	
		Max	**2**
	(ii)	Up to 1 mark per well explained point Not going concern therefore modified opinion Adverse opinion Basis for adverse opinion paragraph, going concern basis not appropriate Opinion paragraph, financial statements not true and fair	
		Max	**3**
Total			**10**

Examiner's comments

Part (a) required going concern audit procedures. Performance was mixed on this question.

Candidates failed to maximise their marks here by providing too brief tests such as 'check cash flow forecasts' and 'obtain management rep' or unrealistic tests such as 'write to the bank and ask if they will require the loan to be repaid', the bank will not answer such a request. In addition some answers focused on audit procedures which would have already been undertaken during the substantive testing stage such as 'perform a receivables circularisation'.

Part (b) (i) for 2 marks required Kiwi's responsibility for reporting going concern to the directors. This question was answered unsatisfactorily.

Many candidates were unable to correctly identify any of the auditors' responsibilities on reporting going concern to the directors. Where candidates did score a mark it was usually with regards to the requirement to inform the directors if the going concern assumption was appropriate. Many candidates focused instead on the directors' responsibilities under going concern; this was not what was required.

Part (b) (ii) for 3 marks required the impact on the audit report if the directors refused to amend the financial statements. This was answered unsatisfactorily.

Many candidates were unable to provide the correct audit opinion and so adopted a scatter gun approach of listing every audit report modification available.

Also many candidates correctly identified that the opinion needed to be modified; however they then suggested an emphasis of matter paragraph. This demonstrates that candidates do not understand when an 'emphasis of matter' paragraph is relevant, and seem to think that it is an acceptable alternative to modifying the opinion. This demonstrates candidates' fundamental lack of understanding of audit reports.

Where candidates were able to correctly identify that an adverse opinion was required they failed to describe the impact on the audit report, many were unable to describe how the opinion paragraph would change and that a basis for adverse opinion paragraph was necessary.

Future candidates are once again reminded that audit reports are the only output of an external audit and hence an understanding of how an audit report can be modified and in which circumstances, is considered very important for this exam.

196 HUMPHRIES *Walk in the footsteps of a top tutor*

Top Tutor Tips

This is a straightforward audit reporting question and the requirement is nicely broken down for you. It gives you an approach to use. Discuss the issue (remember to consider if it is material), describe further procedures and describe the impact on the audit report.

When discussing the impact on the audit report remember that the opinion is only one element of the report. Consider whether there is a need for any further modifications such as a 'basis for' paragraph if you are suggesting the opinion should be modified or an emphasis of matter paragraph if there are material uncertainties which have been adequately disclosed by the client.

*Don't waste time stating the impact on the report if the issue is resolved as the question specifically asks for the impact if it is **not** resolved.*

Receivable

A customer, owing $0.3 million at the year end, is experiencing significant going concern difficulties. This information was received after the year end but provides further evidence of the recoverability of the receivable balance at the year end. Under IAS 10 *Events after the Reporting Period*, if the customer is experiencing cash flow difficulties just a few months after the year end, then it is highly unlikely that the $0.3m was recoverable as at 30 September.

The receivables balance is overstated and consideration should be given to adjusting this balance, if material, through the use of an allowance for receivables or by being written off.

The following audit procedures should be applied to form a conclusion as to the level of the adjustment:

- The correspondence with the customer should be reviewed to assess whether there is any likelihood of payment.
- Discuss with management as to why they feel an adjustment is not required.
- Review the post year-end period to see if any payments have been received from the customer.

The receivable of $0.3 million is not material as it represents 4% of profit (0.3/7.5) and 0.4% of revenue (0.3/78) and therefore, although overstated, it does not require adjustment. However, the $0.3m should be noted in the summary of unadjusted errors.

As the error is immaterial then no amendment is required to the audit opinion.

Lawsuit

A key supplier is suing Humphries Co for $1 million; the company has made contingent liability disclosures. However, subsequent to the year end the supplier agreed to settle at $0.6 million and it is likely the company will agree. Although the settlement was agreed after the year end, it provides further evidence that the company had a present obligation as at 30 September.

The financial statements should be adjusted with the contingent liability disclosures being removed and instead a provision of $0.6 million being recorded.

The following audit procedures should be applied to form a conclusion as to the level of the adjustment:

- The auditor should contact the company's lawyers to ask their view as to whether the settlement is probable and whether $0.6 million is the likely amount.
- Review the correspondence with the supplier to confirm that the amount they are willing to accept is in fact $0.6 million.
- Discuss with management as to whether it is probable that they will pay this sum and obtain a written representation confirming this.

The sum being claimed is $1 million but the probable payment is $0.6 million, this is material as it represents 8% of profit (0.6/7.5) and hence management should provide for this amount.

If management refuse to provide then the audit report will need to be modified. As management has not complied with IAS 37 *Provisions, Contingent Liabilities and Contingent Assets* and the error is material but not pervasive then a qualified opinion would be necessary.

A basis for qualified opinion paragraph would be required and would need to include a paragraph explaining the material misstatement in relation to the lack of a provision and the effect on the financial statements. The opinion paragraph would be qualified 'except for'.

ACCA marking scheme	
	Marks
Up to 1 mark per valid point, overall maximum of 5 marks per event.	
Receivable	
Provides evidence of conditions at the year end	
Receivable to be adjusted via write down or allowance	
Review correspondence with customer	
Discuss with management	
Review post year-end period for cash receipts	
Calculation of materiality	
No audit report modification required	
Max	**5**
Lawsuit	
Provides evidence of present obligation at the year end	
Provision required and not contingent liability disclosures	
Discuss with company lawyer	
Review correspondence with supplier	
Discuss with management and obtain written representation	
Calculation of materiality	
Type of audit report modification required	
Impact on audit report	
Max	**5**
Total	**10**

197 MINNIE *Walk in the footsteps of a top tutor*

Top Tutor Tips

This is a straightforward audit reporting requirement dealing with two separate issues. Each issue has its own mark allocation therefore deal with each in turn.

When discussing the impact on the audit report remember that the opinion is only one element of the report. Consider whether there is a need for any further modifications such as a 'basis for' paragraph if you are suggesting the opinion should be modified or an emphasis of matter paragraph if there are material uncertainties which have been adequately disclosed by the client.

(i) **Wages program**

Minnie Co's wages program has been corrupted leading to a loss of payroll data for a period of two months. The auditors should attempt to verify payroll in an alternative manner. If they are unable to do this then payroll for the whole year would not have been verified.

Wages and salaries for the two month period represents 11% of profit before tax (1.1m/10m) and therefore is a material balance for which audit evidence has not been available.

The auditors will need to modify the audit report as they are unable to obtain sufficient appropriate evidence in relation to a material, but not pervasive, element of wages and salaries and therefore a qualified opinion will be required.

A basis for qualified opinion paragraph will be required to explain the limitation in relation to the lack of evidence over two months of payroll records. The opinion paragraph will be qualified 'except for' – due to insufficient appropriate audit evidence.

(ii) **Lawsuit**

The company is being sued by a competitor for breach of copyright. This matter has been correctly disclosed in accordance with IAS 37 *Provisions, Contingent Liabilities and Contingent Assets.*

The lawsuit is for $5m which represents 50% of profit before tax (5·0m/10m) and hence is a material matter. This is an important matter which needs to be brought to the attention of the users.

An emphasis of matter paragraph would need to be included in the audit report, in that the matter is appropriately disclosed but is fundamental to the users' understanding of the financial statements; this will not affect the audit opinion which will be unmodified in relation to this matter.

An emphasis of matter paragraph should be inserted after the opinion paragraph, the paragraph would explain clearly about the lawsuit and cross references to where in the financial statements the disclosure of this contingent liability can be found.

ACCA marking scheme

			Marks
(i)	**Wages program**		
	Up to 1 mark per valid point, overall maximum of 5 marks		
	Discussion of issue		
	Calculation of materiality		
	Opinion and report modified- material not pervasive		
	Qualified 'except for' opinion		
	Basis for paragraph		
	Position and reason for 'basis for'		
		Max	**5**
(ii)	**Lawsuit**		
	Up to 1 mark per valid point, overall maximum of 5 marks		
	Discussion of issue		
	Calculation of materiality		
	Unmodified opinion		
	Emphasis of matter paragraph		
	Position and reason for 'EOM'		
		Max	**5**
Total			**10**

Examiner's comments

The question required a discussion of two issues in the scenario as well as a description of the impact on the audit report if these issues remain unresolved. Candidates' performance was unsatisfactory on this question.

Each of the issues had a maximum of 5 marks available and in order to score well candidates needed to consider the following in their answer:

- A description of the audit issue; such as lack of evidence to support wages or contingent liability disclosure.
- A calculation of whether the issue was material or not, using the financial information provided in the scenario.
- An explanation of the type of audit report required.
- A description of the impact on the audit report.

With regards to the type of audit report required, many candidates provided a scatter gun approach of suggesting every possible audit report option. Candidates often hedge their bets by saying 'if management will make an amendment then we will give an unmodified opinion, however if they do not make the adjustment then we will give a qualified except for opinion.' Giving every possible audit report option will not allow candidates to score well.

Many candidates used terms such as 'except for', 'modified' or 'qualified' but the accompanying sentences demonstrated that candidates did not actually understand what these terms meant. In addition a significant proportion of candidates do not understand when an 'emphasis of matter' paragraph is relevant, and seemed to think that it was an alternative to an 'except for' qualification. Also candidates are reminded that since the clarified ISAs have been issued the old terminology of 'disagreement' is no longer relevant and instead should refer to 'material misstatement'.

In relation to the impact on the audit report, many candidates were unable to describe how the opinion paragraph would change and that a basis for qualified opinion paragraph was necessary for issue (i).

In addition a significant proportion of candidates provided procedures the auditor would undertake in order to understand or resolve the issues. For example, alternative procedures for verifying wages were given, or the steps to take in contacting lawyers in relation to the lawsuit. Whilst valid procedures, they did not score any marks as they were not part of the question requirement. Candidates must answer the question asked and not the one they wish had been asked.

Future candidates are once again reminded that audit reports are the only output of a statutory audit and hence an understanding of how an audit report can be modified and in which circumstances, is considered very important for this exam.

198 MICKEY *Walk in the footsteps of a top tutor*

Top Tutor Tips

Part (a) is quite tricky but easy marks can be earned by taking a logical and common sense approach. Think about what happens when the auditor identifies misstatements and what they have to do to try and get them resolved.

Part (b) is a straightforward audit reporting requirement. When discussing the impact on the audit report remember that the opinion is only one element of the report. Consider whether there is a need for any further modifications such as a 'basis for' paragraph if you are suggesting the opinion should be modified.

(a) **Misstatements**

ISA 450 *Evaluation of Misstatements Identified During the Audit* considers what a misstatement is and deals with the auditor's responsibility in relation to misstatements.

It identifies a misstatement as being: A difference between the amount, classification, presentation, or disclosure of a reported financial statement item and the amount, classification, presentation, or disclosure that is required for the item to be in accordance with the applicable financial reporting framework. Misstatements can arise from error or fraud.

It also then defines uncorrected misstatements as: Misstatements that the auditor has accumulated during the audit and that have not been corrected.

There are three categories of misstatements:

(i) Factual misstatements are misstatements about which there is no doubt.

(ii) Judgemental misstatements are differences arising from the judgements of management concerning accounting estimates that the auditor considers unreasonable, or the selection or application of accounting policies that the auditor considers inappropriate.

(iii) Projected misstatements are the auditor's best estimate of misstatements in populations, involving the projection of misstatements identified in audit samples to the entire populations from which the samples were drawn.

The auditor has a responsibility to accumulate misstatements which arise over the course of the audit unless they are very small amounts.

Identified misstatements should be considered during the course of the audit to assess whether the audit strategy and plan should be revised.

The auditor should determine whether uncorrected misstatements are material in aggregate or individually.

All misstatements should be communicated to those charged with governance on a timely basis and request that they make necessary amendments. If this request is refused then the auditor should consider the potential impact on their audit report.

A written representation should be requested from management to confirm that unadjusted misstatements are immaterial.

> ***Tutorial note***
>
> *The model answer is more comprehensive than would be expected for 5 marks; this is because ISA 450 is a relatively new auditing standard and the above has been presented as a teaching resource.*

(b) **Depreciation on land and buildings**

Depreciation has been provided on the land element of property, plant and equipment and this is contrary to IAS 16 *Property, Plant and Equipment,* as depreciation should only be charged on buildings.

The error is material as it represents 7% of profit before tax (0·7m/10m) and hence management should remove this from the financial statements.

If management refuse to amend this error then the audit report will need to be modified. As management has not complied with IAS 16 and the error is material but not pervasive then a qualified opinion would be necessary.

A basis for qualified opinion paragraph would need to be included explaining the material misstatement in relation to the provision of depreciation on land and the effect on the financial statements. The opinion paragraph would be qualified 'except for' – due to material misstatement.

ACCA marking scheme

			Marks
(a)	Up to 1 mark per well explained point		
	Definition of misstatements		
	Definition of uncorrected misstatements		
	Factual misstatements		
	Judgemental misstatements		
	Projected misstatements		
	Auditor should accumulate misstatements		
	Consider if audit strategy/plan should be revised		
	Assess if uncorrected misstatements material		
	Communicate to those charged with governance, request changes		
	If refused then assess impact on audit report		
	Request written representation		
		Max	**5**
(b)	Up to 1 mark per valid point		
	Discussion of issue		
	Calculation of materiality		
	Opinion and report modified- material not pervasive		
	Qualified 'except for' opinion		
	Basis for paragraph		
		Max	**5**
Total			**10**

Examiner's comments

Part (a) for 5 marks required an explanation of the term 'misstatement' and a description of the auditor's responsibility in relation to misstatements. This question was unrelated to the scenario, and was not answered well by many candidates. Most candidates were able to gain 1 mark by explaining that a misstatement was an error, however they could not then explain the auditor's responsibility.

ISA 450 *Evaluation of Misstatements Identified During the Audit* provides guidance on this area. This is a relatively new ISA and was issued as part of the clarity project. As this ISA had not yet been tested then this is an area which should have been prioritised by candidates. However, many candidates clearly had not studied this area at all. They therefore provided answers which focused on the auditor's responsibilities to provide an opinion on the truth and fairness of the financial statements or to detect material misstatements. In addition a minority of candidates produced answers which focused on materiality.

Part (b) required a discussion of an accounting issue as well as a description of the impact on the audit report if the issue remains unresolved. Candidates' performance was unsatisfactory on this question.

In order to score well candidates needed to consider the following in their answer:

- A description of the audit issue; such as incorrectly depreciating land.
- A calculation of whether the issue was material or not, using the financial information provided in the scenario.
- An explanation of the type of audit report required.
- A description of the impact on the audit report. A significant minority of candidates stated that it was acceptable to depreciate land, and the issue was that it should have been charged for the prior year as well. This demonstrates a fundamental lack of accounting knowledge. In relation to the materiality calculation, some candidates stated the issue was material but without using the financial information provided. What was required was a calculation, for example, the land depreciation was $0.7m and so represented 7% of profit before tax, and then an explanation of whether this was material or not. The benchmark from ISA 320 *Materiality in Planning* and Performing an Audit of 5% of profit before tax was taken as being material.

With regards to the type of audit report required, many candidates provided a scatter gun approach of suggesting every possible audit report option. Candidates often hedge their bets by saying 'if management will make an amendment then we will give an unmodified opinion, however if they do not make the adjustment then we will give a qualified except for opinion.' Giving every possible audit report option will not allow candidates to score well.

Many candidates used terms such as 'except for', 'modified' or 'qualified' but the accompanying sentences demonstrated that candidates did not actually understand what these terms meant. In addition a significant proportion of candidates do not understand when an 'emphasis of matter' paragraph is relevant, and seemed to think that it was an alternative to an 'except for' qualification. Also candidates are reminded that since the clarified ISAs have been issued the old terminology of 'disagreement' is no longer relevant and instead should refer to 'material misstatement'.

In relation to the impact on the audit report, many candidates were unable to describe how the opinion paragraph would change and that a basis for qualified opinion paragraph was necessary.

In addition a significant proportion of candidates provided procedures the auditor would undertake in order to understand or resolve the issues. Whilst valid procedures, they did not score any marks as they were not part of the question requirement. Candidates must answer the question asked and not the one they wish had been asked.

Future candidates are once again reminded that audit reports are the only output of a statutory audit and hence an understanding of how an audit report can be modified and in which circumstances, is considered very important for this exam.

199 GREENFIELDS CO *Walk in the footsteps of a top tutor*

Online question assistance

Top Tutor Tips

Part (a) asks you to discuss the appropriateness of written representations as evidence for the receivables balance and the warranty provision. You must apply your knowledge to the specific issues described.

Part (b) then introduces a client imposed limitation of scope – refusal to provide written representations. A reasonable mark can be achieved by discussing, in general terms, the impact on the audit report if the auditor cannot obtain sufficient appropriate evidence. To achieve a higher mark a good understanding of the importance of written representations is necessary.

The highlighted words are key phases that markers are looking for.

(a) **Receivables balance owing from Yellowmix Co**

The written representation proposed by management is intended to verify valuation, existence and rights and obligations of a material receivables balance. As management has refused to allow the auditor to circularise the balance and there has been little activity on the account for the past six months then there is very little evidence that has been obtained by the auditor.

This representation would constitute entity generated evidence and this is less reliable than auditor generated evidence or evidence from an external source. If related control systems operate effectively then this evidence becomes more reliable. In addition if the representation is written as opposed to oral then this will increase the reliability as an evidence source.

Overall this representation is a weak form of evidence, as there were more reliable evidence options available, such as the circularisation but this was not undertaken.

Warranty provision

In this case the auditor has performed some testing of the provision in order to obtain auditor generated evidence. The team has tested the calculations and assumptions. None of this is evidence from an external source.

The very nature of this provision means that it is difficult for the auditor to obtain a significant amount of reliable evidence as to the level of future warranty claims. Hence the written representation, whilst being an entity generated source of evidence, would still be useful as there are few other alternatives.

Top tutor tips

Remember that written representations cannot be used to replace more reliable evidence that would normally be expected to exist. Here, in relation to the balance owed from Yellowmix, the auditor would normally obtain written confirmation from a receivables circularisation. A written representation cannot replace this better evidence. Explain why it is better evidence but conclude that a written representation would not be appropriate.

However, the provision relates to future outflow of economic benefit and therefore there is unlikely to be reliable evidence available. It would be normal to obtain a written representation from management confirming the reliability of accounting estimates, such as the provision.

(b) **Steps to take if written representation on warranty provision is not provided**

ISA 580 Written *Representations* provides guidance to the auditor in the case where written representations are requested from management but they refuse to provide.

If management does not provide the requested written representation on the warranty provision the auditor of Greenfields should discuss the matter with management to understand why they are refusing.

In addition the auditor should re-evaluate the integrity of Greenfields' management and consider the effect that this may have on the reliability of other representations (oral or written) and audit evidence in general.

The auditor should then take appropriate actions, including determining the possible effect on the audit opinion.

Impact on audit report

As the auditor is unable to obtain sufficient appropriate evidence to conclude that the warranty provision is free from material misstatement then a modified audit opinion will be required.

The warranty provision is material but not pervasive and therefore a qualified opinion would be appropriate.

The audit report will require a 'basis for' paragraph before the opinion which will describe the reason for the modification; namely that management refused to provide a written representation in relation to the warranty provision and hence we are unable to form an opinion on this balance. The opinion paragraph will be amended to state 'except for'.

ACCA marking scheme			
			Marks
(a)	Up to 2 marks for each discussion of reliability of representations		
	Receivable balance		
	Warranty provision		
			4
		Max	
(b)	Up to 1 mark per point		
	ISA 580 provides guidance		
	Discuss with management		
	Re-evaluate management integrity		
	Consider impact on audit opinion		
	Modified opinion		
	Qualified opinion as not pervasive		
	Additional paragraph describing modification		
	'Except for' opinion		
		Max	6
Total			10

200 GOING CONCERN *Walk in the footsteps of a top tutor*

Top Tutor Tips

Part (a) asks you what procedures you would perform during the audit in respect of going concern. A company will remain a going concern if it has sufficient cash to meet its debts when they fall due. Procedures therefore need to focus on gathering evidence that the company will be able to do this.

Part (b) When discussing the audit report there are two ways it can be modified: by modifying the wording of your opinion or by adding an additional paragraph. The latter is never used to explain the opinion and it has no effect on it.

The highlighted words are key phases that markers are looking for.

(a) **Procedures**

- Obtain the company's cash flow forecast and review the cash in and out flows. Assess the assumptions for reasonableness and discuss the findings with management to understand if the company will have sufficient cash flows.
- Perform a sensitivity analysis on the cash flows to understand the margin of safety the company has in terms of its net cash in/out flow.
- Review any current agreements with the bank to determine whether any key ratios have been breached. Review any bank correspondence to assess the likelihood of the bank providing additional facility.
- Review the company's post year end sales and order book to assess if the levels of trade are likely to increase and if the revenue figures in the cash flow forecast are reasonable.
- Review post year end correspondence with suppliers to identify if any restrictions in credit have arisen, and if so ensure that the cash flow forecast reflects an immediate payment for trade payables.

- Enquire of the lawyers as to the existence of litigation and claims, if any exist then consider their materiality and impact on the going concern basis.
- Perform audit tests in relation to subsequent events to identify any items that might indicate or mitigate the risk of going concern not being appropriate.
- Review the post year end board minutes to identify any other issues that might indicate financial difficulties for the company.
- Review post year end management accounts to assess if in line with cash flow forecast.
- Consider whether any additional disclosures as required by IAS 1 *Presentation of Financial Statements* in relation to material uncertainties over going concern should be made in the financial statements.
- Obtain a written representation confirming the director's view that the company is a going concern.

(b) The directors of Kennedy Co have agreed to make going concern disclosures, however, the impact on the audit report will be dependent on the adequacy of these disclosures.

If the disclosures are adequate, then the audit opinion will be unmodified. However, an emphasis of matter paragraph would be required, therefore the report will be modified.

This will state that the audit opinion is not modified, identify that there is a material uncertainty and will cross reference to the disclosure note made by management, this paragraph would be included after the opinion paragraph.

If the disclosures made by management are not adequate the audit report and opinion will need to be modified due to material misstatement.

The modification required will depend on the materiality of the issue. This will be either a qualified or an adverse opinion.

A 'basis for' paragraph describing the matter giving rise to the modification will be included just before the opinion paragraph.

ACCA marking scheme		
		Marks
(a)	Up to 1 mark per well explained point – If the procedure does not clearly explain how this will help the auditor to consider going concern then a ½ mark only should be awarded: – Review cash flow forecasts – Sensitivity analysis – Review bank agreements, breach of key ratios – Review bank correspondence – Review post year end sales and order book – Review suppliers correspondence – Inquire lawyers any litigation – Subsequent events – Board minutes – Management accounts – Consider additional disclosures under IAS 1 – Written representation	
	Max	**6**

ACCA marking scheme		
		Marks
(b)	Up to 1 mark per point – Depends on adequacy of disclosures – Adequately disclosed – unmodified – Emphasis of matter para – after opinion – Not adequately disclosed – modified – Material misstatement – Basis for paragraph before opinion and impact on opinion paragraph	
	Max	**4**
Total		**10**

201 REPORTING

(a) **Importance of reporting to those charged with governance**

In accordance with ISA 260 *Communication with Those Charged with Governance*, it is important for the auditors to report to those charged with governance as it helps in the following ways:

(1) It assists the auditor and those charged with governance in understanding matters related to the audit, and in developing a constructive working relationship. This relationship is developed while maintaining the auditor's independence and objectivity.

(2) It helps the auditor in obtaining, from those charged with governance, information relevant to the audit. For example, those charged with governance may assist the auditor in understanding the entity and its environment, in identifying appropriate sources of audit evidence and in providing information about specific transactions or events.

(3) It helps those charged with governance in fulfilling their responsibility to oversee the financial reporting process, thereby reducing the risks of material misstatement of the financial statements.

(b) **Matters to be communicated to those charged with governance**

- The auditor's responsibilities with regards to providing an opinion on the financial statements and that they have carried out their work in accordance with International Standards on Auditing.
- The auditor should explain the planned approach to the audit as well as the audit timetable.
- Any key audit risks identified during the planning stage should be communicated.
- In addition, any significant difficulties encountered during the audit should be communicated.
- Also significant matters arising during the audit, as well as significant accounting adjustments.
- During the audit any significant deficiencies in the internal control system identified should be communicated in writing or verbally.

- Those charged with governance should be notified of any written representations required by the auditor.
- Other matters arising from the audit that are significant to the oversight of the financial reporting process.
- If any suspected frauds are identified during the audit, these must be communicated.
- If the auditors are intending to make any modifications to the audit opinion, these should be communicated to those charged with governance.
- For listed entities, a confirmation that the auditors have complied with ethical standards and appropriate safeguards have been put in place for any ethical threats identified.

(c) **Pervasive**

Pervasive in the context of the audit report means the financial statements are materially misstated to such an extent that they are unreliable as a whole.

This may be where there are multiple material misstatements and is therefore not isolated to just one area of the financial statements.

Material misstatements may be isolated to one balance but they represent a substantial proportion of the financial statements that the effect is pervasive.

In relation to disclosures, the effect will be pervasive if a disclosure is fundamental to the users understanding of the financial statements.

(d) **Modified opinions**

Qualified

Used where there is a material, but not pervasive, material misstatement or inability to obtain sufficient appropriate evidence. The wording of the report states that except for the matter giving rise to the modification, the financial statements show a true and fair view.

Adverse

Used where there is material misstatement in the financial statements that has a pervasive effect, for example if the going concern basis of preparation had been used when the company was not a going concern.

Disclaimer of opinion

Used where the auditor has been unable to obtain sufficient appropriate evidence for a substantial proportion of the financial statements and the effects are potentially pervasive, for example if the majority of the client's accounting records had been destroyed and no back-ups were available.

ACCA marking scheme		
		Marks
(a)	Up to 1 mark per well explained point	
	Assists the auditor and those charged with governance in understanding matters related to the audit	
	Obtains information relevant to the audit	
	Helps those charged with governance in fulfilling their responsibility to oversee the financial reporting process	
	Max	**2**
(b)	Up to 1 mark for each example matter to be communicated to those charged with governance.	
	Auditor responsibilities	
	Planned audit approach	
	Key audit risks	
	Significant difficulties encountered	
	Significant deficiencies in internal control	
	Written representations required	
	Other matters significant to oversight of FR process	
	Suspected fraud	
	Expected modifications to the audit report	
	Independence issues (listed entities)	
	Max	**3**
(c)	1 mark per point	
	Renders FS as a whole unreliable	
	Not isolated	
	If isolated, substantial proportion of FS	
	Disclosures which are fundamental to users understanding	
	Max	**2**
(d)	½ mark for naming the opinion and ½ mark for explanation.	
	Qualified – material misstatement/unable to obtain sufficient appropriate evidence	
	Adverse	
	Disclaimer	
	Max	**3**
Total		**10**

AUDIT FRAMEWORK

202 TRUE & FAIR/ISAs/RIGHTS *Walk in the footsteps of a top tutor*

Top Tutor Tips

This is a tricky knowledge based question.

Part (a) is for 4 marks – start by explaining the overall concept of 'true and fair' and then explain each component individually. You will need to make at least four points in total. Be careful to answer only the requirement set and not stray into explaining broader concepts such as materiality.

Be careful to read the requirement in part (b) carefully – you are asked to explain the status of ISAs. This means the authority of ISAs, overall contents, the types of assignments they apply to and how they interact with other legislation.

Part (c) asks you to state the rights of auditors EXCLUDING those relating to resignation. Be careful to read the requirement carefully as any rights that are specific to resignation of auditors will not earn any marks.

The highlighted words are key phases that markers are looking for.

(a) **True and Fair presentation**

Financial statements are produced by management which give a true and fair view of the entity's results. The auditor in reviewing these financial statements gives an opinion on the truth and fairness of them.

Although there is no definition in the International Standards on Auditing of true and fair it is generally considered to have the following meaning:

True – Information is factual and conforms with reality in that there are no factual errors. In addition it is assumed that to be true it must comply with accounting standards and any relevant legislation. Lastly true includes data being correctly transferred from accounting records to the financial statements.

Fair – Information is clear, impartial and unbiased, and also reflects plainly the commercial substance of the transactions of the entity.

(b) **International Standards on Auditing**

International Standards on Auditing (ISAs) are issued by the International Auditing and Assurance Standards Board (IAASB) and provide guidance on the performance of an audit.

ISAs only apply to the audit of historical financial information. They are written in the context of an audit of financial statements by an independent auditor.

The ISAs contain basic principles and essential procedures together with related guidance in the form of explanatory material and appendices. It is necessary to consider and understand the entire text of an ISA to understand and apply the basic principles and essential procedures.

The basic principles and essential procedures of an ISA are to be applied in all cases. If in exceptional cases the auditor deems it necessary to depart from an ISA to achieve the overall aim of the audit, then this departure must be justified.

(c) **Auditors' rights**

- Right of access at all times to the company's books, accounts and vouchers.
- Right to require from an officer of the company such information or explanations as they think necessary for the performance of their duties as auditors.
- Right to receive all communications relating to written resolutions.
- Right to receive all notices of, and other communications relating to, any general meeting which a member of the company is entitled to receive.
- Right to attend any general meeting of the company.
- Right to be heard at any general meeting which an auditor attends on any part of the business of the meeting which concerns them as auditor.

ACCA marking scheme

		Marks
(a)	Up to 1 mark per valid point	
	Accounts produced and auditors give opinion on true and fair view	
	True – factual, conforms with reality	
	True – conforms with standards and legislation	
	True – correctly transferred from accounting records	
	Fair – clear, plain and unbiased	
	Fair – reflects commercial substance	
	Max	**4**
(b)	Up to 1 mark per valid point	
	Issued by IAASB	
	Apply to audit of historical financial information	
	Contain basic principles/essential procedures/explanatory material and appendices	
	If depart from ISA – justify	
	Max	**2**
(c)	Up to 1 mark per valid point	
	Access to books and records	
	Information and explanations	
	Receive written resolutions	
	Notice of and communication relating to general meetings	
	Attend general meetings	
	Be heard at general meetings on audit matters	
	Max	**4**
Total		**10**

203 AUDIT AND ASSURANCE

(a) **Limited assurance**

Limited assurance is a moderate level of assurance. The objective of a limited assurance engagement is to obtain sufficient appropriate evidence that the subject matter is plausible in the circumstances.

With limited assurance, limited procedures are performed, mainly inquiries and analytical procedures.

A statutory audit provides reasonable assurance, which is a high level of assurance, or confidence.

The objective of a statutory audit is to obtain sufficient appropriate evidence that the financial statements conform in all material respects with the relevant financial reporting framework.

More evidence will need to be obtained to provide reasonable assurance, and a wider range of procedures performed, including tests of detail, analytical procedures and tests of controls.

A limited assurance report provides a negative opinion. The practitioner will state that nothing has come to their attention which indicates that the cash flow forecast contains any material errors. The assurance is therefore given on the absence of any indication to the contrary.

The statutory audit report provides a positive opinion; that is the financial statements do (or don't) show a true and fair view.

(b) The purpose of the external audit under International Standards on Auditing is for the auditor to obtain sufficient appropriate audit evidence on which to base the audit opinion. This opinion is on whether the financial statements give a 'true and fair view' (or 'present fairly in all material respects') of the position, performance (and cash flows) of the entity. This opinion is prepared for the benefit of shareholders.

Companies are owned by shareholders but they are managed by directors (in very small companies, owners and managers are the same, but many such companies are not subject to statutory audit requirements).

Those who own the company wish to ensure that those to whom they have entrusted control are looking after their investment. This is known as the 'stewardship' function.

The requirement for an independent audit helps ensure that financial statements are free of bias and manipulation for the benefit of users of financial information.

The requirement for a statutory audit is a public interest issue: the public is invited to invest in enterprises, it is in the interests of the capital markets (and society as a whole) that those investing do so in the knowledge that they will be provided with 'true and fair' information about the enterprise.

(c) **Limitations of external audits**

An external audit has a number of limitations which reduce its usefulness:

Sampling

It is not practical for an auditor to test 100% of transactions and so they have to apply sampling methodologies in selecting balances/transactions to test. Therefore, there could be an error in an item not selected for testing by the auditor.

Subjectivity

Financial statements include judgemental and subjective areas and therefore the auditor is required to use their judgement in assessing whether the financial statements are true and fair.

Inherent limitations of internal control systems

An internal control system is operated by people and hence is liable to human error. In addition, there is the possibility of controls override by management and of collusion and fraud. It is impossible to remove all of these inherent limitations and as the auditor relies on the internal control systems, this can reduce the usefulness of the audit.

Evidence is persuasive not conclusive

The opinion is based on audit evidence gathered; however, while this evidence can indicate possible issues affecting the audit opinion, evidence involves estimates and judgements and hence does not give a definite conclusion.

Audit report format

The format of the opinion is determined by International Standards on Auditing. However, the terminology used is not usually understood by non-accountants. This means that users may not actually understand the audit opinion given.

Historic information

The audit report is often issued some time after the year end, and so the financial information can be quite different to the current position. In the current marketplace where companies' financial positions can change quite quickly, the audit opinion may no longer be relevant as it is out of date.

ACCA marking scheme			
			Marks
(a)	Up to 1 mark per well explained point Limited assurance = moderate assurance Subject matter is plausible Limited procedures performed Audit gives reasonable assurance = high level Subject matter conforms with suitable criteria More evidence required inc TOC Ltd assurance – negative conclusion Nothing has come to our attention... Audit – positive opinion		
		Max	**5**
(b)	Up to 1 mark per well explained point Provide opinion on FS – TFV Separation of ownership and control Efficient capital markets		
		Max	**2**
(c)	Up to 1 mark per well explained limitation Sampling Subjectivity Inherent limitations of internal control systems Evidence is persuasive not conclusive Audit report format Historic information		
		Max	**3**
Total			**10**

204 CHANGE OF AUDITOR

(a) **Steps**

- A meeting must be arranged giving special notice to vote in favour of the auditor's removal.
- At least 51% of the shareholders must vote in favour of the removal.
- The auditor must submit a statement of circumstances to the registered office.
- The auditor must return any books and records that belong to the client.
- The auditor can choose to speak at the general meeting of the shareholders to communicate any issues they wish the shareholders to be aware of.
- The auditor should respond promptly to any requests for information.

(b) **Professional clearance**

- Request permission from the entity to contact the outgoing auditor.
- If permission is not given, consider refusing the engagement as this may cast doubt over management integrity.
- If permission is given, write to the outgoing auditor asking for any professional reasons they should be aware of for the change of auditor that may affect their acceptance decision.
- If no response is received, a follow up letter should be sent.
- If a response is still not received the auditor should consider carefully whether they should accept the engagement. The lack of response may indicate issues with the entity.
- The outgoing auditor will also need to obtain permission from the client to respond to the new auditor's request for information.
- If permission is not given, the outgoing auditor should inform the new auditor of this fact.

ACCA marking scheme		
		Marks
(a)	Up to 1 mark per well explained point	
	Meeting with special notice	
	Majority vote in favour	
	Statement of circumstances	
	Return books and records belonging to the client	
	Speak at general meeting	
	Respond promptly to requests from incoming auditors	
	Max	**5**
(b)	Up to 1 mark per explained point	
	Incoming auditor request permission from entity	
	Consider refusing if permission not given	
	Write to outgoing auditor if permission given	
	Follow up if no response	
	Consider acceptance carefully if no response received after follow up	
	Outgoing auditor request permission from entity	
	Inform new auditor if permission is not given	
	Max	**5**
Total		**10**

Fundamentals Level – Skills Module

Audit and Assurance

Specimen Exam applicable from December 2014

Time allowed
Reading and planning: 15 minutes
Writing: 3 hours

This paper is divided into two sections:

Section A – ALL TWELVE questions are compulsory and MUST be attempted

Section B – ALL SIX questions are compulsory and MUST be attempted

Do NOT open this paper until instructed by the supervisor.

During reading and planning time only the question paper may be annotated. You must NOT write in your answer booklet until instructed by the supervisor.

This question paper must not be removed from the examination hall.

The Association of Chartered Certified Accountants

Paper F8

ACCA

Section A – ALL TWELVE questions are compulsory and MUST be attempted

Please use the space provided on the inside cover of the Candidate Answer Booklet to indicate your chosen answer to each multiple choice question.

1 **Which of the following sampling methods correctly describes systematic sampling?**

A A sampling method which is a type of value-weighted selection in which sample size, selection and evaluation results in a conclusion in monetary amounts

B A sampling method which involves having a constant sampling interval, the starting point for testing is determined randomly

C A sampling method in which the auditor selects a block(s) of contiguous items from within the population

(1 mark)

2 An audit junior has been assigned to the audit of bank and cash balances of Howard Co. He has obtained the following audit evidence:

1 Bank reconciliation carried out by the cashier
2 Bank confirmation report from Howard's bankers
3 Verbal confirmation from the directors that the overdraft limit is to be increased
4 Cash count carried out by the audit junior

What is the order of reliability of the audit evidence starting with the most reliable first?

A 4, 2, 1 and 3
B 2, 1, 4 and 3
C 4, 3, 2 and 1
D 2, 4, 1 and 3

(2 marks)

3 Fellaini Co operate a large department store and have a large internal audit department in place. The management of Fellaini Co are keen to increase the range of assignments that internal audit undertake.

Which of the following assignments could the internal audit department of Fellaini Co be asked to perform by management?

A Internal audit department members could undertake 'mystery shopper' reviews, where they enter the store as a customer, purchase goods and rate the overall shopping experience

B Internal audit could be asked to assist the external auditors by requesting bank confirmation letters

C Internal audit could be asked to implement a new payroll package for the payroll department

D Internal audit could be asked to assist the finance department with the preparation of the year end financial statements.

(2 marks)

4 Application controls are manual or automated procedures that operate over accounting applications to ensure that all transactions are complete and accurate

Which TWO of the following are application controls?

1 Password protection of programs
2 Batch controls
3 One for one checking
4 Regular back up of programs

A 1 and 4
B 3 and 4
C 1 and 2
D 2 and 3

(2 marks)

5 Which TWO of the following are fundamental principles as stated in the ACCA's *Code of Ethics and Conduct*?

1 Objectivity
2 Independence
3 Confidentiality
4 Professional skepticism

A 1 and 4
B 1 and 2
C 2 and 3
D 1 and 3

(2 marks)

6 Auditors usually carry out their audit work at different stages known as the interim audit and the final audit.

Which of the following statements, if any, is/are correct?

1 Carrying out tests of control on the company's sales day books would normally be undertaken during an interim audit.
2 Review of aged receivables ledger to identify balances requiring write down or allowance would normally be undertaken during a final audit.

A Neither 1 nor 2
B Both 1 and 2
C 1 only
D 2 only

(2 marks)

7 Which of the following statements relate to review engagements?

1 Subject matter is plausible
2 Reasonable assurance
3 Nothing has come to our attention which would indicate that the subject matter contains material misstatements
4 Positive assurance

A 1 and 3
B 2 and 4
C 2 and 3
D 1 and 4

(2 marks)

8 When placing reliance on the work of an expert is the following statement true or false?

In order to place reliance, the auditor is required to evaluate the work performed by the expert.

A True
B False

(1 mark)

9 An emphasis of matter paragraph is used in an audit report to draw attention to a matter affecting the financial statements.

Which TWO of the following are correct in relation to an Emphasis of Matter Paragraph in the Auditor's Report?

1 It is used when there is a significant uncertainty
2 It constitutes a qualified audit opinion
3 The audit report is referred to as an unmodified report
4 The matter is deemed to be fundamental to the users understanding of the financial statements

A 1 and 2
B 1 and 4
C 1 and 3
D 2 and 4

(2 marks)

10 During the planning stages of the final audit, the auditor believes that the probability of giving an inappropriate audit opinion is too high.

How should the auditor amend the audit plan to resolve this issue?

A Increase the materiality level
B Decrease the inherent risk
C Decrease the detection risk

(1 mark)

11 The audit of Giggs Co's financial statements for the year ended 31 October 2014 has been completed; the audit report and the financial statements have been signed but not yet issued.

The finance director of Giggs Co has just informed the audit team that he has received notification that a material receivable balance has become irrecoverable and Giggs Co will not receive any of the amounts owing.

What actions, if any, should the auditor now take to satisfy their responsibilities under ISA 560 *Subsequent Events*?

A No actions required as the audit report and financial statements have already been signed
B Request management to adjust the financial statements, verify the adjustment and provide a new audit report
C Request management to make disclosure of this event in the financial statements
D Request that management adjust for this event in the following year's financial statements as it occurred in year ending 31 October 2015.

(2 marks)

12 ISA 315 *Identifying and Assessing the Risks of Material Misstatement through Understanding the Entity and Its Environment* sets out the five components of internal control.

Which of the following is NOT set out as a component of internal control within ISA 315?

A Control environment
B The information system relevant to financial reporting
C Human resource policies and practices

(1 mark)

Section B – ALL SIX questions are compulsory and MUST be attempted

1 The audit engagement partner for Hazard Co (Hazard), a listed company, has been in place for approximately six years and her son has just accepted a job offer from Hazard as a sales manager. This role would entitle him to shares in Hazard as part of his remuneration package.

Hazard's directors are considering establishing an internal audit department, and the finance director has asked the audit firm, Remy & Co about the differences between internal audit and external audit.

If the internal audit department is established, and Remy & Co is appointed as internal as well as external auditors, then Hazard has suggested that the external audit fee should be renegotiated with at least 20% of the fee being based on the profit after tax of the company as they feel this will align the interests of Remy & Co and Hazard.

Required:

(a) Using the information above:

(i) Explain the ethical threats which may affect the independence of Remy & Co in respect of the audit of Hazard Co; and (3 marks)

(ii) For each threat explain how it might be reduced to an acceptable level. (3 marks)

(b) Distinguish between internal and external audit. (4 marks)

(10 marks)

2 **(a)** Auditors are required to obtain sufficient appropriate audit evidence. Tests of control and substantive procedures can be used to obtain such evidence.

Required:

Define a 'test of control' and a 'substantive procedure'. (2 marks)

(b) Balotelli Beach Hotel Co (Balotelli) operates a hotel providing accommodation, leisure facilities and restaurants. Its year end was 31 October 2014. You are the audit senior of Mario & Co and are currently preparing the audit programmes for the year end audit of Balotelli. You are reviewing the notes of last week's meeting between the audit manager and finance director where two material issues were discussed.

Depreciation
Balotelli incurred significant capital expenditure during the year on updating the leisure facilities for the hotel. The finance director has proposed that the new leisure equipment should be depreciated over 10 years using the straight-line method.

Food poisoning
Balotelli's directors received correspondence in September from a group of customers who attended a wedding at the hotel. They have alleged that they suffered severe food poisoning from food eaten at the hotel and are claiming substantial damages. Balotelli's lawyers have received the claim and believe that the lawsuit against the company is unlikely to be successful.

Required:

Describe substantive procedures to obtain sufficient and appropriate audit evidence in relation to the above two issues.

Note: The total marks will be split equally between each issue. (8 marks)

(10 marks)

3 (a) You are the audit manager of Savage & Co and you are briefing your team on the approach to adopt in undertaking the review and finalisation stage of the audit. In particular, the audit senior is unsure about the steps to take in relation to uncorrected misstatements.

Required:

Describe the auditor's responsibility in respect of misstatements. (2 marks)

(b) You are the audit manager of Villa & Co and you are currently reviewing the audit files for several of your clients for which the audit fieldwork is complete. The audit seniors have raised the following issues:

Czech Co

Czech Co is a pharmaceutical company and has incurred research expenditure of $2·1m and development expenditure of $3·2m during the year, this has all been capitalised as an intangible asset. Profit before tax is $26·3m.

Dawson Co

Dawson Co's computerised wages program is backed up daily, however for a period of two months the wages records and the back-ups have been corrupted, and therefore cannot be accessed. Wages and salaries for these two months are $1·1m. Profit before tax is $10m.

Required:

For each of the clients above:

(i) Discuss the issue, including an assessment of whether it is material; and (4 marks)

(ii) Describe the impact on the audit report if the issue remains unresolved. (4 marks)

(10 marks)

4 (a) Explain FOUR financial statement assertions relevant to account balances at the period end. (4 marks)

(b) Torres Leisure Club Co (Torres) operates a chain of health and fitness clubs. Its year end was 31 October 2014. You are the audit manager and the year-end audit is due to commence shortly. The following matter has been brought to your attention. Torres's trade receivables have historically been low as most members pay monthly in advance. However during the year a number of companies have taken up group memberships at Torres and hence the receivables balance is now material. The audit senior has undertaken a receivables circularisation for the balances at the year end; however, there are a number who have not responded and a number of responses with differences.

Required:

Describe substantive procedures you would perform to obtain sufficient and appropriate audit evidence in relation to Torres's trade receivables. (6 marks)

(10 marks)

5 You are the audit senior of Holtby & Co and are planning the audit of Walters Co (Walters) for the year ended 31 December 2014. The company produces printers and has been a client of your firm for two years; your audit manager has already had a planning meeting with the finance director. He has provided you with the following notes of his meeting and financial statement extracts.

Walters's management were disappointed with the 2013 results and so in 2014 undertook a number of strategies to improve the trading results. This included the introduction of a generous sales-related bonus scheme for their salesmen and a high profile advertising campaign. In addition, as market conditions are difficult for their customers, they have extended the credit period given to them.

The finance director of Walters has reviewed the inventory valuation policy and has included additional overheads incurred this year as he considers them to be production related.

The finance director has calculated a few key ratios for Walters; the gross profit margin has increased from 44·4% to 52·2% and receivables days have increased from 61 days to 71 days. He is happy with the 2014 results and feels that they are a good reflection of the improved trading levels.

Financial statement extracts for year ended 31 December

	DRAFT 2014 $m	**ACTUAL 2013 $m**
Revenue	23·0	18·0
Cost of sales	(11·0)	(10·0)
Gross profit	12·0	8·0
Operating expenses	(7·5)	(4·0)
Profit before interest and taxation	4·5	4·0
Inventory	2·1	1·6
Receivables	4·5	3·0
Cash	–	2·3
Trade payables	1·6	1·2
Overdraft	0·9	–

Required:

(a) Using the information above:

(i) Calculate an additional THREE ratios, for BOTH years, which would assist the audit senior in planning the audit; and (3 marks)

(ii) From a review of the above information and the ratios calculated, describe SIX audit risks and explain the auditor's response to each risk in planning the audit of Walters Co. (12 marks)

(b) Describe the procedures that the auditor of Walters Co should perform in assessing whether or not the company is a going concern. (5 marks)

(20 marks)

6 Garcia International Co (Garcia) is a manufacturer of electrical equipment. It has factories across the country and its customer base includes retailers as well as individuals, to whom direct sales are made through their website. The company's year end is 30 September 2014. You are an audit supervisor of Suarez & Co and are currently reviewing documentation of Garcia's internal control in preparation for the interim audit.

Garcia's website allows individuals to order goods directly, and full payment is taken in advance. Currently the website is not integrated into the inventory system and inventory levels are not checked at the time when orders are placed. Inventory is valued at the lower of cost and net realisable value.

Goods are despatched via local couriers; however, they do not always record customer signatures as proof that the customer has received the goods. Over the past 12 months there have been customer complaints about the delay between sales orders and receipt of goods. Garcia has investigated these and found that, in each case, the sales order had been entered into the sales system correctly but was not forwarded to the despatch department for fulfilling.

Garcia's retail customers undergo credit checks prior to being accepted and credit limits are set accordingly by sales ledger clerks. These customers place their orders through one of the sales team, who decides on sales discount levels.

Raw materials used in the manufacturing process are purchased from a wide range of suppliers. As a result of staff changes in the purchase ledger department, supplier statement reconciliations are no longer performed. Additionally, changes to supplier details in the purchase ledger master file can be undertaken by purchase ledger clerks as well as supervisors.

In the past six months Garcia has changed part of its manufacturing process and as a result some new equipment has been purchased, however, there are considerable levels of plant and equipment which are now surplus to requirement. Purchase requisitions for all new equipment have been authorised by production supervisors and little has been done to reduce the surplus of old equipment.

Required:

(a) In respect of the internal control of Garcia International Co:

(i) Identify and explain SIX deficiencies;

(ii) Recommend a control to address each of these deficiencies; and

(iii) Describe a test of control Suarez & Co would perform to assess if each of these controls is operating effectively.

Note: The total marks will be split equally between each part (18 marks)

(b) Describe substantive procedures Suarez & Co should perform at the year end to confirm plant and equipment additions. (2 marks)

(20 marks)

End of Question Paper

Answers

Section A

Question	Answer	See Note
1	**B**	1
2	**D**	2
3	**A**	3
4	**D**	4
5	**D**	5
6	**B**	6
7	**A**	7
8	**A**	8
9	**B**	9
10	**C**	10
11	**B**	11
12	**C**	12

Notes:

1 The descriptions are correct but relate to alternative sampling methods. A is monetary unit sampling and C is block selection method of sampling.

2 Audit evidence is often described in terms of the degree of reliability. Third party as most reliable followed by auditor generated, company documentation and least reliable verbal evidence.

3 B is incorrect as external auditors alone would request bank confirmation letters, this is not something they would expect internal audit to perform. C is incorrect since internal audit would not retain their independence if they implemented accounting packages; their role is to review how the package operates once implemented. D is incorrect as internal audit should not help prepare financial statements.

4 The controls given at 1 and 4 are incorrect as they are general IT controls that relate to many applications and support the overall IT system.

5 Professional skepticism refers to the state of mind the auditor should maintain whilst conducting the audit. With regards to independence there is an overriding requirement to be independent rather than it being a specific principle.

6 Tests of control are typically undertaken at the interim audit stage. Reviewing the aged receivables would be undertaken on the year end balances and hence at the final audit.

7 Statements 2 and 4 are incorrect as they relate to the level of assurance provided by an external audit rather than a review engagement.

8 The auditor can only rely on the work undertaken by an expert if this has been evaluated.

9 Statement 2 is incorrect since an emphasis of matter does not result in a qualified opinion. Statement 3 is incorrect as an emphasis of matter results in the report being modified but the opinion is unqualified.

10 It is inappropriate to adjust materiality levels to determine audit risk. Inherent risk is not under the auditor's control. Audit risk depends on inherent risk, control risk and detection risk. Only detection risk can be changed by the auditor to reduce audit risk.

11 A is incorrect as even though the financial statements have been signed the auditor has an on-going responsibility. C is incorrect as this is an adjusting event and so must be adjusted for as opposed to just disclosed. D is incorrect as the event requires adjustment in the current year financial statements even though it occurred in year ending 31 October 2015.

12 Human resource policies and practices is an element of a control environment which is itself a component of internal control.

Section B

1 **(a) Ethical threats and managing these risks**

Ethical threat	Managing risk
A familiarity threat arises where an engagement partner is associated with a client for a long period of time. Remy's partner has been involved in the audit of Hazard Co for six years and hence may not maintain her professional skepticism and objectivity.	Remy & Co should monitor the relationship between engagement and client staff, and should consider rotating engagement partners when a long association has occurred. In addition, ACCA's *Code of Ethics and Conduct* recommends that engagement partners rotate off an audit after five years for listed and public interest entities. Therefore consideration should be given to appointing an alternative audit partner.
The engagement partner's son has accepted a job as a sales manager at Hazard Co. This could represent a self-interest/familiarity threat if the son was involved in the financial statement process.	It is unlikely that as a sales manager the son would be in a position to influence the financial statements and hence additional safeguards would not be necessary. If it was believed that additional safeguards were required then consideration should be given to appointing an alternative audit partner.
A self-interest threat can arise when an audit firm has a financial interest in the company. In this case the partner's son will receive shares as part of his remuneration. As the son is an immediate family member of the partner then if he holds the shares it will be as if the partner holds these shares, and this is prohibited.	In this case as holding shares is prohibited by ACCA's *Code of Ethics and Conduct* then either the son should refuse the shares or more likely the engagement partner will need to be removed from the audit.
A self-review threat can arise when an audit firm provides an internal audit service to an audit client.	Remy & Co should have appropriate safeguards by ensuring the audit team is not involved in the internal audit service and also ensuring client staff remain responsible for the internal audit activities and approve all the work done.
Fees based on the outcome or results of work performed are known as contingent fees and are prohibited by ACCA's *Code of Ethics and Conduct*. Hence Hazard's request that 20% of the external audit fee is based on profit after tax would represent a contingent fee.	Remy & Co will not be able to accept contingent fees and should communicate to Hazard that the external audit fee needs to be based on the time spent and level of work performed

(b) Differences between internal and external audit

External Audit	Internal Audit
Objective The main objective of the external auditor is to express an opinion on the truth and fairness of the financial statements.	The main objective of internal audit is to improve a company's operations, by reviewing the efficiency and effectiveness of the company's internal controls.
Reporting External auditors report to the shareholders or members of the company. External audit reports are contained within the financial statements and hence are publicly available.	Internal auditors normally report to management or those charged with governance. Internal audit reports are not publicly available and are only intended to be seen by the addressee of the report. The reports are normally provided to the board of directors and those charged with governance such as the audit committee.
Scope of work The external auditor's work is limited to verifying the truth and fairness of the financial statements of the company.	The internal auditor can have a wide scope of work and it is determined by the requirements of management or those charged with governance. Commonly internal audit focus on the company's internal control environment, but any other area of a company's operations can be reviewed.
Relationship with company External auditors are appointed by the company's shareholders. They are independent of the company.	Internal auditors are appointed by management. As internal auditors are normally employees of the company they lack independence. However, the internal audit department can be outsourced and this can increase their independence.

2 (a) Tests of control and substantive procedures

Tests of control test the operating effectiveness of controls in preventing, detecting or correcting material misstatements.

Substantive procedures are aimed at detecting material misstatements at the assertion level. They include tests of detail of transactions, balances, disclosures and substantive analytical procedures

(b) Substantive procedures

Depreciation

- Review the reasonableness of the depreciation rates applied to the new leisure facilities and compare to industry averages.
- Review the capital expenditure budgets for the next few years to assess whether there are any plans to replace any of the new leisure equipment, as this would indicate that the useful life is less than 10 years.
- Review profits and losses on disposal of assets disposed of in the year, to assess the reasonableness of the depreciation policies.
- Select a sample of leisure equipment and recalculate the depreciation charge to ensure that the non-current asset register is correct.
- Perform a proof in total calculation for the depreciation charged on the equipment, discuss with management if significant fluctuations arise.
- Review the disclosure of the depreciation charges and policies in the draft financial statements.

Food poisoning

- Review the correspondence from the customers claiming food poisoning to assess whether Balotelli has a present obligation as a result of a past event.
- With the client's permission, send an enquiry letter to the lawyers of Balotelli to obtain their view as to the probability of the claim being successful.
- Review board minutes to understand whether the directors believe that the claim will be successful or not.
- Review the post year-end period to assess whether any payments have been made to any of the claimants.
- Discuss with management as to whether they propose to include a contingent liability disclosure or not, consider the reasonableness of this.
- Obtain a written management representation confirming management's view that the lawsuit is unlikely to be successful and hence no provision is required.
- Review the adequacy of any disclosures made in the financial statements

3 (a) Misstatements

As per ISA 450 *Evaluation of Misstatements Identified during the Audit* the auditor has a responsibility to accumulate misstatements which arise over the course of the audit unless they are very small amounts.

Identified misstatements should be considered during the course of the audit to assess whether the audit strategy and plan should be revised.

The auditor should determine whether uncorrected misstatements are material in aggregate or individually.

All misstatements should be communicated to those charged with governance on a timely basis and the auditor should request that they make necessary amendments. If this request is refused then the auditor should consider the potential impact on their audit report.

A written representation should be requested from management to confirm that unadjusted misstatements are immaterial.

(b) Audit reports

Czech Co

Czech Co has incurred research expenditure of $2·1m and development expenditure of $3·2m and this has all been capitalised within intangible assets. This is contrary to IAS 38 *Intangible Assets*, as research expenditure should be expensed to profit or loss account rather than capitalised.

The error is material as it represents 8% of profit before tax (2·1m/26·3m) and hence management should adjust the financial statements by removing the research expenditure from intangibles and charging it to profit or loss account instead.

If management refuse to amend this error then the audit report will need to be modified. As management has not complied with IAS 38 and the error is material but not pervasive then a qualified opinion would be necessary.

The basis of opinion paragraph would need to include a paragraph explaining the material misstatement in relation to the provision of depreciation on land and the effect on the financial statements. The opinion paragraph would be qualified 'except for'.

Dawson Co

Dawson Co's wages program has been corrupted leading to a loss of payroll data for a period of two months. The auditors should attempt to verify payroll in an alternative manner. If they are unable to do this then payroll for the whole year would not have been verified.

Wages and salaries for the two month period represents 11% of profit before tax (1·1m/10m) and therefore is a material balance for which audit evidence has not been available.

The auditors will need to modify the audit report as they are unable to obtain sufficient appropriate evidence in relation to a material, but not pervasive, element of wages and salaries and therefore a qualified opinion will be required.

The basis of opinion section will be amended to explain the limitation in relation to the lack of evidence over two months of payroll records. The opinion paragraph will be qualified 'except for'.

4 (a) Financial statement assertions for balances at the period end.

(i) Existence – Assets, liabilities and equity interests exist.
(ii) Rights and obligations – The entity holds or controls the rights to assets, and liabilities are the obligations of the entity.
(iii) Completeness – All assets, liabilities and equity interests that should have been recorded have been recorded.
(iv) Valuation and allocation – Assets, liabilities and equity interests are included in the financial statements at appropriate amounts and any resulting valuation or allocation adjustments are appropriately recorded.

(b) Substantive procedures receivables

- For non-responses, with the client's permission, the team should arrange to send a follow up circularisation.
- If the customer does not respond to the follow up, then with the client's permission, the senior should telephone and ask whether they are able to respond in writing to the circularisation request.
- If there are still non-responses, then the senior should undertake alternative procedures to confirm receivables.
- For responses with differences, the senior should identify any disputed amounts, and identify whether these relate to timing differences or whether there are possible errors in the records of Torres.
- Any differences due to timing, such as cash in transit, should be agreed to post year-end cash receipts in the cash book.
- The receivables ledger should be reviewed to identify any possible mis-postings as this could be a reason for a response with a difference.
- If any balances have been flagged as disputed by the receivable, then these should be discussed with management to identify whether a write down is necessary.

5 (a) (i) Ratios to assist the audit supervisor in planning the audit:

	2014	2013
Operating margin	4·5/23 = 19·6%	4/18 = 22·2%
Inventory days	2·1/11 * 365 = 70 days	1·6/10 * 365 = 58 days
Payable days	1·6/11 * 365 = 53 days	1·2/10 * 365 = 44 days
Current ratio	6·6/2·5 = 2·6	6·9/1·2 = 5·8
Quick ratio	(6·6 – 2·1)/2·5 = 1·8	(6·9 – 1·6)/1·2 = 4·4

(ii) Audit risks and responses:

Audit risk	Audit response
Management were disappointed with 2013 results and hence undertook strategies to improve the 2014 trading results. There is a risk that management might feel under pressure to manipulate the results through the judgements taken or through the use of provisions.	Throughout the audit the team will need to be alert to this risk. They will need to carefully review judgemental decisions and compare treatment against prior years.
A generous sales-related bonus scheme has been introduced in the year, this may lead to sales cut-off errors with employees aiming to maximise their current year bonus.	Increased sales cut-off testing will be performed along with a review of post year-end sales returns as they may indicate cut-off errors.
Revenue has grown by 28% in the year however, cost of sales has only increased by 10%. This increase in sales may be due to the bonus scheme and the advertising however, this does not explain the increase in gross margin. There is a risk that sales may be overstated.	During the audit a detailed breakdown of sales will be obtained, discussed with management and tested in order to understand the sales increase.
Gross margin has increased from 44·4% to 52·2%. Operating margin has decreased from 22·2% to 19·6%. This movement in gross margin is significant and there is a risk that costs may have been omitted or included in operating expenses rather than cost of sales.	The classification of costs between cost of sales and operating expenses will be compared with the prior year to ensure consistency.
There has been a significant increase in operating expenses which may be due to the bonus and the advertising campaign but could be related to the misclassification of costs.	

Audit risk	Audit response
The finance director has made a change to the inventory valuation in the year with additional overheads being included. In addition inventory days have increased from 58 to 70 days. There is a risk that inventory is overvalued.	The change in the inventory policy will be discussed with management and a review performed of the additional overheads included to ensure that these are of a production nature. Detailed cost and net realisable value testing to be performed and the aged inventory report to be reviewed to assess whether inventory requires writing down.
Receivables days have increased from 61 to 71 days and management have extended the credit period given to customers. This leads to an increased risk of recoverability of receivables.	Extended post year-end cash receipts testing and a review of the aged receivables ledger to be performed to assess valuation.
The current and quick ratios have decreased from 5·8 to 2·6 and 4·4 to 1·8 respectively. In addition, the cash balances have decreased significantly over the year. Although all ratios are above the minimum levels, this is still a significant decrease and along with the increase of sales could be evidence of overtrading which could result in going concern difficulties.	Detailed going concern testing to be performed during the audit and discussed with management to ensure that the going concern basis is reasonable.

(b) Going concern procedures

- Obtain Walters' cash flow forecast and review the cash in and out flows. Assess the assumptions for reasonableness and discuss the findings with management to understand if the company will have sufficient cash flows.
- Review any current agreements with the bank to determine whether any key ratios have been breached with regards to the bank overdraft.
- Review the company's post year-end sales and order book to assess the levels of trade and if the revenue figures in the cash flow forecast are reasonable.
- Review post year end correspondence with suppliers to identify whether any restriction in credit have arisen, and if so ensure that the cash flow forecast reflects an immediate payment for trade payables.
- Inquire of the lawyers of Walters as to the existence of litigation and claims; if any exist then consider their materiality and impact on the going concern basis.
- Perform audit tests in relation to subsequent events to identify any items that might indicate or mitigate the risk of going concern not being appropriate.
- Review the post year end board minutes to identify any other issues that might indicate financial difficulties for the company.
- Review post year end management accounts to assess if in line with cash flow forecast.
- Consider whether any additional disclosures as required by IAS 1 *Presentation of Financial Statements* in relation to material uncertainties over going concern should be made in the financial statements.
- Obtain a written representation confirming the director's view that Walters is a going concern.

6 (a) Garcia International's (Garcia) internal control

Deficiency	Control	Test of control
Currently the website is not integrated into inventory system. This can result in Garcia accepting customer orders when they do not have the goods in inventory. This can cause them to lose sales and customer goodwill.	The website should be updated to include an interface into the inventory system; this should check inventory levels and only process orders if adequate inventory is held. If inventory is out of stock, this should appear on the website with an approximate waiting time.	Test data could be used to attempt to process orders via the website for items which are not currently held in inventory. The orders should be flagged as being out of stock and indicate an approximate waiting time.
For goods despatched by local couriers, customer signatures are not always obtained. This can lead to customers falsely claiming that they have not received their goods. Garcia would not be able to prove that they had in fact despatched the goods and may result in goods being despatched twice.	Garcia should remind all local couriers that customer signatures must be obtained as proof of delivery and payment will not be made for any despatches with missing signatures.	Select a sample of despatches by couriers and ask Garcia for proof of delivery by viewing customer signatures.

Deficiency	Control	Test of control
There have been a number of situations where the sales orders have not been fulfilled in a timely manner. This can lead to a loss of customer goodwill and if it persists will damage the reputation of Garcia as a reliable supplier.	Once goods are despatched they should be matched to sales orders and flagged as fulfilled. The system should automatically flag any outstanding sales orders past a predetermined period, such as five days. This report should be reviewed by a responsible official.	Review the report of outstanding sales orders. If significant, discuss with a responsible official to understand why there is still a significant time period between sales order and despatch date. Select a sample of sales orders and compare the date of order to the goods despatch date to ascertain whether this is within the acceptable predetermined period.
Customer credit limits are set by sales ledger clerks. Sales ledger clerks are not sufficiently senior and so may set limits too high, leading to irrecoverable debts, or too low, leading to a loss of sales.	Credit limits should be set by a senior member of the sales ledger department and not by sales ledger clerks. These limits should be regularly reviewed by a responsible official.	For a sample of new customers accepted in the year, review the authorisation of the credit limit, and ensure that this was performed by a responsible official. Enquire of sales ledger clerks as to who can set credit limits.
Sales discounts are set by Garcia's sales team. In order to boost their sales, members of the sales team may set the discounts too high, leading to a loss of revenue.	All members of the sales team should be given authority to grant sales discounts up to a set limit. Any sales discounts above these limits should be authorised by sales area managers or the sales director. Regular review of sales discount levels should be undertaken by the sales director, and this review should be evidenced.	Discuss with members of the sales team the process for setting sales discounts. Review the sales discount report for evidence of review by the sales director.
Supplier statement reconciliations are no longer performed. This may result in errors in the recording of purchases and payables not being identified in a timely manner.	Supplier statement reconciliations should be performed on a monthly basis for all suppliers and these should be reviewed by a responsible official.	Review the file of reconciliations to ensure that they are being performed on a regular basis and that they have been reviewed by a responsible official
Changes to supplier details in the purchase ledger master file can be undertaken by purchase ledger clerks. This could lead to key supplier data being accidently amended or fictious suppliers being set up, which can increase the risk of fraud.	Only purchase ledger supervisors should have the authority to make changes to master file data. This should be controlled via passwords. Regular review of any changes to master file data by a responsible official and this review should be evidenced.	Request a purchase ledger clerk to attempt to access the master file and to make an amendment, the system should not allow this. Review a report of master data changes and review the authority of those making amendments.
Garcia has considerable levels of surplus plant and equipment. Surplus unused plant is at risk of theft. In addition, if the surplus plant is not disposed of then the company could lose sundry income.	Regular review of the plant and equipment on the factory floor by senior factory personnel to identify any old or surplus equipment. As part of the capital expenditure process there should be a requirement to confirm the treatment of the equipment being replaced.	Observe the review process by senior factory personnel, identifying the treatment of any old equipment. Review processed capital expenditure forms to ascertain if the treatment of replaced equipment is stated.
Purchase requisitions are authorised by production supervisors. Production supervisors are not sufficiently independent or senior to authorise capital expenditure.	Capital expenditure authorisation levels to be established. Production supervisors should only be able to authorise low value items, any high value items should be authorised by the board.	Review a sample of authorised capital expenditure forms and identify if the correct signatory has authorised them.

(b) **Substantive procedures additions**

- Obtain a breakdown of additions, cast the list and agree to the non-current asset register to confirm completeness of plant and equipment (P&E).
- Select a sample of additions and agree cost to supplier invoice to confirm valuation.
- Verify rights and obligations by agreeing the addition of plant and equipment to a supplier invoice in the name of Garcia.
- Review the list of additions and confirm that they relate to capital expenditure items rather than repairs and maintenance.
- Review board minutes to ensure that significant capital expenditure purchases have been authorised by the board.
- For a sample of additions recorded in P&E, physically verify them on the factory floor to confirm existence.

			Marks
Section A			
		Questions 1–12 multiple choice	20
		Total marks	**20**
Section B			
1	**(a)**	Up to 1 mark per well explained threat and up to 1 mark for method of managing risk, overall maximum of 6 marks.	
		Familiarity threat – long association of partner Self-interest threat – son gained employment at client company Self-interest threat – financial interest (shares) in client company Self-review threat – audit firm providing internal audit service Contingent fees	6
	(b)	Up to 1 mark per well explained point	
		Objective Whom they report to Reports – publicly available or not Scope of work Appointed by Independence of company	4
			10
2	**(a)**	1 mark for each definition	
		Definition of test of control Definition of substantive test	2
	(b)	Up to 1 mark per relevant substantive procedure, maximum of 4 marks for each issue.	
		Depreciation Review the reasonableness of the depreciation rates and compare to industry averages Review the capital expenditure budgets Review profits and losses on disposal for assets disposed of in year Recalculate the depreciation charge for a sample of assets Perform a proof in total calculation for the depreciation charged on the equipment Review the disclosure of depreciation in the draft financial statements	
		Food poisoning Review the correspondence from the customers Send an enquiry to the lawyers as to the probability of the claim being successful Review board minutes Review the post year-end period to assess whether any payments have been made Discuss with management as to whether they propose to include a contingent liability disclosure Obtain a written management representation Review any disclosures made in the financial statements	8
			10

			Marks
3	(a)	Up to 1 mark per well described point	
		Auditor should accumulate misstatements Consider if audit strategy/plan should be revised Assess if uncorrected misstatements material Communicate to those charged with governance, request changes If refused then assess impact on audit report Request written representation	2
	(b)	Up to 1 mark per valid point, overall maximum of 4 marks per client issue.	
		Discussion of issue Calculation of materiality Type of audit report modification required Impact on audit report	8
			10
4	(a)	Up to 1 mark per assertion, ½ mark for stating assertion and ½ mark for explanation.	
		Existence – explanation Rights and obligations – explanation Completeness – explanation Valuation and allocation – explanation	4
	(b)	Up to 1 mark per relevant substantive procedure	
		For non-responses arrange to send a follow up circularisation With the client's permission, telephone the customer and ask for a response For remaining non-responses, undertake alternative procedures to confirm receivables For responses with differences, identify any disputed amounts, identify whether these relate to timing differences or whether there are possible errors in the records Cash in transit should be vouched to post year-end cash receipts in the cash book Review receivables ledger to identify any possible mis-postings Disputed balances, discuss with management whether a write down is necessary	6
			10

				Marks
5	**(a)**	**(i)**	½ mark per ratio calculation per year Operating margin Inventory days Payable days Current ratio Quick ratio	3
		(ii)	Up to 1 mark per well explained audit risk, maximum of 6 marks for risks and up to 1 mark per audit response, maximum of 6 marks for responses Management manipulation of results Sales cut-off Revenue growth Misclassification of costs between cost of sales and operating Inventory valuation Receivables valuation Going concern risk	12
	(b)		1 mark per well explained point – If the procedure does not clearly explain how this will help the auditor to consider going concern then a ½ mark only should be awarded: Review cash flow forecasts Review bank agreements, breach of key ratios Review post year-end sales and order book Review suppliers correspondence Inquire of lawyers for any litigation Subsequent events Board minutes Management accounts Consider additional disclosures under IAS 1 Written representation	5
				20
6	**(a)**		Up to 1 mark per deficiency, up to 1 mark per well explained control and up to 1 mark for each well described test of control, maximum of 6 marks for deficiencies, maximum of 6 marks for controls and maximum of 6 marks for tests of control. Website not integrated into inventory system Customer signatures Unfulfilled sales orders Customer credit limits Sales discounts Supplier statement reconciliations Purchase ledger master file Surplus plant and equipment Authorisation of capital expenditure	18
	(b)		Up to 1 mark per substantive procedure Additions Cast list of additions and agree to non-current asset register Vouch cost to recent supplier invoice Agree addition to a supplier invoice in the name of Garcia to confirm rights and obligations Review additions and confirm capital expenditure items rather than repairs and maintenance Review board minutes to ensure authorised by the board Physically verify them on the factory floor to confirm existence	2
				20